Authentic Managerial Leadership

Learning the essential leadership principles

and management skills

for ministry effectiveness

Robert A. Orr, Ph.D.

Authentic Managerial Leadership
Condensed Version of *The Essentials for Effective Christian Leadership Development*
by Robert A. Orr

Printed in the United States of America

ISBN 9781613796092

Unless otherwise indicated, Bible quotations are taken from the Authorized King James Version.

Desktop publishing, graphics: Carol Y. Abbott, B.R.Ed.
Software used: Adobe: Illustrator CS3, InDesign CS3, Photoshop CS3; Broderbund: ClickArt Christian Graphics Deluxe and ClickArt Infinity; Corel Gallery 1,000,000; CorelDraw X4; Hemera: The Big Book of Art (MAC and Windows); IMSI Masterclips 35,000

Canadian Cataloguing in Publication Data
Orr, Robert A. (Robert Alexander), 1940-
    Authentic Managerial Leadership
Includes Bibliographical References
ISBN: 9781613796092
    1. Leadership   2. Christian Leadership
I. Title.
HD38.077 1994   685.4'092   C94-900858-3

www.xulonpress.com

TABLE OF CONTENTS

A Note to My Readers Around the World

Teachers and Trainers:

This summary of *Authentic Managerial Leadership* is the result of extensive research, input from contemporary leadership and management trainers, valuable insight from many authors on the subject, as well as personal training and experience in this field. This book brings together authentic leadership principles and management skills and forms one workable concept that I call, "Authentic Managerial Leadership". It fills a vacuum that exists in today's theories of leadership and management. Teach this and you will put a strong foundation under the lives of present leaders and those leaders-in-the-making that the world so desperately needs. This book makes many references to the Holy Scriptures as the source of what God thinks about the character of leadership.

Students:

Just think about it... you won't need to obtain 20 to 50 or more other books to get the essentials covered here! It's all between the front and back cover! A student bargain for the price! For further study you are encouraged to follow-up on the documented quotes and references and their sources listed in the endnotes and additional books listed in the bibliography. You have begun your journey to becoming a godly and authentic leader!

Executives, Leaders and Managers:

Keep this book on your desk. The table of contents and index will enable you to locate the help you need for many difficult and different situations you face daily in your responsible role. The section on functions has a number of tools and worksheets that you will find useful.

Ministry Leaders and Clergy:

This summarized manual will challenge and enable you to mentor and pass the leadership torch more effectively to younger disciples, your potential "leaders-in-the-making"!

Friends:

Many of you are in different and unique cultures. How can I serve you better within your sphere of influence? Give me some feedback after **you have studied the contents. Let me know by dropping a note to** *robertalexorr@yahoo.ca.*

It's a privilege and honour to serve you!

Robert A. Orr

Give a man a fish

and he will eat for a day.

Teach a man to fish

and he will eat for a lifetime.

I. THE CRISIS

"In those days Israel had no king (leader); everyone did that which was right in his own eyes" (Judges 17:6). *"The reason I left you in Crete was that you might straighten out what was left unfinished and appoint elders (leaders) in every town, as I directed you"* (Titus 1:5).

Authentic Leadership is Missing!

The time has come to scrutinize and re-evaluate leadership. Exemplary, effective authentic leadership is often the missing link in management theory. Many organizations such as churches, charities, ministries, businesses and governments, are led by "status quo", money-hungry, self-centered, greedy individuals who focus their efforts on managing their own little (some aren't so little) kingdoms. Even many "efficient" and frugal organizations are not effective in fulfilling their so-called purpose and reaching their objectives. Their vision (if it exists) does not become a reality. People heavy-heartedly whisper, "We have a leadership crisis! We are floundering! We have lost our way!"

The missing link in management theory

"And the things that you have heard me say in the presence of many witnesses entrust to reliable (faithful, trustworthy) men and women who will also be QUALIFIED (ABLE, COMPETENT) to teach others also." (II Tim. 2:2)

A Leadership Crisis – Why?

"We are over-managed and under-led"! Leadership training and development is not a priority. Why? It threatens the "establishment". Other hindrances to leadership development are:

a. Traditions, status quo (*the customary, bureaucratic or traditional manner in which we do things*), and old paradigms – We are not ready or willing for change.

b. "Security" ("Don't rock my/our boat!") – A false sense of security.

c. Prestige, arrogance, "little kingdoms", status, old structures – God's purpose is absent.

d. Old rule books, policy manuals, technologies

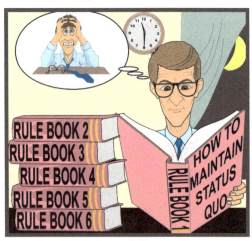

e. Complicated theology and excessive emphasis on intellectual knowledge; bigoted doctrinal perspectives.

This crisis calls for urgent change. Why has this change been delayed?

a. People fear change. "*Those who are the most resistant to change are the ones who need to change the most!*" (Mark Orr) One person may welcome change wholeheartedly while another in the same circumstance is "paralyzed" with fear.

b. People fear losing control. "If others are trained, they may appear to be better or do a better job than I".

c. Change requires creative thinking and that often clashes with the "establishment", church or "leader" at the top!

Consequences of Failed Leadership

a. Organizations bog down. They fail to produce successive authentic and competent leaders. They become ineffective (no fruit) – lots of motion without meaning. They become meeting-oriented – yet no action!

b. Biblical values, vision, purpose, passion, motivation, a clear conscience, integrity are weak or lost.

c. Gifts, talents, skills are not developed and used.

d. People lose their own purpose for living. Complacency and false security becomes the norm. People become unmotivated "robots".

e. Institutions, organizations, churches and ministries no longer serve people. People give their allegiance to organizations. They become *prisoners of habits*, practices and rules that make them ultimately ineffective individually and collectively.

Victims of Old Paradigms

A paradigm is *a way of doing things*. An old or obsolete paradigm (*an outdated way of doing things*) is rooted in the minds of the people who belong to a particular organization or system. Such a paradigm no longer functions. It is not effective or productive and no longer meets real and actual needs. However the outdated paradigm continues to be dogmatically practiced even without any positive results. A new vigorous, authentic leadership is needed to shake off the binding chains of old, ineffective paradigms! Are you a victim of old paradigms? Will you change?

The Myths of Leadership

Myth 1: *"Leaders are born, not made"*. False! Leaders are not ready-made; they must be discipled, trained, and made. Jesus said, "I will make you…" (Matt. 4:19)

Myth 2: *Leaders exist only at the top*. False. Authentic and effective leaders must exist at every level.

Myth 3: *Leadership and management are the same*. False. They are different but must work together synergistically in unity.

We need to get out of our "rut" and accept the challenge to change the way we think and do things.

Perceived Success

We often fail to grow, make, develop, prepare and raise up authentic leaders. Why?

We become overly "spiritual" and overly "theological" concerning how God provides for this need. We tend to think that God "snaps" His fingers and lo-and-behold we have a leader! He can but He rarely does!

The momentum at the beginning of a worthwhile endeavor often gives a false sense of success. Why? It lacked quality leadership training. Was Jesus successful? Yes! He completed the work His Father gave Him to do (John 17). He prepared leaders to continue the work – He passed the leadership torch! Then He left.

Acts 6:1-7 – The apostles initiated, delegated and incorporated a plan for leadership development. The result of this new wave of leadership was that God's Word spread and the Church grew.

The excitement of initial (perceived growth) and momentum can cause a false sense of success that leads to failure when there is no preparation of new leaders for the present and the future. This must change!

Perceived success without successful successive successors is failure!

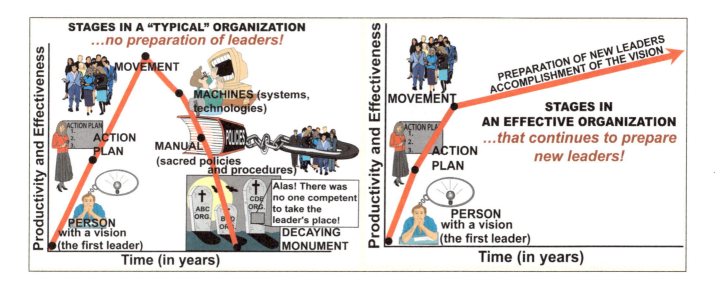

Donkey Leadership

When conflict arises within our organization, how do we handle it? Sometimes conflict resolution stalls at step three and the conflict is not resolved properly—a symptom of poor leadership. True resolution can begin only when step four occurs. Effective leadership creates a workable solution to the conflict whereby both parties win! But it must not stop 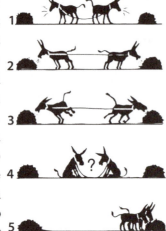 there! This workable solution is ineffective until it is put into action. Steps five and six must take place! Authentic leadership is necessary to make this happen!

Activating Potential Skills

Often people assume they are leaders but the great majority of their group lack enthusiasm, direction and purpose. They are inactive and unmotivated.

The leader has not been a catalyst in converting the potential force of the group into an active, effective force. Effective leaders activate and unleash the potential force around them; they make something of people.

"The laity are not passengers on a ship, but members of a crew." (Elton Trueblood)

Leadership Training and Church Growth

The misconception of the roles of the congregation and the pastor is at the root of ineffective growth.

INEFFECTIVE CHURCH GROWTH

Role of the Congregation: Watch the pastor do everything

Role of the Pastor: "He must do everything!"; doer; employee; shepherd; chaplain; manager; benevolent dictator (sometimes not so benevolent!)

EFFECTIVE CHURCH GROWTH

Role of the Congregation: Trained to do ministry

Role of the Pastor: Equipper; leader; trainer; motivator, mentor

The role of the members of the congregation is to do the work of *ministry*. The role of the pastor with his group of "leadership trainees" is to be a *leader, mentor, equipper, trainer, motivator and enabler* so as to empower the larger group to do the ministry.

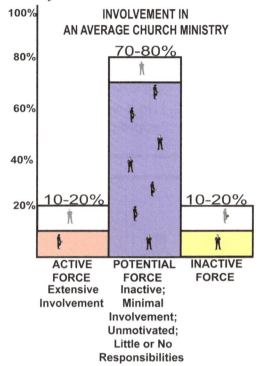

Too often the active 10-20% are very busy doing all the work themselves instead of delegating the work to the other 70-80%. They have failed to train, develop and allow the 70-80% to use their God-given abilities, gifts and talents.

The active 10-20% should be leading the other 70-80% in doing the work of ministry. However, has this 10-20% been trained to become "competent" themselves?

> An equipper is a leader who actively sets goals for a congregation according to the will of God, obtains goal ownership from the people, and sees that each church member is properly motivated and equipped to do his or her part in accomplishing the goals. (Peter Wagner)

More than ever there is a need for people to seize opportunities to lead us to greatness. Yet there seems to be a reluctance to answer the cry for leadership. Why? We believe this cautiousness results not from a lack of courage or competence, but from outdated notions about leadership.

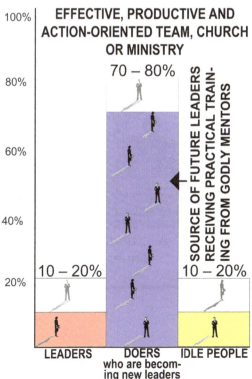

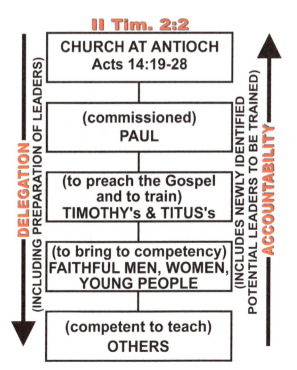

How to Lose Your Job!

We need leaders—not theories about leaders—but leaders who function in the real world rather than in some artificial setting or theological—"cocoon"—authentic leaders of godly character and integrity that train others. We need leaders who will train others to do the work and who will "let go" and allow new leaders to do the job. Such an effective leader can expect a promotion to a new area of service that God has planned for him or her! He/she passed the torch!

1. I do it and I give a good example of it.

2. I do it with another person. People do what they see!

3. The other person learns and does it. I praise and coach him.

4. The other person does it and gives a good example.

5. The other person does it with another person.

6. ...and the process continues without me...!

7. ...and the process continues without me...!

8. ...and the process continues without me...!

Perceived success without successful successive successors is failure!

Titus 1:5 – Titus had forgotten his job description! Paul reminded him that he was to prepare leaders for every city. And you? Are you developing competent leaders?

Yet sometimes we find "leaders" who are actually "theological monsters". A diploma or degree in theology or any other discipline does not make a leader! A theological monster takes something simple and makes it complicated! An equipper takes a complicated matter and makes it simple to understand!

An equipper spends time to make winners out of the lay people. Truth is applied, not sermonized! He must work with a vision and a purpose. To that end he must discover the gifts of "potential leaders in the making" and prioritize the church ministries. He influences and mobilizes people and instills the commitment to change, to develop new strategies and to focus energy and resources on the right objectives.

Are you a "theological monster" or an equipping leader training other potential leaders?

A lack of model leaders

We need leaders who understand that they must "walk the talk" if the long range results are to be realized.

> The day was cold and bleak. George Washington, starting out from his headquarters, drew on his greatcoat, turned up the collar, and pulled his hat down to shield his face from the biting wind. As he walked down the road to where the soldiers were fortifying a camp, no one would have known that the tall, muffled

figure was the Commander-in-Chief of the Army. As he came near the camp he stopped to watch a small company of soldiers, under the command of a corporal, building a breastwork of logs. The men were tugging at a heavy log. The corporal, important and superior, stood at one side giving orders. "Up with it!" he cried. "Now all together! Push. Up with it, I say!" The men gathered new strength. A great push and the log was nearly in its place, but it was too heavy. Just before it reached the top of the pile it slipped and fell back. The corporal shouted again. "Up with it! What ails you? Up with it!" The men tugged

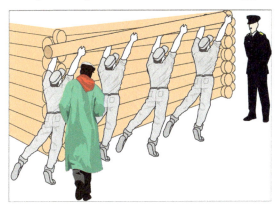

and strained again. The log nearly reached the top, slipped, and once more rolled back. "Heave hard!" cried the corporal. "One, two, three—now push!" Another struggle and then, just as the log was about to roll back for the third time, Washington ran forward, pushed with all his strength, and the log rolled into place on top of the breastwork. The men, panting and perspiring, sought to thank him, but he turned toward the corporal. "Why don't you help your men with this heavy lifting, when they need another hand?" he asked. "Why don't I?" asked the man. "Don't you see I am a corporal?" "Indeed," replied Washington, throwing open his greatcoat and showing his uniform. "I am only the Commander-in-Chief. Next time you have a log too heavy for your men to lift, send for me!"

Next time you have a log too heavy for your men to lift, send for me!

Oh, for this kind of leadership today!

What Must We Do?
WE MUST CHANGE—change our outdated thinking, our definition of character, our strategy, ways, and direction. We must free ourselves from old binding paradigms.

Finally! I have been wanting these changes for such a long time! Let's celebrate!

Here is the list of changes.

Often two different people in the same circumstances will react very differently to change—

one may wel-come change *wholeheart-edly while the other may be-come "para-lyzed" with fear.*

What? Changes? I detest changes! Why do we need these changes?

Here is the list of changes.

We are often "stuck in a rut" caused by perceptions and misconceptions.

Change our thinking to godly thinking
Understand the concept, definitions and roles of leadership, management, and managerial leadership. Renew enthusiasm, passion and purpose.

It is not enough to teach only theology and academics—that makes only theologians and scholars. How does God define authentic leadership?

Change our character to godly character
Avoid "nit-picking, self-serving, authoritarian 'leadership', the slave-master legalistic know-it-all theological monster" approach. Are we preaching the gospel of Jesus? Or are we preaching the "gospel" of wealth, prosperity and success rather than the gospel that saves the soul?

We must understand servant leadership which is often falsely equated with weakness and therefore undesirable. (Was Jesus weak when He washed Peter's feet? John 13:3-17). We need to model Jesus, beginning with a servant's heart.

We must become effective godly leaders of integrity, honesty, willing to pay the price, focused on God, family, people development, and leadership training.

Change our strategy
We need to change our ways and strategies to comply with what God desires us to change.

Many training processes and programs don't work; this must change! They are not sacred!

We must establish clear values, vision and purpose. Implement an action plan so that you can fulfill the purpose for which God created and saved you.

Develop teams with a clear purpose that accomplish what one individual alone cannot do.

We must prepare and train individuals to fill the gap (Ezekiel 22:30).

We must unleash the tremendous potential in people! We need leaders (young and old) who can turn challenging opportunities into remarkable successes.

Train and challenge younger leaders to implement new ideas, strategies, challenges, methods and new organizations that fit today's reality. Stand back and give them a chance!

The migration of the Canada geese – even nature teaches leadership principles and management skills!

ORGANIZING THEMSELVES!
LEADER
TEAM
The young ones are given an opportunity to lead!

The Supreme Biblical Model

Our Saviour and Lord Jesus, our Perfect Model Leader implemented a strategy.

He *envisioned* the future and how to fulfill the mandate God gave Him while here on earth (which was to proclaim the Kingdom) John 7:16.

He *acknowledged* the lives and contributions of those patriarchs of the Old Testament. He loved the Scriptures; yet was hard on the status quo religiosity of the day. He challenged the process. He brought back meaning and purpose to life.

He *had a following*; communicated His vision to His disciples; enlisted others; initiated action; motivated, enabled, and empowered others to action. He transformed doubters into trusters.

He knew that leaders who are chosen and empowered by God must be *trained and equipped*. He accepted the responsibility to discover and develop them. He challenged the disciples to greater work. He was a mentor and teacher. He trained people to do the same with others.

He *taught* His disciples in live situations (on-the-job training).

He *built a strong team*. He set goals. He defined the duties.

He *delegated* responsibility. He allowed growth, mistakes, and failures *to bring about maturity*.

He knew His followers well. He did not push His disciples into situations they were not prepared to handle. He was patient. He inspired, encouraged, motivated and challenged His disciples to stretch their capabilities. He recognized individual contributions.

He *anticipated problems* and prevented petty problems from becoming major problems. He maintained wise control.

He *entrusted* disciple-making to those He discipled.

He said, "**Follow Me** and **I will make** you to become fishers of men" ("I will make you to become something worthwhile and productive!") and then "**go ye** into all the world" (Matt. 4:19; Matt. 28:19,20 and Mark 16:15).

"A Christian leader is someone who is called by God to lead; leads with and through Christlike character; and demonstrates the functional competencies that permit effective leadership to take place".

Jesus
2
4
12
70
500
3000
8000

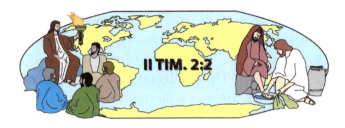

A Revolution

Our approach to leadership development needs to be revolutionary.

A shortage of leaders creates a shortage of followers. And a shortage of followers produces a shortage of future leaders.... The shortage of leaders in the Christian community is already taking an alarming toll. (Myron Rush)

Abigail Adams, back in 1790, wrote a letter to President Jefferson. He said, "Great necessities call forth great leaders." His words are just as applicable now as they were then—and even more so today!

It has been well said that middle management must be replaced by leaders who can destroy the status quo, become people-oriented and personally transmit values. This sounds revolutionary but many organizations have become useless bureaucracies with too many managers and few, if any, leaders. Godly values are not being taught to the people nor are the people being led to a place of personal success. It is this status quo bureaucracy that needs to be destroyed.

Bramble Leadership

Was Gideon a spiritual man? Yes. Was he called of God? Yes. Was he a good leader? (Israel had peace for 40 years.) Yes and no! After Gideon died, Israel experienced total anarchy and chaos. Why? Gideon failed to train and prepare leaders to take his place. Judges 9:7-15. The trees decided to anoint a king to rule over them. The grape vine, the olive and fig trees all declined the position. They were able but unwilling, content in their prosperous ways to follow a corrupt leader. The thorn bush accepted the noble position, but replied, "If you anoint me king, then come and shelter in my shade. If not, fire will come from the thorn bush and consume the cedars of Lebanon (the best trees)."

The bramble begins his reign by lying and making promises it could not keep—a bramble cannot provide shade! The bramble planned to be the biggest and meanest, to bully and destroy anything that got in his way.

JUDGES 9:7-15

When good leaders are slow to come forward to lead their people, evil ones rush in to take their place. Why? Trained leaders of godly character are not available to fill the positions of leadership. The leadership torch was not passed! No training! No people development!

"Shirtsleeves Christians" or "Roll-up-Your-Shirtsleeves Christians"

Shirtsleeves Christians are the kind who believe in wearing their Christianity on their shirtsleeves, who spend more time belly-aching about how immoral and godless the world is rather than making the world a better place to live. They worry about how high the steeple is on their church rather than if people really pray there or if a room can be used to tutor underprivileged children. ON THE OTHER HAND, Rollup-Your-Shirtsleeves Christians dig into life, teach their children values, and support good causes... (they) believe Christianity is faith and action. They try to get things done in a real world in a Christian way.... Convictions aren't just religious beliefs, though most good principles come from the Scriptures. Convictions also means staying true to your principles—whether you're in business, a community organization, or a single parent... I've learned the biggest successes are usually built from the grassroots up... (Dave credits his grandmother, Minnie Sinclair, for strongly influencing and motivating him.) She prayed much. She worshipped God, loved Jesus, and read the Bible every day. She also was a motivator. From Grandma Sinclair I learned seven lessons for living.

- don't waste
- work hard
- don't cut corners
- have fun doing things
- be strict, but caring
- tackle problems head-on
- pray

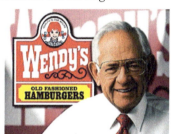

Dave Thomas, Founder Wendy's Fast-Food Restaurants

Summary

Leadership is influence, its key is priorities, its most important ingredient is integrity, and its ultimate test is creating change. The quickest way to gain leadership is by problem-solving, its extra plus is attitude, and its most appreciable asset to be developed is people. Leadership's indispensable quality is vision, its price-tag is self-discipline, and its most important lesson is staff development.
My question is: Are we teaching and developing this kind of leadership?

A sower went forth to sow. I like that. Forth to sow. Not to discuss the soil; not to compute his pension; not to count the

days to his next vacation; ...not to introspect his psyche; not to puzzle why some like him a little, some a lot and others not at all. A sower went forth to sow! A teacher went forth to teach! A leader went forth to lead! A preacher went forth to preach! Jesus took a towel. Jesus said, "Follow Me!" They also serve who lead. Let neither modesty nor intimidation find you holding back. Go with God. (Ernest T. Campbell, 1978 Commencement Address, Princeton Theological Seminary)

Stop loosely uttering the word "leadership" as a meaningless buzz word! Live what it means to be an authentic leader.

W. Stanley Mooneyham, former President of World Vision International, wrote the "Forward" to Ted Engstrom's book, *The Making of a Christian Leader*. He commented,

Sadly... tragically... the Church has been so slow to train and qualify those on whom it has thrust leadership.... He [a youthful friend who had assumed the leadership of an organization with great potential] asked me if I knew of an organization or school that was "turning out" Christian leaders. My answer was: Nobody "turns out" Christian leaders. Certificates, degrees and diplomas don't make leaders. They can't be mass-produced like hothouse plants. Rather they are like rare wild flowers, discovered growing sometimes in the least likely places. Fortunate is the movement or organization which, on finding such a promising example of the species, is able to transplant and cultivate it for maximum benefit and use.

Jesus Christ was not content just to acquire followers. He didn't believe a leader was simply one who leads followers. He felt His job as a leader was not complete until He had actually reproduced Himself in the lives of His twelve disciples and turned them from followers into leaders. He actually redefined effective leadership. (Myron Rush)

Leadership is the courage to admit mistakes, the vision to welcome change, the enthusiasm to motivate others and the confidence  to stay out of step when everyone else is marching to the wrong tune. (E.M. Estes)

Assignment

1. List 3 reasons why "Leadership Training and People Development" was crossed off this list. Are you or your organization guilty of this?

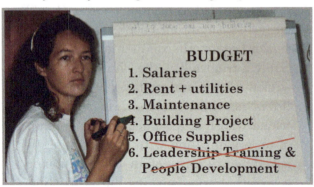

2. What consequences of incompetent leadership (bramble leadership) have you experienced in the past or are presently experiencing?

3. How well do you know your people? Do you take care of them? Are you training them? "Know your flocks' conditions well; take good care of your herds" (Prov. 27:23, Jerusalem Bible).

Leaders must be the conscience for the organization and the people they lead.

Are you passing the leadership torch?

Are you trustworthy?

Are you qualified?

Are you able?

Are you competent?

Are they trustworthy?

Are they qualified?

Are they able?

Are they competent?

"Be diligent in these matters; give yourself wholly to them, so that everyone may see your progress" (I Tim.4:15, NIV).

5. In today's reality, in order to be more effective in accomplishing your organization's vision and purpose, what old paradigms do you need to abandon or wisely adjust? What new paradigms do you need to embrace?

6. Are you training your replacements or will there be an engraving on your tombstone, "Alas! There is no one to take his place!"

"We constantly change the world, even by our inaction. Therefore, let us change it responsibly." (Benjamin Franklin)

II. THE DEFINITION

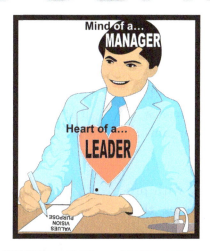

"The only way to lead people is to show them a future. A leader is a dealer in hope."
(Napolean Bonaparte)

"Authentic leadership is seeing further down the road than those around me can!"
(Author unknown)

"And the things that you have heard me say in the presence of many witnesses entrust to reliable (faithful, trustworthy) men and women who will also be QUALIFIED (ABLE, COMPETENT) to teach others also." (II Tim. 2:2)

Authentic Leadership is...

There is much to learn about leadership! This section is only a beginning!

> Leadership is not optional. It is the ingredient essential to the success of any organization. Take away leadership and confusion replaces vision. (Charles Swindoll)

> The leader, whenever possible, strives for consensus and commitment rather than the tyranny of the majority of one vote.

> Leadership is a MULTIPLIER FACTOR. Its aim is to produce results that surpass the ordinary expectations of the organization.

Good leadership has to do primarily with producing people of vision and developing their skills by using their varied and numerous abilities and talents.

> The sign of outstanding leadership appears primarily among the followers. Are the followers reaching their potential? Are they learning? Serving? Do they achieve the required results? Do they change with grace? Manage conflict?... The art of leadership requires us to think about the leader-as-steward in terms of relationships: of assets and legacy, of momentum and effectiveness, of civility and values... People are the heart and spirit of all that counts. Without people, there is no need for leaders....

The focus must shift from a bureaucratic status quo towards a people-oriented leadership that promotes the growth of people and shows them a better future.

...People-oriented

"Leadership involves a set of actions for dealing with people-related issues". Leaders are pacesetters.

Carnegie's Epitaph
"Here lies a man who put in his service men better than himself."

An effective leader pushes and grows others, even if it means that those trained and equipped appear to be more successful than himself.

An effective leader assists in the development of the individual's gifts, abilities and skills so that he or she becomes successful and fulfilled as a person of purpose.

> Fail to honour people, they fail to honour you; but of a good leader, who talks little, when his work is done, his aim fulfilled, they will all say, "We did this ourselves!" (Lao Tzu)

This is the *acid test of leadership*! I reach my objective but those who helped me *claim the credit*! I invest, train, mentor and develop another person but the "trainee" becomes more successful than I! It's contrary to human nature to humbly accept this with gladness! Yet, if you are going to be an authentic leader, claim to be one, aspire to be one, or have been asked to be one—gladly accepting this challenging aspect of leadership is exactly how you will know whether you are an authentic leader. Receiving no credit is part of the price!

An authentic leader "is willing to develop people to the point that they eventually surpass him or her in knowledge and ability."

"A leader is a person who knows the road, can keep ahead and pull others along, with no map and sign posts. Middle management must be replaced by leaders who can destroy the status quo, become people-oriented and personally transmit values" (Author Unknown). The focus must shift from bureaucratic status quo management towards people-oriented leadership.

Leaders create a climate in which it is possible for others to do their best. They serve as models for what followers are expected to be and do.

Leaders must be concerned with human values. "Too many people who know all about financial values know nothing about human values" (Roy L. Smith).

...Future-oriented

"The task of a leader is to get his people from where they are to where they have not been" (Kissinger).

Future oriented leadership must possess a clear vision of what is possible. This will stimulate and encourage the effort to fulfill that future objective, goal and purpose.

> A leader is a visionary that energizes others...creating a vision of the future and inspiring people to make the vision reality ...leaders appeal to the hearts of their followers—not their minds. Vision is therefore the first critical dimension of effective leadership. Without vision

there is little or no sense of purpose in an organization. Efforts drift aimlessly. The loss of purpose leads to a lack of coordination between work units and divisive infighting among executives"...including church and ministry leaders!

...the most significant contributions leaders make (are)... to the long-term development of people and institutions who (adapt), prosper and grow.

...Purpose-oriented

Leaders influence those around them to successfully achieve the vision and purpose of the organization and its people, making both successful.

Leadership is the art of combining vision, ideas, people, resources, technology, organization, administration, management, faith, love and the training of future leaders to accomplish the established vision, objectives and goals with passion and clarity.

Leaders have a sense of direction and purpose beyond the moment. They enlist others to a common purpose. They are in touch with those they lead and foster collaboration. They build effective teams.

Leadership is knowing where you are, where you are supposed to be going, and then marshalling the resources necessary to get there.

A leader must possess a compelling vision, purpose, passion and dedication. He needs to transfer that vision ("transvisioning") by influencing, challenging, motivating, energizing, empowering and coaching another person or a group of persons (a team) to accomplish the organization's purpose in such a way as to make the individual or group of persons successful and fulfilled, becoming significant, purposeful team members.

Leadership is the capacity and the will to rally men and women to a common purpose, and the character which inspires confidence. (Lord Montgomery).

...Change and Development-oriented

Leaders work to gain participation and commitment, to harness diversity, and to build consensus... they improve them. Leaders...develop the organization and each other.

Leadership is the instrument by which intended, real change (that meets people's needs) is accomplished.

Good leaders are not restricted by the way 'things have always been done'. Their leadership is a continuing search for the best way, not the most familiar. (Paul J. Meyer)

Leaders are change-agents!

...Influence and Motivation-oriented

"Leadership is influence." (John Maxwell)

Leadership is the ability to get a man (or woman) to do what you want him (or her) to do, when you want it done, in a way you want it done, because he (she) wants to do it! (Dwight D. Eisenhower)

"Leadership is motivating (inspiring, influencing) others toward a specified goal for the purpose of making them feel successful" (and fulfilled). Leadership is a relationship.

"Leadership is not so much what you do as what you cause to be done!" (Mark Orr)

Leadership involves creating meaning, inflaming the heart with human passion, and translating intention into reality and then sustaining it.

Leadership is
 ...the ability to make things happen—to act

in order to help others work in an environment within which each individual serving under him finds himself encouraged and stimulated to a point where he is helped to realize his fullest potential to contribute meaningfully. Outstanding results cannot be forced out of people. They occur only when individuals collaborate under a leader's stimulation and inspiration in striving toward a worthy common goal.

"Leadership is
'a learnable set of practices' thus demystifying the issue and showing that it is within all of us to lead in our spheres of influence. Leaders are learners. Yes! They are born to learn the art of leadership!" (Kouzes and Posner).

Leadership is not the private reserve of a few charismatic men and women!

To determine your effectiveness as a leader, "turn around and see if anyone is following you" (John Maxwell) and what is being accomplished!

...Action-oriented
"Leadership is action, not position".

Leadership "bridges the gap between knowing and doing and makes things happen". Leaders take people from knowing to doing; from stagnation to creativity; from the past to the future.

Christian Leadership is...
Christian leadership is "the exercise of one's spiritual gifts under the call of God to serve a certain group of people in achieving the goals God has given them toward the end of glorifying Christ". (Kenneth Gangel)

Christian leaders are motivated by genuine godly love for their Model Leader and Master, and for others. They must be willing to submit to Christ's leadership and His purpose and objectives for the Church, for themselves, and for those around them—and then work within such parameters. Christian leaders must allow the Holy Spirit to change them into the godly persons He desires them to be. Christian leaders trust God to enable them to accomplish what needs to be done and to give them wisdom in their leadership roles.

A Christian leader, therefore, "...is a person with God-given capacity and responsibility to influence a specific group of God's people toward God's purposes for the group".

Leadership is the ability to translate vision into reality through human participants in dependence upon God, regardless of who is credited.

The leader must know the distinctiveness of a Christian organization—its purpose and motivation (to give glory to God by serving Him), allegiance to Jesus Christ, biblical values, character requirements (I Tim.3:1-7), and accepting the final authority of God.

What do Christian leaders do?
- Challenge the process.
- Search for opportunities.
- Envision the future.
- Enlist and enable others to act.
- Transvision the dream.
- Build a strong team.
- Model the way.
- Mentor others.

- Encourage the heart.
- Trust God for wisdom.
- Recognize individual contributions.
- Celebrate accomplishments.
- Give their lives for others (sacrificial dedication).
- A competent yet humble leader can actually lead others without needing formal organizational power, authority or position, yet exert notable influence.

Leaders are decisive, credible and focused. They have strong personalities and demonstrate courage. They have a clear vision and a simple message. They are good communicators and manifest modest charisma. They mobilize followers. They are in the right place at the right time. They are "winners" at fulfilling their purpose.

Management is…

Management is a distinct process consisting of planning, organizing, actuating, and controlling, performed to successfully accomplish and fulfill the stated objectives and purpose, to pursue one or more goals through human assistants and other resources.

Management is "a set of activities directed at the efficient and effective use of resources in the pursuit of one or more goals".

Managers oversee the tasks and ensure the efficient use of technology, systems, tools, instruments, education, etc. to accomplish the work that needs to be done so that the vision can be accomplished. Effective managers are concerned with the efficiency of the procedures, technologies and systems to accomplish the vision, purpose, objectives and goals.

A manager is backed by formal organizational power and authority of position. He is responsible for technologies and systems, other people and their work and who attempts to accomplish the established vision, purpose, objectives, and goals.

Management's focus is "WORK", getting things done through people who can function individually and collectively to accomplish the work. In Christian circles, management seeks to utilize efficiently the talents and spiritual gifts of those persons entrusted to the leader's care.

What is the difference?

Leadership and management cannot function separately if the organization is to be successful in accomplishing its purpose and vision. Although their characteristics, roles and functions are different, they are equally important. An imbalance will result in inefficiency and lack of effectiveness. They must complement each other.

Leadership captures concepts, visions, and overall direction. Once those are established, management sees that it is done.

An organization can develop into a useless bureaucracy when there are too many managers and too few leaders.

Management is concentrated in systems, equipment and technologies. Leadership is focused on values, vision, purpose and people.

Most people confuse leadership with a position or role—a leader is usually thought

A Leader ...	A Manager ...
... exercises optimistic faith	... emphasizes the importance of facts
... is concerned about effectiveness and development	... strives for efficiency and stability
... follows intuition	... seeks credible data
... inspires and motivates followers; focuses on "what" and "why"	... manages through policies, procedures (the "how"), technologies, chain of command
... takes calculated risks	... guards and conserves standards
... originates and experiments	... follows efficient procedures
... is respected and obeyed without official title or position	... is respected and obeyed based on official title and position
... is concerned about doing the right things	... is conscientious about doing things right
... is uncomfortable with the status quo; he/she brings about changes	... seeks stability and consistency
... is a visionary concerned with long-term results	... focuses on short-term results

of as the head of all or part of an organization. The people in charge are likely to be more administrators, managers, technologists, or bosses rather than true leaders. Leadership is reflected in the ability to initiate action and move others to a shared goal… persuasion (motivation) not position power. Its product is the will to win, the desire to belong. Technology and management are critical elements. If you want to capitalize on them, you need a firm foundation… authentic leadership.

Managerial Leadership is…

It is a concept that must be developed in every level of the organization.

…managers should not be required to become more like leaders; nor should leaders be required to be more like managers. Rather, both should come to value and emphasize the unique strengths of each other in order to tap the natural tension between them to produce a 'one-plus-one-equals-three' outcome. This requires blending strong management and

strong leadership into one integrated whole where the strengths of leaders combine with, rather than clash with, the strengths of managers…. Managers or leaders who have achieved some of this balance and integration have guided their organization to greater heights.

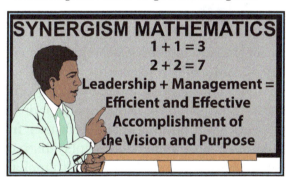

Synergism is the simultaneous action of separate but related parts to produce a sum greater than that of its separate components.

We need to blend leadership principles and management skills into one ideal approach – managerial leadership that is people-oriented, task-oriented, purpose-oriented, knowledge-oriented, learning-oriented and training-oriented.

We blend the process of management, using systems, technologies, "know-how" to get things done, and the process of influential leadership, influencing others to want to do the work.

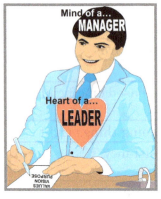

Leaders and managers play distinctly different roles yet cooperate and work together! They complement each other's work. The concept of principled leadership and skilled management in action must be obvious at all organizational levels!

It is the "marriage" of leadership and management into a unified concept that is noticeably functioning throughout the entire organization. You cannot lead without good management nor can you manage without good leadership.

Many of the authors of books on business management and leadership use the terms leadership and management interchangeably. This suggests that leaders and managers do the same work—yet, nothing could be farther from the truth! Leaders and managers play distinctly different roles and require different emphases in their training. Then, there is "MANAGERIAL LEADERSHIP"! It "marries" leadership and management into one truly effective function which we will explore later. In effective organizations, leaders and managers complement each others' work in a fashion which might be compared to the two legs of a person. Two healthy legs function in harmony and are synchronized to enable the person to walk, run, jump, swim, climb, engage in sports or do whatever a good pair of legs should do. When the roles of lead-ers and managers are in balance, the organization runs smoothly, goals and objectives are achieved efficiently.

Christian Managerial Leadership

The union of leadership and management is glued/fused together (like a marriage) by a common vision, purpose, and Biblical values.

It is the process of motivating and empowering people to use their skills, abilities, and God-given talents to implement technologies and procedures within the organization's guidelines and policies to accomplish a common purpose.

The management process (planning, organizing, staffing, directing, and controlling) and the elements of leadership (envisioning, people development, equipping, team building, learning, etc.) function together in harmony. If organizations want to be effective and efficient, all these elements must be evident and exemplified.

Recognizing the need for godly leadership and management, effective Christian managerial leaders EMPOWER new leaders and managers to produce the necessary changes and increased productivity to fulfill God's plan.

The result will be faithful, successful, fulfilled team members with a sense of individual significance who are accomplishing God's purpose in their lives and ministries, and who train faithful men and women to train others also. (II Tim. 2:2)

Key words are "commit", "able" and "teach". Are we "committing" the work and task in such a way that the individual becomes "able" (competent) to accomplish the advice of the Apostle Paul so that he/she will repeat the process and pass it on… "to faithful men (and women) who shall be able to "teach" others also?" Leaders must be competent to teach and train in their role of leadership, ensuring that other leaders in the organization do the same.

A CHRISTIAN MANAGERIAL LEADER...
...is enabled by the Holy Spirit,
...serves with passion and purpose,
...models godly character, scriptural values and ethics,
...possesses and transfers a compelling vision

...TO WHOM?...
...to another person or group of people (a team)
...HOW?...
...by influencing, delegating, discipling,
(Equipping, training, coaching, encouraging, enabling, facilitating, energizing, empowering, committing, challenging, inspiring, motivating, edifying, developing, mentoring)
...BY WHAT MEANS?...
...by the 7 fundamental functions
(envisioning, planning, organizing, controlling, team building, leading, learning)
...practised within the parameters of the Holy Scriptures
...WHY?...
...to accomplish the vision, purpose, objectives & goals in an effective, efficient manner, while overcoming the perils & enjoying the blessings and experiencing fulfillment and success together as a team.

2 Tim. 2:2 Christ centered

A manager is not automatically a leader nor is a leader automatically a manager. Managers need some knowledge of leadership principles in order to motivate subordinates to be productive and leaders need some knowledge of management or at least be convinced of its impor-

KEEP BALANCED! BOTH LEADERSHIP AND MANAGEMENT ARE NEEDED!

tance so that they see that the work gets done effectively and efficiently.

Summary

(A leader is) one who guides the activities of others and who himself acts and performs to bring those activities about. He is capable of performing acts which will guide a group in achieving objectives. He takes the capacities of vision and faith, has the ability to be concerned and to comprehend, exercises action through effective and personal influences in the direction of an enterprise and the development of the potential into the practical and/or profitable means. To accomplish this, a true leader must have a strong drive to take the initiative to act— a kind of initial stirring that causes people and an organization to use their best abilities to accomplish a desired end.

One could define a leader as one who "makes things happen" in a competent and efficient way, being decisive in his actions, recognizing and anticipating problems and their solutions before they become emergencies, without becoming a passive puppet of another person, system, tradition, status quo, bureaucracy, hierarchy or an organization. Jesus looked for this in His disciples when He taught them that to follow Him meant leaving all, even family (Matt.19:5; Mk.10:7). This is hard to understand!

As we face the third millennium, we need to have new paradigms in the fast changing world in which we live.

The global economy continues to be one of the strongest forces pushing organizations to rethink how they do business, providing great opportunities as well as challenges. Interestingly, these changes have only increased the need to create leaders, at all levels of the organization.

"I can't do it" never accomplished anything;
"I'll try" has performed wonders!
(George P. Burnham)

Some of these leaders bear the organizational title of manager; others are called team leaders; still others are members of autonomous work teams where everyone is called upon to play leadership roles. Regardless of title, more and more organizations are calling for employees at all levels to take on responsibilities that were previously reserved only for upper-level managers, and this has in turn changed the nature of managerial work.

The most valuable asset an organization has and needs are people. We can organize the machinery of "things" and we call that management and organization, but humans are a different matter, they need leaders to organize and lead them! We need LEADERS—not theo-ries about leaders—LEADERS who function in the real world rather than in some artificial setting or "cocoon." We have been waiting for some "born leaders" BUT we will wait until the fourth millennium! LEADERS ARE MADE, NOT BORN. They are taught, trained, and developed to lead—not to be driven. They are people of purpose, vision, planning, motivation and transvisioning (they pass the vision to someone else). To grow this type of leader takes patience, perseverance, and the eradication of every trace of laziness in this task.

Assignment

1. What steps will you take to ensure an effective, efficient, stable and healthy balance of management and leadership will be evident in your organization?

2. Who will teach this subject and train others?

"To know and not to do (not acting on learned and practical knowledge and wisdom) is not to know at all." (Howard Hendricks)

III. THE CHARACTER

"The crucible for silver and the furnace for gold, but the Lord tests the heart." (Proverbs 17:3)

"...As the clay is in the potter's hand, so are you in My hand." (Jeremiah 18:4,6)

"O Lord, You are our Father. We are the clay. You are the Potter, we are all the work of Your hand." (Isaiah 64:8)

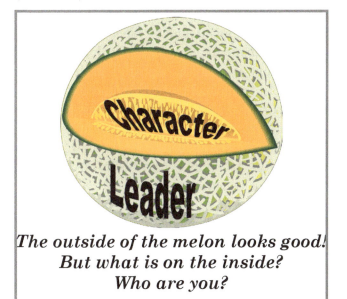

The outside of the melon looks good!
But what is on the inside?
Who are you?

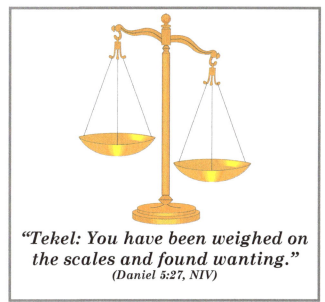

"Tekel: You have been weighed on the scales and found wanting."
(Daniel 5:27, NIV)

"And the things that you have heard me say in the presence of many witnesses entrust to reliable (faithful, trustworthy) men and women who will also be QUALIFIED (ABLE, COMPETENT) to teach others also." (II Tim. 2:2)

Character is a heart issue! (See Jeremiah 17:9.10). The quality of one's character will define his performance as a leader. Become the vessel that God planned for you!

Character is what you are in the dark.
"The law of the harvest is to reap more than you sow.
Sow an act, and you reap a habit;
Sow a habit and you reap a character;
Sow a character and you reap a destiny."
(G.D. Boardman)

The ultimate effectiveness (or lack of it) of our leadership will be largely determined by the quality of our inner character. Don't be fooled by the outside appearance. It is the core of the melon that matters. Is it rotten or good? Followers often take on the characteristics of their leaders–whether good or bad. Godly leaders who continually grow, develop, learn and improve demonstrate the following characteristics.

Purpose-oriented Characteristics

Real joy comes not from ease or riches or from the praise of men, but from doing something worthwhile. (Sir Wilfred Grenfel, Canadian explorer)

The people who get on in this world are the people who get up and look for the circumstances they want, and, if they can't find them, make them. (George Bernard Shaw)

Visionary, Purposeful, Action-oriented

"Vision is what you will seek to achieve within the parameters of your calling" (George Barna).

Vision is an act of seeing an imaginative perception of things, combining insight and foresight.

"Where there is no vision the people perish" (Proverbs 29:18).

Even if you are on the right track...

...you'll get run over if you sit there! **(Oliver Wendell Holmes)**

Vision brings dynamism, enthusiasm, and a sense of usefulness to God and the world. It energizes every effort and provides a force that pushes through problems...creating purpose!

Turn vision, deep think-time and prayer into **action**. Organizational activity must be focused on the values, vision, purpose and objectives. It was not sufficient for Moses to dream and pray about the Promised Land which flowed with "milk and honey". It was not enough for Nehemiah to dream and pray about a rebuilt wall at Jerusalem. It was not enough for the Apostles to dream and pray about the gospel being announced to the entire world; it was not enough for Jesus to dream and pray about having disciples to follow Him. Each one did something to turn their dreams into reality–ACTION WAS ESSENTIAL! Vision and purpose became a reality.

Courageous Risk-taker

One does not discover new continents without consenting to lose sight of the shore for a very long time. (André Gide)

The greatest achievements in the history of the church and of missions have been the outcome of some leader in touch with God taking courageous, carefully calculated risks.

An effective leader takes wise, calculated risks (not

recklessly)! He keeps going in spite of opposition.

"Failure is not the crime; low aim is" (John Wooden). You may fall as you try, but don't give up (Prov. 24:16).

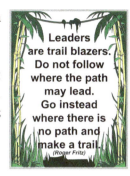

Leaders are trail blazers. Do not follow where the path may lead. Go instead where there is no path and make a trail.
(Roger Fritz)

Change Agent

Don't be satisfied with the traditional, status quo, bureaucratic lifestyle. Move through chaotic situations and manage vital change in order to fulfill the vision and purpose of the organization. You may be labelled a "courteous rebel" but those who are resistant to change may be the true "rebels"!

Committed, Disciplined, Responsible

Be committed to the call of God, the vision, the purpose. Grace, peace and wisdom from God can keep you disciplined and committed to your calling.

Be an example of high standards, conviction, godly ethics.

Carefully manage your life, time, relationships. Seek out effective, long-range solutions to problems.

Take life seriously; don't shirk your responsibilities. But don't fail to take those necessary little breaks!

"You can only lead others where you yourself are willing to go" (Lachlan Mclean).

"To lead others one must be master of oneself" (Sanders). Difficulties and stress reveal character!

Tenacious, Persistent and Motivated

"For though the virtuous man falls seven times, he stands up again" (Prov. 24:16).

"Persistence prevails when all else fails. ...The

difference between a successful person and others is not a lack of strength, not a lack of knowledge, but rather in a lack of will" (Successories Inc.). Keep others motivated to fulfill the task even when the going gets tough. Difficulties reveal and test one's character.

"The heights by great men reached and kept were not attained by sudden flight; but they, while their companions slept, were toiling upward in the night."
(Author unknown)

"Satan will not bother a man (or woman) who has quit fighting. But the cost of quitting will be a life of peaceful stagnation. We sons of eternity just cannot afford such a thing. (A. W. Tozer)

Although vision brings with it dynamism, enthusiasm, and a sense of usefulness to God and the world, the path travelled in seeing the vision come to fruition is often very lonely.

"Anyone can hold the helm when the sea is calm" (Successories); however, a calm sea does not produce a skilled sailor.

The real leader has the resilience to take setbacks in stride, the tenacity to overcome fatigue and discouragement, and the wisdom to 'turn stumbling blocks' into stepping stones." (John R. W. Stott)

Maintain a balanced sense of the urgent and the importance of the task burning within your soul. Be inspired and passionate about your call, purpose and mission.

"There was a very cautious man who never laughed or played. He never risked; he never tried. He never sang or prayed. And when one day he passed away, his insurance was denied – for since he never really lived, they claimed he never died!" (author unknown)

Effective and Efficient
"Efficiency" focuses on the process only" (*doing things the right way*)–management.

"Effectiveness" focuses on the results, the overall objective (*doing the right thing*)–leadership. Practise wise common sense–the ability of *"seeing things as they are, and doing things as they ought to be done"* (Stowe).

Optimistic and Principled
"Leaders need to be optimists. Their vision is beyond the present. Some call it stubbornness. I call it principled leadership" (Rudy Guiliani). "I run so as to win" (Apostle Paul, I Cor. 9:24).

Transvisionary
Transvisionary is that quality which enables a person to motivate others in such a way that the vision is transferred to them and they possess the vision as their own. Visions must be shared for people to feel useful and fulfilled.

Decisive
Do not be afraid to make hard, costly, unpopular decisions; trust God to help you make wise decisions. "No problem can withstand the assault of sustained thinking." (Voltaire) At some point, decisive action must be taken.

Uncomplicated
"Plan it BIG and plan it SIMPLE!" (James Orr) Jesus uncomplicated life and ministry (especially theological issues. (Matt. 22:37-40; John 14:6; Matt. 12:11,12; Luke 13:11-17; Luke 14:5. Read about the donkey story!)

Don't let the "Pharisees" and theologians complicate the issue! Do what needs to be done!

People-oriented Characteristics
"The worst sin toward our fellow creatures is not to hate them, but to be indifferent to them–that is the essence of inhumanity." (George Bernard Shaw)

"You will never be a leader unless you first learn to follow and be led" (Tiorio). Treat others as you want to be treated (Matt.7:12).

An effective leader collaborates, leads and works together with others for the greater good of the entire team and organization.

Exemplary and Able to Teach
Model the way; lead by example (I Tim. 4:12). Be consistent with God's standards, your values and level of responsibility. What you expect of others, require the same of yourself–and more!

"You can preach a better sermon with your life than with your lips" (Goldsmith). Be slow to anger!

Listens and Communicates Well

Listen. Keep silent long enough to get all the facts before you speak or act. Articulate your thoughts clearly, concisely, non-threateningly. By listening, you can develop the ability to understand and relate to the people and the culture in which you find yourself—whether that be a national, church, ministry or business culture.

Diplomatic, Tactful and Peace-Maker

"If it be possible, as much as lieth in you, live peaceably with all men" (Rom 12:18, KJV). Be a peace-maker rather than a trouble-maker who creates issues and problems among others. Handle matters without raising antagonism and hostility. "Blessed are the peacemakers..." (Matt.5:9).

Sensitive/Discerning, Fair/Just

Be keenly conscious, alert and consistent to the culture and environment you work in.

Be sensitive to people and their needs.

Discern your own strengths and weaknesses as well as those you work with; be considerate.

Evaluate with empathy, sympathetic understanding, wisdom, compassion, meekness.

Be fair, just, non-manipulating in dealing with people regardless of their position or status.

Serving with Humility, Compassion and Generosity

Serve, not your own interests, but the interests of others and ultimately God's interests with compassion, sensitivity and kindness—open heart and home (Phil.2:4; John 13:3-7).

Mother Teresa and Princess Diana are two examples of people who cared for the poor and the lepers.

Avoid excessive individualism, extreme isolation, self-serving, self-centered "empire-building", wealth-seeking.

Live and demonstrate a spirit of meekness. Serve by providing good leadership. Those who serve others serve best in a team. Servanthood, meekness, humility aren't weak characteristics! Jesus washed Peter's feet!

Lonely

"Leaders are much like eagles. ...They don't flock, you find them one at a time".

Do not betray, compromise or deny your calling, values and responsibility, even though it may cost you your friends or co-workers.

> "When the system is all important, in church or state, it is likely that the man who criticizes any part of it will be branded a heretic or a traitor... and yet perhaps the most important people in history are the courteous rebels. They are the mature and creative people" (Stephen Neill).

Oh, my friend, it's not what they take away from you that counts, it's what you do with what you have left! (Hubert Humphrey)

If a man does not keep pace with his companions, perhaps it is because he hears a different drummer. Let him step to the music which he hears, however measured or far away.

The path travelled in seeing the vision come to fruition is often very lonely. Leaders can be stripped of everything they have—often because they stood their ground when they could not compromise or deny their calling, values, purpose and responsibility—but they can pick up the pieces that are left over and build again—growth through adversity, pain and betrayal!

Loyal, Loving, Patient and Forgiving

Loyalty is something you give! Be true and loyal to others—they may become more loyal to you. However, do not compromise your values and purpose.

Be tolerant of people and their human natures. Accept delays, setbacks, etc. as part of life. See the reality and humanity of life. View each other's weaknesses and strengths from God's perspective.

The leader demonstrates loyalty through both good and bad times. He cannot walk away when a colleague fails in his/her responsibilities or suffers a setback in life.

"A friend loves at all times, and a brother is born for adversity" (Prov. 17:7). He cares and stands by that person.

"When you meet a man you judge him by his clothes. When you leave a man you judge him by his heart." (Old Russian Proverb)

Flexible, Versatile and Creative

Change is inevitable! Adjust your behavior and adapt to changing needs—of people, tasks, situations, team, environment, circumstances. If you have difficulty, determine and evaluate why. It may be that the proposed changes need to be modified or that you need to address your own fear of change.

You cannot direct the wind, but you can adjust the sails!

Be creative and original in solving problems; determine and implement alternatives as you envision what needs to be done, motivating people

to fulfill the purpose and to reach the objectives and goals.

Complimentary, Encourager, Empowerer

Encourage by telling people they are needed and their work is valuable. This motivates and reassures them, makes them feel significant, and builds confidence and the desire to do their best.

"Catch people doing something right! Then tell everyone about it!" Focus on strengths; buttress weaknesses. Expect and show high expectations.

Keep hope alive. Leaders are dealers in realistic hope (not false hope nor utopian)!

Provide necessary resources and authority; energize, edify and empower your followers. They will be encouraged and motivated to become competent along with a healthy self-esteem.

Influential, Attractive, Balanced

Motivate people to do better, to accomplish the vision and purpose, and to feel fulfilled.

Don't use manipulative, destructive power. Seek "win-win" situations (both sides benefit).

A leader is catalytic, capping the latent energy in his organization and activating the potential. He knows how to find the correct stimulus, energizes and motivates people, gives them a will to win and

a desire to belong to the group and turns the potential energy into active, productive, and exciting work! He knows the "match" to strike! Are you reflecting Jesus? Exude a positive attitude. Love, encourage, edify. Avoid gossip.

Integrity (the Heart of Character)

Be honest, credible and trustworthy. Keep your promises; be consistent; tell the truth; build trust. Degrees, titles, wealth, certificates, prestige, etc. don't make you credible–your character does!

Create credibility by...

- ... equipping, training, giving opportunities for your followers to lead and use their gifts and talents,
- ... encouraging them to develop their gifts, skills,
- ... giving credit where credit is due! Do it sincerely!
- ... exposing them to other successful leaders.

Do the right thing, no matter how inconvenient, unpopular or painful it may be.

"Blowing out your followers' candles won't make yours any brighter.

But as you use yours to light theirs, you not only provide light for them, but multiply the light of your own candle many times over." (Myron Rush)

Set high standards and values based on biblical principles and teachings. Live by them!

Create a good reputation rather than an image.

Lead with integrity, not craftiness or deceit.

God-oriented Characteristics

Success in life is not determined by position, but by character. Do you understand and know *God's purpose* for your life? It starts with God-awareness.

God-awareness with Gratitude

Resolve your own personal relationship with God. Accept Jesus Christ as the true Messiah, the Son of God, Saviour and Lord of your life.

Be continually aware of and follow the Holy Spirit's leading. It needs to be as natural as breathing. Listen to and obey the still, small voice deep within.

Have the faith that overcomes the emotional ups-and-downs, doubts, and discouragements.

Learn what the Bible teaches; how it relates to your life today; meditate on God's Word. Analyze the opinions of man-made denominations or religious organizations to ensure they are not in conflict with God and His inspired Word.

Keep in fellowship with God through prayer.

Have a quiet time with God. "The prayer of a righteous man is powerful and effective" (James 5:16). Don't get behind in your think-time!

Self-awareness/Self-esteem

What does God think of me? Have a proper perspective of yourself, based on God's viewpoint.

You were created in God's image! He prepared a unique plan and purpose for your life! Prayerfully discover it! It must not be self-centered!

When God wants to drill a man
And thrill a man
And skill a man,
When God wants to
mold a man
To play the noble's
part;

When He yearns with all His heart
To create so great and bold a man
That all the world should be amazed,
Watch His methods, watch His ways!
How He ruthlessly perfects
Whom He royally elects!
How He hammers him and hurts him
And with mighty blows converts him
Into trial shapes of clay which
Only God understands
While his tortured heart is crying,
And he lifts beseeching hands!
How He bends but never breaks
When his good He undertakes;
How He uses whom He chooses
And with every purpose fuses him;
By every act induces him
To try His splendor out–
God knows what He is about! (Oswald Sanders)

Common sense is your guide,
Veneered over with Christian sentiment.
But if once you receive a commission from
     Jesus Christ,
The memory of what God wants will always
     come like a goad;
And you will no longer be able to work for
     Him on the common sense basis.
                              (Oswald Chambers)

"Faithful is He that calls you who also will do it" (I Thess. 5:24). Enjoy life! "The joy of the Lord is your strength." (Neh. 8:10; John 10:10b)

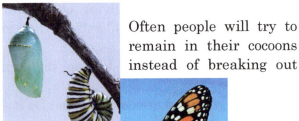

Often people will try to remain in their cocoons instead of breaking out of the cocoon and becoming the beautiful "butterfly" God intended the "caterpillar" to become!

God-given Intuitiveness

Use your five senses… and your intellect. Sharpen your memory! Balance it with verifiable facts, logic, emotions etc. "Examine all things; retain that which is good" (I Thess. 5:21). Trust God's inner voice!

Called

You know you are called and set apart by God for a particular purpose and mission. His divine assignment provides an anchor when turbulent storms of life try to overwhelm us.

It is easier to serve God without a vision,
Easier to work for God without a call;
Because then you are not bothered by
what God requires.

Leaders are people who cultivate a positive expression even when the going gets tough, for that is when the tough get going and demonstrate a positive expression.

Teachable and Emotionally Stable

Constantly learn new things that God teaches through His Word, nature, life, experience and other people. Avoid thinking you know it all!

Learn from good and bad experiences, adversity, mistakes and bad decisions. These create opportunities for new understanding, growth and change.

Keep well-grounded on God's Word. Know His peace, promises, and wise counsel. Maintain an attitude of prayer.

Stages and Development in Life's Journey

The following are stages in our journey as we become authentic leaders in our spheres of influence. Jesus said, "In the world ye shall have tribulation, but be of good cheer, I have overcome the world!" (John 16:33). As you come to the end of this study on the character of managerial leadership, where do you find yourself on your journey of a purposeful life – a life of growth as a leader?

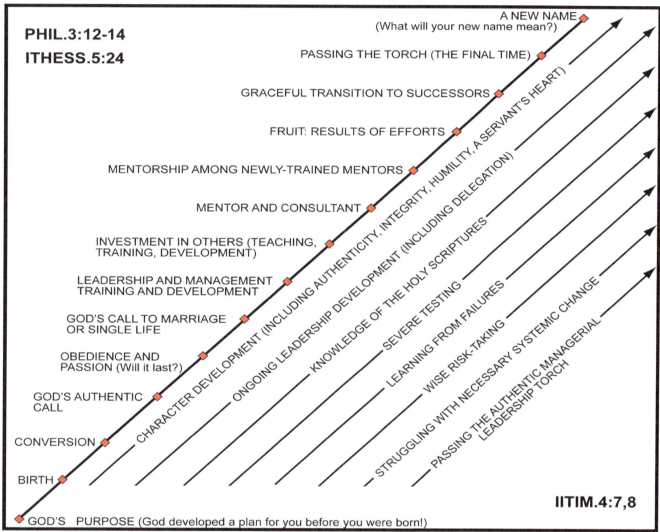

While travelling life's journey to fulfill God's purpose for you, beware of the dangers, pitfalls and snares that can bring you down. Some pitfalls and snares are:

1. Diverted vision
2. Loss of first love for God
3. Discouragement
4. Loneliness
5. Excess idealism
6. Joining the wrong crowd
7. Sexual temptation; marital conflicts; failure to maintain a healthy relationship with God and family
8. Lack of godly character such as godly ethics, honesty, integrity, humble heart; the development of ungodly characteristics such as: pride, arrogance and self-centeredness infiltrate one's life; setting a bad example
9. Love of money, possessions, covetousness
10. Failure to maintain your health
11. Abuse of authority and power; reckless and foolish risk-taking; impulsiveness
12. Failure to get up when you fall

(You can read about more pitfalls and snares in Section VI. The Snares.)

Realistic World-awareness

What does God think of His creation, the world? Learn all you can about the world (cultures, people groups, perspectives). Evaluate. "Examine all things; retain that which is good". (I Thess. 5:21; Eph. 1:17; Phil.4:8; I John 4:6; John 16:13a) Read. Listen. What is God doing?

Summary

The leader needs to have a servant's heart, but he remembers that he/she "serves" best by effectively and competently leading well! Godly character involves the development of servant leadership and living by a higher set of standards.

My friend Chester, told me of a recent survey in which persons 95 and over were asked, "What three things would you do differently if you had your life to live over again?" The participants of the survey almost unanimously came up with the following answer:
• I would reflect (think) more.
• I would risk more.
• I would be sure to do something that would outlive me and would benefit others.

Shouldn't this be the desire of each one of us as leaders—to leave a mark on history and to benefit those who followed us and to benefit the generations that followed ours after we have passed on? We are stewards of God's gifts and talents which He loans us and we will have to give an account as to what was accomplished in life and what was accomplished after death that benefited others because of our use of these gifts and talents.

Remember that character has a lot to do with whether you can persevere with tenacity *after the moment has passed.* Winston Churchill in his inspiring "Battle of Britain" radio broadcast challenged the British to win and

saved Britain and the free world in the process—but he told them that it would first take blood, toil, sweat and tears to win. He didn't promise them the battle would be easy, but he did promise victory—and they won!

"I have a dream that my four children will one day live in a nation where they will not be judged by the color of their skin but by the content of their *character*." (From speech given by Martin Luther King Jr., on the steps at the Lincoln Memorial in Washington D.C. USA, on August 28, 1963)

Jesus our Model Leader left His disciples to continue the work which He had begun and provided the Holy Spirit to be the Resource they could count on to get the job done and passed on to the next generation. We need to take the "torch" and pass it on to the next generation also—just as the leaders in the Holy Scriptures did to their next generations.

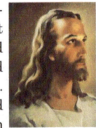

Assignment

1. What characteristics are strengths in your life, church, ministry, your leaders?

2. Which characteristics are weak or missing?

3. How are you going to strengthen the strong characteristics and buttress the weaknesses?

An authentic godly leader must know, study and understand the nine foundational pillars of the Holy Scriptures. Study carefully the next section.

Those who are the most resistant to change are the ones who need to change the most. (Mark Orr)

IV. THE NINE PILLARS OF THE HOLY SCRIPTURES

Every authentic Christian leader must have a clear understanding of the nine basic biblical doctrines or pillars of the Holy Scriptures upon which our true faith is built.

As a "Christian" leader, what do you believe? Why? Our doctrinal security and safety lie only in the Holy Scriptures inspired by God.

"All Scripture is God-breathed and is useful for teaching, rebuking, correcting and training in righteousness, so that the man of God may be thoroughly equipped for every good work." (II Timothy 3:16,17)

"Study to show thyself approved unto God, a workman that needeth not to be ashamed, **rightly** dividing the word of truth." (II Timothy 2:15)

Strong godly leaders are clear on what they believe. They interpret the Scriptures "**rightly**".

"*And the things that you have heard me say in the presence of many witnesses entrust to reliable (faithful, trustworthy) men and women who will also be QUALIFIED (ABLE, COMPETENT) to teach others also.*" (II Tim. 2:2)

Introduction
Theological Soundness and the 9 Dot Puzzle

Join these 9 dots with only 4 straight lines without lifting your pencil from the paper or without backing up.

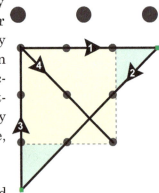

To solve it you had to go outside the imaginary box you created in your mind. Did you destroy the 9 dots? No! Often the solution to our practical problems lies outside of our imaginary box (tradition, culture, old paradigms).

Likewise we have to find new ways to fulfill God's purpose for us and our organizations and to get His work done while keeping the 9 dots (pillars of the faith) intact.

Liberty and grace create a new fence surrounding both God's established doctrinal absolutes and the additional area in which to work creatively. We must consider new situations and realities. We adapt new methodology, strategy, the 7 functions of managerial leadership, leadership training and development, etc. We have a new working reality in and outside the traditional box—but we keep the absolutes of the Holy Scriptures!

You don't have to be a theologian or seminary graduate to know the uncomplicated essence of what God teaches in His Word. A degree, diploma or clergy certificate does not guarantee that you know what these nine pillars are. So here they are to get you started in your study of God's Word. Look up and study the biblical references listed for each pillar. If you know these, you know the essentials of theology! Now, go and teach your followers!

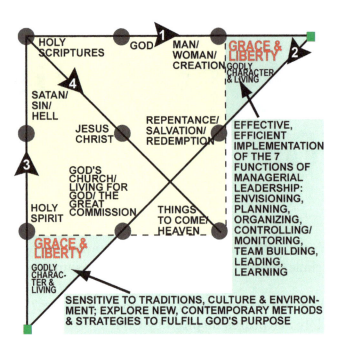

The Biblical Absolutes

Pillar 1: The Inspired Word of God, the Bible (the Holy Scriptures)...

It was originally written inspired directly by God the Holy Spirit. Its inspired writers came from different backgrounds and experience; yet it is completely consistent (II Tim. 3:16).

It is perfect, true, authoritative, eternal (Ps. 18:30; Ps. 119:89).

It is the book about God. It gives us His wisdom (Ps. 119:99,105,130; Matt.7:24,25; II Tim. 3:16).

It can be trusted as God's words to us (Ps. 33:4).

It reveals truth. It can be understood by anyone through the Holy Spirit that indwells every believer in Jesus Christ. (John 14:6; Psalms 119:30; Psalms 25:2)

It is the Christian's spiritual weapon. (Eph. 6:17). It must be read, honored, properly interpreted and obeyed. It helps us grow spiritually (Heb. 4:12; II Tim. 3:14-16).

It reveals God's rescue plan for man's salvation (Is. 9:6; Luke 19:10; I John 4:14).

It reveals what we should believe (John 20:30-31) and how we should live and behave (I Tim. 3:15).

It is relevant and cross-cultural to all people throughout all ages (Heb. 1:1; Act 18:28; II Cor. 2:12-16).

It is divided into the Old Testament that points to the coming Saviour and Messiah, and the New Testament that reveals Jesus Christ as the promised Messiah, Saviour and Lord (Is. 9:6; Rom. 1:2).

Note: Avoid the trap of complicating God's Holy Word. Christians have the propensity to go beyond what the Bible is really teaching. They complicate spiritual and Biblical matters. They often fail to consider the context in which God's Word is written. They bring in twisted interpretation influenced by their own carnal and biased thinking with fads that come and go in the Church. The Pharisees in Jesus' day were a prime example of this. Jesus was constantly facing this problem as He intermingled with those church leaders and theologians. It is no different today. We have many examples of pastors and ministry leaders twisting the Holy Scriptures to fit their thinking, fads, and even to promote and enrich themselves by misguiding their followers! Those who do so will face very *serious consequences* when they stand before a holy God to give an account. God's Word says, "Study to show thyself approved unto God, a workman that needeth not to be ashamed, RIGHTLY dividing the Word of Truth" (II Tim. 2:15). Jesus uncomplicated theology and Bible teaching and made its teachings clear! Today we still have theologians and preachers complicating it! Jesus identified what was important and taught in an uncomplicated, easy-to-understand manner. Examples: "Thou shalt love the Lord

thy God..." (Matt. 22:37-40; Luke 10:27); the donkey story (Luke 14:1-6); the woman at the well (John 4:1-30); the woman caught in adultery by the "religious leaders" (John 8:1-11); Thomas' question answered (John 14:6); etc.

Pillar 2: God

God is eternal ("In the beginning God...") and unchangeable. He is a spirit and alive. (Ps. 90:2; Is. 40:28; Mal. 3:6; John 4:24; Heb. 11:3)

God created all and He provides for and sustains His creation. (Heb. 11:3; Acts 14:17; Ps. 19:1; Jer. 32:17; Ps. 71:5)

God's handiwork is seen in creation and very specially in the creation of man/woman in His image! (Gen. 1:26; Ps. 19:1; Ps. 50:1)

God is concerned with the least as well as the greatest and cares about each. He loves you! (I John 4:8-10; Ps. 8:2)

God is at work restoring a fallen world to freedom and perfection—a new heaven and a new earth. (Heb. 10:17,18; John 3:16; Rom. 11:33; Rev. 21:1)

God is omnipotent (meaning "all-powerful") and omniscient (meaning "He knows everything"). God is King of Kings. Note: There are a few things God cannot do. For example, He cannot lie, sin, or remember forgiven sin! (Ps. 147:5; Deut.

32:4; Luke 1:37; I Tim. 6:15; Heb. 10:17,18; Rev. 15:3)

God is holy, just, hates sin and unrighteousness and will judge. Yet, in His very nature, God is love. (Is. 6:3; Deut. 32:4)

God is intimate. He is our Father. A man or woman can be adopted by Him. He is approachable—the father of those who come back to him in repentance and through the mediation of Jesus Christ. ("Our Father Who art in heaven, hallowed be Thy name..." Matt. 6:9-13). A believer can approach God with freedom and confidence. (Gen. 17:1; Rom. 8:15; John 3:16; Eph. 1:5; I Tim. 4:10)

God's person and character is shown supremely through Jesus Christ His Son. (I John 4:8-10; Rom. 5:8; John 3:16)

God is three in one: Father, Son and Holy Spirit. He reveals Himself in three distinct and inseparable ways. (Eph. 1:17; Rev. 1:8; Matt. 28:19)

God is pleased to be worshipped by His creation; for He alone is the only true and living God.

God is good and helps His people when they are in trouble. He is our rock! He is our hope! (Ps. 19:14; Ps. 8:2; Ps. 34:8; Ps. 46:1; Ps. 62:6; Deut. 32:4)

God chooses believers to be co-workers with Him! (I John 4:8-10; I Cor. 3:9)

Note: No man can take the place of God. If man tries he will eventually suffer very *serious consequences.* No church leader, ministry leader, government nor secular authority can play God. God alone is to be the focus of our worship and praise. He alone is to be the center of our lives. (Ps. 97:6; Ps. 99:9; James 4:12)

Pillar 3: Man and Woman—God's special creation...

We are unique—the pinnacle of God's creation. (Gen. 1:26,27; Ps. 139:14-16)

We can know and relate with our Creator, God. He planned our existence before our conception. (Gal. 4:6,7; John 10:14,15)

 We were created in God's image (Gen. 1:26,27). We are both spiritual and physical beings (Ps. 139:14-16).

We were given orders to care for God's creation. (Gen. 2:15; Ps. 8:3-8)

We fell into a state of moral rebellion against God. We became separated from Him as a result of the Fall. (Rom. 3:23)

We have sinned and strayed away from God's original plan for man. (Is. 53:6)

We can come back to God through the mediator He provided in His Son, Jesus Christ. (I Cor. 15:22; I John 5:13)

We were created equal. We are to live within a structure God ordained for family order and work. (Eph. 5:22-33)

We were created to love, to be loved, and to meet each other's needs and live purposeful lives. (I John 3:11, 16-18)

Pillar 4: Satan, Sin and Hell
Satan...

Satan is a fallen angel. His final dwelling will be Hell (Is. 14:12; Rev. 12:7-9; 20:2,10). Satan is a real personality. His powers and wicked purposes are real (Eph. 6:12). Satan is a deceiver, tempter, schemer and betrayer. He often appears as an "angel of light". (Matt. 16:23; II Cor. 11:14; I Thess. 3:5; II Thess. 2:9,10)

Satan is the enemy of God. Satan has a grip on the whole world. Our struggle is against Satan's spiritual forces of evil—but God is greater! (I John 5:19; Eph. 6:12; Ps. 91:1)

Satan is at work in the world and creates much evil. He knows his time is short. He's already condemned. (I John 3:8; John 14:30; 16:11)

Satan will be vanquished for all time at the end—in the lake of fire, hell. (Rev. 20:2,10)

Satan is the Christian's enemy and the deceiving monster of the heavens and the earth (I Peter 5:8,9; Rev. 12:9; 20:2). Satan constantly tries to deceive us and even uses Scripture to distort God's true word. He confuses and tries to blind us from God's truth. (I Tim. 4:1,2)

Sin...
Sin has contaminated all mankind. (Rom. 3:23)

Sin is the barrier that cuts us off from God and puts us under God's judgment. (Is. 59:2)

Sin has deadened our hearts' attitude and conscience towards obeying God's commands. (Eph. 4:17-19; 1 Tim. 4:1,2)

Sin is defined through God's ten commandments which are the moral standards that show how impossible it is to meet God's requirements—hence the need for a Saviour, the sacrificial Lamb. (Exod. 20:1-17; Heb. 9:28; 10:12; I Peter 3:18)

Hell, The Lake Of Fire...
It was prepared for Satan and his fallen angels (II Peter 2:4), It will be the final place of all those who reject God and His solution for man's redemption through Jesus 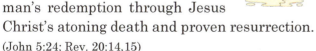 Christ's atoning death and proven resurrection. (John 5:24; Rev. 20:14,15)

> How do we get back to God? Can we be restored and meet God's requirements? Yes, through Jesus Christ, God's Son. Jesus came to destroy the devil's control and to redeem us to God.

Pillar 5: Jesus Christ—God's Son, God's Gift, our Saviour and Redeemer...

He is God, a member of the Trinity—Father, Son and Holy Spirit. He existed at the beginning with God. Jesus is in nature both God and man. This is why His sacrifice is perfect. (John 1:1,2; Phil.2:9,10; Heb. 9:28)

He is the Messiah promised in the Old Testament Scriptures. He fulfilled the Law's requirements for us. (Is. 7:14; 53:5,6)

He was born by supernatural conception through the virgin Mary. Her pregnancy was not the result of any human action, but by the direct action of the Holy Spirit. He was her first born and born without sin. (Matt. 1:18; Luke 1:31,34-35)

He was sent to earth by God to make possible our way back to Him. Jesus lived as a man, died for mankind, rose again and returned to His Father. He is our mediator! (John 3:16,17; John 5:24; Rom. 6:23; I Tim. 2:5,6)

He invites us to accept Him as our Saviour and calls us to follow and obey Him—yet doesn't force us. (Matt. 16:24)

His life reveals God's character. (John 14:8,9; Heb. 7:26)

He is the head of the church. He is the highest authority. He is sinless and holy. He is coming again. (Eph. 5:23; Heb. 4:15; Heb. 7:26)

His death and resurrection broke the control of Satan over creation. Jesus Christ provides a way back to God and the remedy for our salvation. (John 5:24, 26: 14:6)

He will return for the redeemed church and also as the Judge of the whole earth. (Matt. 24:30:

Mark 13:26; Titus 2:13; Acts 10:42)

He made it clear that judgement hinges on our acceptance or rejection of Him. (John 3:16,17; John 14:6)

He enables and strengthens the believers to fulfill His purpose and calling, and to accomplish all tasks, ministry and responsibilities approved by God. (Is. 35:5,6; Phil. 4:13)

He is truly the greatest leader that ever lived. He led with a "servant's heart". His aim as a leader was to transform and make something out of His followers. "I will make (a process) you (to become) fishers of men..."–something useful of your life... being a part of Jesus' work by learning to have a servant's heart to do His work or as Jesus put it to Peter, "If you don't let Me give you an example by washing your feet, you will have no part with me!" (John 13:1-17). Peter learned this lesson! He wanted to be a part of Jesus' work by demonstrating a servant attitude and heart!

Pillar 6: Repentance and Salvation

Salvation is found in Jesus Christ alone (Acts 4:12; Titus 3:4-7). First of all, we must accept Jesus Christ as the true Messiah, the Son of God, Saviour, Mediator and Lord of our lives. This is the only way back to God!

Sin's pardon is provided through the death and resurrection of Jesus Christ, our Savior and Mediator. (Rom. 6:5-10; I Peter 3:21,22; I Tim. 2:5)

God's plan and provision for salvation spans eternity. (Eph. 1:11; II Peter 3:9)

God made man for Himself. He wants him back in fellowship with Him. He wants our worship. We worship, not only by praising, but by doing

the work He purposed for us before we were born! (John 14:6; 4:23; Rom. 3: 21-24; Matt. 24:46)

God's way to salvation is provided through Jesus Christ alone. Through Him we are born again. (Acts 16:31-33; Eph. 1:17; Eph. 2:8,9; John 3:3-7)

Jesus' death and resurrection brings forgiveness of our sin and breaks down the barrier between God and man. By faith we must accept this forgiveness by trusting in Jesus Christ. (Col. 1:13,14)

Jesus' resurrection brings us new life. He is a living Saviour whom we can know and trust. He mediates for us (John 1:12). He understands us.

Salvation restores our relationship with God. We cannot be separated from the love of God. We are made free from any charge against us. We have been bought with a price. We belong to God. We can rejoice in our redemption and forgiveness. (Rom. 8:25-39; I Cor. 12:27; I Cor. 6:19,20)

We must determine to live for Him and to be obedient to His call. (Acts 2:38; Luke 3:7,8; Luke 13:35; Eph. 4:1; Rev. 3:20,21)

There is rejoicing in heaven when a sinner repents and is saved. Fellowship with God is restored (Luke 15:7). "...he is a new creation; the old has gone, the new has come!" (2 Cor. 5:17,NIV)

To become a godly leader you must first make your peace with God! Then you can sing, "It is well with my soul!"

Pillar 7: The Holy Spirit

He is God, equal to God the Father and God the Son. (John 15:26; John 16:13-15)

After Pentecost He indwells every born-again believer. He never leaves him. He fills and empowers him for service and fruit bearing. (Acts 1:8; Matt. 7:19,20; I

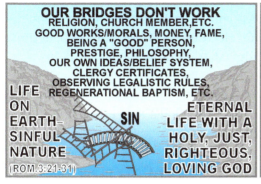

Adapted from the original chalk art of James Orr

Cor. 12:1,4-11; Luke 3:16; Titus 3:5; Gal. 5:22,23—nine fruits!)

He glorifies Christ. He convicts of sin. He regenerates and commissions the believer for productive service (Acts 5:3,4; John 16:7-14). He teaches, guides, empowers, sanctifies and opens our spiritual eyes. He is involved in our salvation. He lives within us. (Rom. 8:11; Rom. 15:16; I Cor. 2:10; 6:19)

He is the Comforter sent by God the Father to teach us all things (John 14:26; John 15:26). He brings to remembrance what Jesus taught while on this earth. (John 14:26)

He gives gifts to Christians for service to benefit others (serving, teaching, encouraging, giving money, leadership, management, mercy, wisdom, knowledge, faith, healing, miracles, prophecy, distinguishing between spirits, speaking in tongues, interpretation of tongues, apostles, prophets, helps, administration, evangelists, pastors). No one possesses all the gifts. But we all have a part—a special purpose. No one is left out of helping to build God's church here on earth. (Rom. 12:6-8; I Cor. 12:4-11; Eph. 4:11-13; I Peter 4:10,11)

Pillar 8: Things to come, Heaven
God is in control of His world and creation. He will bring it to an end in His own time. (II Chr. 20:6; Mark 13:32,33; Matt. 24:36)
God will bring all humankind to face final judgment. (Heb. 9:27: Rev. 7:9-12)
God will send Jesus Christ again as King and

Judge. (Matt. 16:27; Matt. 25:32; I Cor. 4:5)

God will separate His own redeemed creation to be united with Himself. There will be a new heaven and a new earth. Pain, betrayal, trials, sin, suffering and death will be no more! (Rev. 22:14,15; Matt 25:32; Rev. 21:1-4; Rev. 7:17; Col. 3:1-5; II Peter 3:13)

God's Son, Jesus Christ, is preparing a glorious place for believers. (John 14:1-3)

God will give His redeemed children a new special name! What will yours mean? It may describe how you lived for Him. (Rev. 2:17; 3:12)

Jesus Christ will be declared by all to be Lord and Christ. (Phil. 2:10,11)

By accepting Jesus Christ as your Saviour, you are guaranteed citizenship in Heaven! (John 14:6; Phil. 3:20; John 3:3). All races will be welcomed equally in heaven (Rom. 10:12,13); it is for the forgiven. No sin or suffering will be present in  heaven. It has no sun or sea. It is forever eternal. (Rev. 15:2; 21:1,23; Rev. 21:4; Rev. 22:5)

Pillar 9: God's Church, Living for God and the Great Commission
The Church...
The Church is the bride of Christ, God's people

through all ages, a family dependent on one another. (Rev. 21:2; Acts 2:42-47)

It will be fully united with Christ when He comes to rapture it for Himself. God the Father will determine when the appropriate time will be. We must occupy (do God's business) until He comes. (Matt. 24:36, 44-47; Acts 1:10,11)

It was established by God, with Christ as the head. It is a spiritual building made up of living stones. Jesus died for and cares for His Church. (I Peter 2:4,5; Eph. 2:20-22; Acts 20:28 Matt. 16:16-19; John 14:6)

It is to be God's people on earth, living for His glory and representing Him well. God is pleased when we meet together as believers to learn about His Word, to praise Him, to fellowship together, and to encourage one another in the faith. (Matt. 22:37-40; Matt. 28:19-20)

It is to be constantly preparing competent leaders (Titus 1:5; II Tim. 2:2).

Note: God's Church is not a particular denomination. No one can be an owner of God's Church, nor act as the god of a church. There is only one owner and one God, the God Almighty of the Holy Scriptures. He said, "I will build MY Church..." Religious denominations are man-made structures that have been set up throughout history. They come and go; they rise and fall. Some have accepted God's truth as written in the Holy Scriptures; others only a portion of God's Word; and others have departed completely from God's Word. Before joining a religious group, we must ensure it teaches the *whole* Word of God; otherwise we should not join it. We need to be sure man-made "pet ideas" and practices are not added to God's Word as doctrines. Arrogant religious leaders in Jesus' day twisted the Scriptures to fit their own "pet notions" so that they could keep their power, prestige and popularity along with their

"better-than-you" attitude (this even happens today!)—but He rebuked them for their actions and attitude. (Matt. 23:13-15, 27; Rev. 22:18,19)

Living for God
We are called to be God's special people (I Peter 2:9,10; John 15:16)

We are sinners saved by God's grace. (Eph. 2:8.9)
We are born of God therefore Satan cannot touch us (I John 5:18).
We are members together of God's family. (Rom. 8:16; Gal. 3:28)

We are His Church, citizens of heaven temporarily living on earth as His ambassadors and servants. (Phil. 3:20)

We have a guidebook, the Holy Scriptures. Our link to God is through prayer. (Ps. 119:9; John 2:1)

If we are born-again believers, we are indwelt by the Holy Spirit who enables us to grow more like Jesus. God keeps improving the work He is doing in us and comforts us as He works in our lives and character. (John 3:1-8; I Cor. 6:17-20)

After conversion comes the symbol of baptism which is an outward witness of the inward reality that the experience of being born-again did indeed take place in your life. The symbol of baptism alone does not save us. It is a testimony after conversion, after you received Jesus as your Saviour. (I Cor. 11:28,29; Rom. 6:3,4; Matt. 26:26-28; Matt. 28:19)
We must observe the Lord's Supper to remind us of His death and resurrection and the blood He shed for us.

We are to reflect God's love and character. "Be ye holy as He is holy". (I John 3:17; James 1:27; 1 Peter 1:16)

We are not to tolerate racial prejudice and inequality. (John 4:1-42) We are not to tolerate false cults and teachings that violate the truth taught in God's word. (Acts 20:28-30; I Thess. 5:21; Matt. 7:15)

We are to bear fruit, show spiritual growth, service, giving and godly character (Gal. 5:22,23; Gal. 6:9,10).

We will meet Jesus face to face when God raptures the Church and be held accountable as to whether the purpose for which God placed you on earth was faithfully well done. (Matt. 25:21; I Thess. 4:17)

We will face trials and tribulations as we serve Him on earth. We are promised grace and mercy in time of need and God will even send angels in physical, voice or spirit form to serve Christians in times of distress. Warning: Angels are God's messengers and obey His biding. They don't save our souls nor do they mediate between God and man. That role belongs only to Jesus Christ, our only Savior and Mediator. (Matt. 11:29,30; II Cor. 1:3,4; John 16:33; Heb. 4:16; Rev. 22:8,9; I Cor. 6:3; I John 4:14)

We receive special gifts, talents and skills from God through the Holy Spirit that empower us to fulfill His particular and unique purpose for us individually and collectively in our organizations, churches and ministries. (I Cor. 12:1-11)

Fulfilling The Great Commission

The Great Commission is God's overall purpose for us. Go into all the world (Matt. 28:18-20).

Go into towns/villages—Jesus' compassion (Matt. 9:35-38).

Make (It's a time-taking process!) disciples (Matt.28:18). Make fishers of men ("I will MAKE"—Matt. 4:19).

Make competent leaders (II Tim. 2:2).

Be ambassadors for God (II Cor. 5:20)

Be competent to teach others (Titus 1:5; II Tim. 2:2)

Declare His glory unto all nations. (Is. 66:19; Matt. 5:16; John 15:8: I Cor. 6:20)

"Love the Lord your God with all your heart... Love your neighbor as yourself." (Matt. 22;34-40; Mark 12:28-31; Luke 10:25-27)

Occupy (do God's business) until I come. (Luke 19:13 KJV; John 4:35-38)

Become what God created you to be. You have the responsibility to discover His purpose for your life! Then take appropriate action to go about fulfilling that purpose. In prayer ask God to reveal His purpose for you. The Holy Scriptures and prayer will help you a lot!

For example, it tells you that you were planned by God for His pleasure, to be a part of His family, to become like Jesus, molded and shaped to serve God in fulfilling a purposeful mission or calling. He has already endowed you with special talents, abilities and gifts that makes you a unique personality (Ps. 139:15,16).

Life becomes meaningful when you discover and implement His purpose. "What am I here on earth in this location to accomplish?" You don't have to spend time on other things. You become focused. You become motivated. You enjoy preparing to give a good account when you arrive in eternity. Remember the "parable of the talents"? (Matt. 25:20-21)

Warning: It is fatal to think that God's goal for your life is only prosperity and earthly material success; those are self-centered, temporary goals which are not scripturally based. However, He did promise to provide all your needs as you fulfill His purpose. (Phil.4:19)

In God's eyes you are a success when you please Him by fulfilling His purpose for your life. Obedience glorifies Him. This obedience is the act of truly worshipping God and you will not only receive His smile but He will call you His friend (John 15:15; Phil. 2:5-11). This friendship means you care about what God cares about. For example, God cares about people. When you step into eternity and give your account, God will not ask about your material possessions and prestige you gained, but about how you treated other people and how you used your talents and resources to help others. Did you love them and share focused time with them and build them up? Serving God and others is the only path to real significance. A vision without the anchor of purpose is like building on sand.

> He (God) created the church to meet your 5 deepest needs: a purpose to live for, people to live with, principles to live by, a profession to live out, and power to live on. ...God's purpose for His church is identical to His five purposes for you. Worship helps you focus on God; fellowship helps you face life's problems; discipleship helps fortify your faith; ministry helps find your talents; evangelism helps fulfill your mission. God has called you to do something that matters, something that makes a difference. In obeying that call you choose significance instead of worldly material success and prestige.

> Not to listen to your call is a self-inflicted spiritual crime of omission. Not to allow others to act on theirs is a victim-inflicted spiritual crime of commission.

We will not be able to withstand the severe tests of resistance or opposition with only the vision! Passion comes with purpose—something towards which you are always striving to accomplish that is significant.

Help those around you who are slowly dying inside (including Christians) because they have no meaningful purpose in life and work. They have not discovered it even though God planned their existence and purpose before they were conceived! Discover it! (Psalm 139:1-16)

The Supreme Biblical Model...

Our Saviour and Lord Jesus, our Perfect Model Leader fulfilled God's calling and exemplified godly character.

He was commissioned by God. He received confirmation before He began to lead publicly (Matt. 3:13-17). He received power through obedience and service to the Father (John 4:34; Phil.2:5-11).

He was purpose-oriented and completed the work God gave Him to do (John 17:4). Jesus said on the cross, "It is finished" (John 19:30)

He was a servant of His Father (John 4:34; John 5:30; John 6:36). He served others by leading well, in obedience to His Father. (John 10:11-18)

He demonstrated that only truly strong leaders can be truly gentle. (Mark 14:43-50)

He was a rugged pioneer. A pioneer works alone at first and faces unfamiliar, unexpected circumstances. He is motivated with the burning inner prodding to blaze a trail for others to follow.

He was a risk-taker. He searched for opportunities. He invested His major resources in 12 men.

He left all His heavenly privileges to live as a humble servant in obedience to His Father until death (Phil. 2.5-11).

He was people-oriented. He placed human needs before the status quo, traditions, and customs. He loved people and spoke the truth in love. He forgave others. He expressed anger in healthy ways.

He established communication with His fellow-men and with God. He related to the lowly as well as those of status.

He modelled the way. He left a "legacy" for everyone throughout the ages to follow.

He demonstrated courage to cope in spite of criticism, opposition and the "bitter cup". He was the "cross-bearer". He did not ask anyone to do or to endure what He Himself was not willing to do or endure.

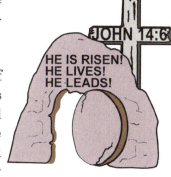

He gave generously of Himself. He gave His all. He gave His all for you and me. He mediates for you and me. He left the Holy Spirit to be the counsellor, empowerer, guide, protector…for you and me.

In Jesus' strategy there were no secrets. He did His work without complicating the Holy Scriptures and without creating divisions and destruction in God's work!

These doctrines and themes make up the 9 pillars of our faith! We cannot destroy or weaken any one of these pillars. We cannot add our traditions, customs and pet ideas and call them doctrines; the **consequences** are serious! True Christian leaders know what these pillars are and embrace them. They ensure their followers know and are faithful to them. However we must use contemporary methods and strategies to be effective in accomplishing the Great Commission. We must get out of our old "boxes" without denying the "Nine pillars" of truth—the absolutes that support our faith! Step out of the crowd! Discover God's purpose for you; then live it out for God and others as you demonstrate godly character by example and integrity.

Invest in Training Godly Leaders

God was constantly looking for, finding, choosing and training men and women to take on leadership challenges. "I looked for a man to stand in the gap…" (Ezek. 22:30).

Intensive training and preparation went into the lives of Bible characters; none were "born" with some special leadership "genes"! God did not "snap" His fingers and lo-and-behold He had an effective, tenacious leader of character and integrity. They were "made" in "the school of hard knocks" where God's gifts, talents and character-building were developed in their lives.

Pressure often reveals flaws, defects, weaknesses in our character. It also reveals our strengths, giftedness and maturity of character.

Consider the following biblical characters.

Joseph: the Prime Minister with godly conviction & ethics
- He endured pressure and unpopularity.
- He was a man of godly conviction.
- He was a man of sound judgment, shrewd, and intelligent (Genesis 41:39,40)
- He was industrious and not afraid of hard work.
- He could dream, imagine, and be creative.
- He was a first-class administrator, and a good organizer.
- He was a man of conviction.
- He learned by experience.
- He was distinctively different.
- He was a man that suffered even when he was right.
- Above all, he was a man of moral integrity.

Nehemiah: the Persistent Architect
- He determined the need.
- He sought the will of God.
- He was a teambuilder who enlisted others. He

organized the work and delegated the necessary authority to accomplish the task.

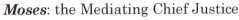

- He transmitted the vision to others and motivated others.
- His deep-rooted commitment to God's calling was essential to withstand his enemies and opposing forces.
- He set the example for the people to follow.
- He remained focused on the task. The goal was accomplished without compromise in 52 days!

Joshua: the Optimistic Commander-in-Chief
- He proved he was first a follower.
- He was a well-tried and prepared soldier, having Moses as his teacher and mentor.
- He was no defeatist or pessimist. In spite of what the majority of the group said, he was the man who said, "We can do it!"
- He knew God! He chose to follow and to serve God. "As for me and my house, we will serve the Lord."
- He believed in the power of God to accomplish the impossible.

Samson: the Tenacious Resistance Leader
- He accepted the task God had matched for him.
- He was a man who did not surrender to the tides of drift, faint endeavour, or feeble impulse. He faced the real enemy with the power of the Spirit of God.
- He was very human.
- Although he tragically failed in careless conduct, he proved God's forgiveness and made a comeback.
- He knew the source of his strength—Almighty God—rather than believing he had the power alone.
- He knew his moment to act and went through with it.

Moses: the Mediating Chief Justice

Field-Marshal Montgomery described Moses as the greatest leader that ever lived. Sir Winston Churchill said Moses was the greatest of the prophets who spoke in person to the God of Israel.
- He was a man of God, matched to the moment of God.
- He made mistakes.
- Although he had exceptional good education, he was ultimately trained in the solitude and loneliness of the desert. Often this is where the quality and fine-tuning of character occurs. He had to mature and ripen for the responsibility and moment of God.
- He was in constant touch with God.
- He was a very human man who learned to conquer his temptations and outgrow his weaknesses; he learned self-mastery.
- He admitted his weaknesses.
- He learned to use authority and power in a tolerant and responsible way.
- He had a forgiving heart.
- Little noticed about Moses' character was that he was the "attorney" and "advocate" of the people even though they "got under his skin" so often.

Esther: the Courageous Mediator
- She was a woman of faith and moral courage.
- She was a woman trained successfully by a mentor, Mordecai.

- She was a woman who knew, felt, and did the will of God under great risk.
- She was a woman gripped by the true value of life and death.
- She understood the principle of continuity—concern for the next generation.
- She was a woman who made a significant impact on her people.

Rebecca: A Beloved Wife (Gen. 22:23; chapters 24-27)

Sarah: A Century of Marriage! (Gen. 12-23; 46:17; Num. 26:45)

Daniel: the Competent Spokesman
- He was a man of moral and physical power.
- He was mentally sharp, alert, teachable, well-informed.
- He was not "hung up" on whether a Christian should be part of the political life of the country—if God willed it, he did it!
- He was a man of discernment and good judgment.
- He worshipped his God in private and served His Creator in public.
- He was proficient socially, and knew how to relate to others.
- Compromise or a "double standard" were not part of his lifestyle.
- He was spiritually and physically attractive.
- He was a man who could not be "bought." He was not "for sale."
- He was able to stand alone.
- He was a man of faith and principles.
- He was a decision-maker.
- He was a man of good habits and maintained good health.
- Although he was not popular, he had some close quality friends who provided encouragement and fellowship during his lonely times.

David: the Humble King
- He inspired affection; people identified with him.
- He was a man of the people; he led from within the group.
- He was human and natural.
- He was vulnerable; the people saw a reflection of themselves in his weaknesses.
- He was courageous.
- He was sympathetic and under-

stood the problems of others.
- He was a man of magnanimity, no hint of vindictiveness or personal triumph when his enemy finally fell.
- He was a man after God's own heart! What a crown to wear! In spite of many personal failures which had far-reaching consequences, he always returned to the Lord he loved.

Deborah: A Discerning, Competent Judge (Judges 4 & 5)

Ruth: Submission with godly character (Book of Ruth)

Naomi: A loving, gracious and influential mentor (Book of Ruth)

Abigail: An astute and wise politician (I Sam. 25; 2 Sam. 3:3)

Eve: A suitable helper and partner (Gen. 2:18)

Samuel: the Obedient Archbishop

- He prayed for his people.
- He was a reformer.
- He was a counsellor.
- He mixed with the people.
- He was a learner and respected the training of a leader.
- He went along with God's subtle and wisely crafted plan to find and anoint David.
- He was an influencer and respected young people. However, he died before he could see how the young boy, David whom he anointed to become the chosen king of Israel, would reign.
- He had family problems.
- He was a man who could unite people, retaining their honour from their hearts and without demand. He was respected by the people.

John the Baptist: the Frugal Reformer
- He was a trailblazer for greater men!

- He was a bold, uncompromising, significant, meaningful voice influencing the moral, social and spiritual life of his country.
- He was disgusted with the religiosity of the day and had hard words even for the bullying clergy of the day.
- He wielded great influence, although he never had a "position" of power. Influence was the result of his character that went to a deeper level than power.
- A man with both authority and profound humility, he could recognize the greatness of another—a rare combination these days.
- He humbly recognized the One to replace him.
- He was a man of simple lifestyle—materialism was not for him. He did not consider a high lifestyle was owed to him as so many clergy and so-called missionaries and Christian workers require today!
- He paid dearly for his godly convictions by being executed.

Timothy: the Godly Equipper

- Timothy was weak physically, timid, and shy.
- He was an ordinary individual through whom God did extraordinary things.
- He exemplified godly character in speech, conduct, love, faith, and purity.
- God was great, supreme, and sovereign to Timothy.
- He committed (truly delegated) the continuance of the ministry to competent men. (2 Tim.2:2)

Simon Peter: the Courageous Businessman

- Peter was a hard-working, prosperous fisherman who was made great by his Master.
- Whenever Peter would fall, he would rise again.
- In spite of his compulsive, spontaneous verbiage, his hot-headedness, his impulsive and fiery nature, and all his failures, Simon Peter developed a personal relationship with his Lord.
- His strong, unmovable faith was an example for the other disciples and converts after Jesus' resurrection and ascension.
- In spite of persecution, opposition, and hardship, Peter's faith and deep commitment to his Lord were an anchor in the storms of life.
- Peter gave his life in martyrdom.

Anna: Prophetess working in the temple; possessed the extraordinary gift of prophecy (Luke 2:36-38)

Dorcas, (Tabitha): A kind and serving woman full of good works; a deaconess who ministered by giving and serving; an early Mother Teresa (Acts 9:36-43)

Euodia & Syntyche: Hard-working church leaders (Phil. 4:2,3)

Phoebe: A faithful deaconess (Romans 16:1,2)

Lydia: A businesswoman, charter member of the church in Philippi (Acts 16:13-15)

Philip's four daughters: all four were prophetesses, pioneers in church-planting (Acts 21:8,9)

Priscilla: a risk-taker; fellow-worker and labourer for Christ; research studies indicate she was an evangelist and teacher (Rom.16:3)

Tryphena and Tryphosa: slaves who laboured in the Lord (Rom.16:12)

Mary, mother of Jesus: Courageous, obedient, and faithful. She believed and accepted God's plan (the four Gospels—Matthew, Mark, Luke, John)

Paul the Apostle: a Bold Missionary Explorer
The Apostle Paul knew keenly what it was like to be lonely, hungry, and deprived of the essentials of life. He took beatings, persecution, dangers, and all kinds of perils as a perpetual accompaniment in his ministry.

- He was a delegator.
- He truly had a saint's and pastor's heart.
- He was an equipper of others.
- He was one of the greatest strategists in Christian work since Christ walked this earth. He had an eye for the grand design, yet was a tactician with skill for detail. He had exceptional skill at being a dogmatist and a pragmatist combined.
- Paul never looked back.
- He was flexible, practical, reasonable, and consistent. He had a sense of discretion and self-adaptation. He had no class, color, race or culture barriers. He was at home with master or servant and with men of different races and peoples. His strategy and tactics are hard to match!

Jesus said to his disciples, "I will 'make' you to become fishers of men". It is a "making" process—sometimes a very long one! Risks were taken. A high price was always paid; yet the investment was always well worth it.

We need to develop an action-oriented working strategy, act on it and obey God in this matter. We need to invest in men and women on a personal level who will begin to resolve this crisis of leadership training that exists in our churches, ministries, societies and governments.

Leadership training is not glamorous. It demands a personal price to be paid. The loneliness, sacrifice, personal cost and passion involved is often misunderstood by well-meaning Christians who demand instant visual and glamorous results... but long-range you get leaders like the examples listed! God is procuring men and women who

will invest their lives and financial resources in this. Will you be one of them? God is looking for men and women who will pray for and encourage those who do the training and for those who finance the cost. Will you be one of them? God is looking for those who have the tenacity to be involved in this tedious endeavor. It will be fruitful long-range! Will you be one of these investors? Where are the men and women to be trained? They are all around you!

Straying from the Nine Pillars
The Bypass
Authentic Christianity teaches substitutionary atonement (John 3:16; Romans 3:23; Romans 6:23; Romans 5:1-21). However, many people choose to bypass the basics of Christianity. It becomes fluffy, self-centred, egotistical, hypocritical (faking) "Christianity".

Legalism
(Turning customs, ideas and personal habits into false doctrines and dogmas)

Another deviation from the nine pillars is the thinking that there are more "pillars". In oth-

● *The red dots show some of the many "doctrines" men have added.*

er words, the false belief is that God's Word is not sufficient and that men know better than God what needs to be added! This can be just as "dangerous" as the bypass.

Jesus did not waste His divinity on stupidity! The Pharisees and theologians of his time tried to trap Him and to complicate theology. They thought they had cornered Him when they told Jesus that a donkey had fallen into a pit on the Sabbath. The donkey might die before the next day when they could "lawfully" remove it from the pit. Jesus could have performed a miracle to keep the donkey alive until the next day or maybe give the donkey enough strength and power to get out by itself. Jesus could have formed a committee to discuss all the various ways to deal with the situation! The Pharisees were very certain that they had trapped Him. Instead, Jesus told them to pull the donkey out of the pit! What a simple, uncomplicated answer! Did He break the law or was He applying the law in a practical, realistic manner that would bring the balance between law and grace?

On another occasion, the courageous, yet still confused Thomas, asked the question, "What is the way to eternal life?" Instead of sending him to the "School of the Prophets" for four years of theological study, Jesus gave Thomas a short answer, "I am the way, the truth and the life. No one comes to the Father but by Me." (John 14:6). This answer has uncomplicated and impacted millions of men and women who have needed an uncomplicated and direct answer to their spiritual needs!

Don't let the modern-day Pharisees, theologians and religious leaders complicate the issues. Don't let legalistic idealism control and dominate. If you have studied and embraced the nine pillars of God's inspired Holy Scriptures you know the essentials of theology!

Materialism

Another deviation from the nine pillars is the worship of materialism. God commanded that there be no other gods before Him. However, in

some cultures or regions, there is more importance on materialistic endeavors. Material things are of greater importance. This is a very subtle deviation because those who have fallen into the trap do not believe that they could be worshipping a god in their lives whom they have placed before God Himself. Don't be guilty of choosing a greedy materialistic lifestyle instead of God's purposes. You cannot take any of it with you to eternity! Money in itself is not evil; worshipping money and possessions becomes a priority over God and His purpose for your life. "The love of money is the root of many evils" (I Tim. 6:10, NIV)

Summary

"The only thing that walks back from the tomb with the mourners and refuses to be buried is character." God loves to do uncommon feats through common people.

Assignment

1. Discuss theological soundness and its absolutes.
2. Study each pillar and Biblical references.
3. Accept, believe, understand, and teach these nine basic Biblical doctrines. Study I Tim. 4:12-16.
4. Evaluate your own life. Are you straying away from the nine pillars by bypassing the cross, or adding to God's doctrines as taught in His Holy Scriptures?
5. Is your religion materialism? Do you worship material things?

V. THE FUNCTIONS

FUNCTION #1: ENVISIONING

Why am I here? What need must be met?

"When a man does not know what harbour he is making for, no wind is the right wind!" (Seneca)

"Where there is no vision, the people perish." (Proverbs 29:18)

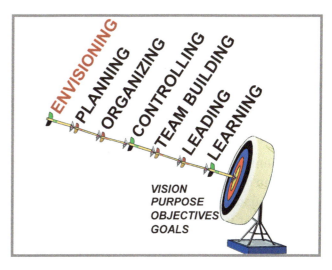

"And the things that you have heard me say in the presence of many witnesses entrust to reliable (faithful, trustworthy) men and women who will also be QUALIFIED (ABLE, COMPETENT) to teach others also." (II Tim. 2:2)

An effective leader will ensure the essential seven functions, tools and skills that are discussed in this section are implemented in his/her organization(s). As a result, the leader will cause *the right things to happen* and the managers will *do those things right.*

Effective leadership resulting in action and growth begins with **envisioning**. This function must be in sync with the values, mission and purpose of both the organization and the leader. This avoids inconsistency and double standards.

Envisioning Defined

Envisioning involves the creation of a clear picture of what the leader sees himself and his group doing and becoming. It meets a need.

It is a mental image of a possible desirable future state of an organization, team, or individual. It is seeing ahead and conceptualizing in the mind. "With men it is impossible, but not with God; for with God all things are possible" (Mark 10:27).

It is future-oriented, looking forward, thinking ahead, so that the purpose can be established and that planning and implementing the intended activities can make the vision a reality.

It is the "glue" that binds people together in a common effort and purpose.

It is collective in nature – enlisting others who share the vision, values, mission and purpose.

Envisioning is unique – being different. God has set you apart for a specific purpose and a vision to fulfill. With the vision that God implants within the depths of our being, we can become the persons He planned and will use – full of possibility!

The Source of Vision

Vision comes softly through the quiet voice of God speaking in the most inner part of your being (sometimes called "intuition").

Vision often originates from one individual then it is transvisioned to others and matures within the group that accepts the vision (Acts 16; Neh2:17; 6:15).

True vision cannot be shaken, even when you are severely criticized, mocked, put down, condemned or even betrayed. This heart conviction is the result of listening to God's still, quiet, assuring, persistent inner voice (godly intuition) deep within your being. It comes from the heart. (Neh.2:17; 6:15)

Ingredients that "Sprout" Vision

+ Word of God
+ Prayer/Fellowship
+ Heart Conviction
+ Biblical Values, Insight
+ Interaction and input from others
+ Patience, Test of Time
+ Clear Focus on Need (not want)
+ Circumstances/Crisis

} Development of a clear, well-defined vision

Why is Vision Important?

A clear and godly vision with action brings forth what God intends for us and those we serve.

It provides staying power, tenacity, motivation to see the situation from God's perspective and to keep going in spite of difficulties and opposition.

It is alive, contemporary, on the "cutting edge" and meets the real needs of an aimless society. Vision reveals our part in God's plan for a better future.

It is a strategic function that meets real needs of those served and focuses on priorities.

It captures the imagination, energizes, gives hope and stimulates the spirit of the participants.

A vision is full of possibilities; it motivates and gives others a sense of direction and the will to serve.

Without vision, there is no vitality and life; there is no organized effort to accomplish the common purpose. The people have no hope. They become unrestrained and perish. They live lives of peaceful stagnation. "Where there is no vision, the people perish" Prov 11:14; 29:18, KJV).

> A vision with a purpose is far more capable of withstanding severe tests of resistance than a vision alone (without purpose) ...purpose is a bedrock from which to build our lives.

Man's Vision

Something is missing in this structure. It is hollow! Brain dead! In a coma! No needs met. No meaningful progress. No results—no souls saved, no church planting, no glory to God, no

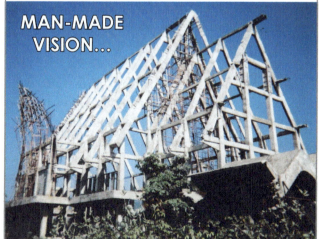

TRADITION, STAGNANT, AUTOCRATIC SELF-CENTERED BUREAUCRATIC MANAGEMENT POWER HUNGRY, SELF-CENTERED AUTHORITARIAN "LEADERSHIP"

MAN-MADE VISION...

UNFINISHED AND ABANDONED CHRISTIAN CATHEDRAL, EAST TIMOR (PHOTO BY ROBERT ORR)

leadership training, no godly leaders emerging, no purpose... a useless structure in decay! *Did God intend the above structure to be the vision ...or rather a vision to build and train people?*

God-Given Vision

The vision must be realistic, meet a need, and be effective. There must be growth – not stagnation, decay and ego-building agendas.

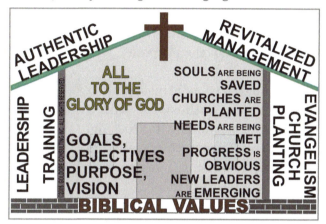

The Price of Envisioning

The high cost of a vision includes great personal sacrifice and a large investment of time and resources. Having a vision and strong tenacity will help you get through the tough times.

Sense of "Security"

Envisioning creates a state of transition and unpredictability. This can create the lack of a sense of perceived "security". Yet often the desired "sense of security" is a false sense of security resulting from complacency and mediocrity. You will experience true security only by doing what God determines (obeying His call).

Friendships and Relationships

Often the call of God involves loneliness and a lack of understanding on the part of those who do not share the vision and are not committed to the call of God in their own lives. Leaders normally have a much greater capacity to cope with loneliness and would rather follow God's vision and purpose for them than stay with the group.

Satisfaction and Contentment

Dissatisfaction, restlessness and discontentment with the status quo can rage within one's inner being until the God-given vision is accomplished—the need and purpose are met.

Setbacks and Hindrances

Once there is a clear vision resulting from God's calling, Satan will try to do everything possible to hinder the accomplishment of the vision and the fulfillment of the purpose.

Although vision brings with it dynamism, enthusiasm, and a sense of usefulness to God and the world, the path travelled in seeing the vision come to fruition is often very lonely.

Transvisioning

Transvisioning is the process of transferring a vision to another person in such a way that he or she embraces the vision as his or her own.

When transvisioning...
- Know your people.
- State the vision in several different ways to ensure clarity.
- Begin by stating the need and difficulties; then state your vision positively and hopefully.
- Do not promise that it will be easy—it probably will not be easy! There is a price to pay!
- Shift from using "I" to "we" part way through the discussion.
- Do not be afraid to express your vision with emotion, passion and a sense of urgency to see the vision become a reality.
- Inform the other team members of the probability of necessary risk-taking. Envisioning always involves risk.
- Be sure to listen to the other person. Input from others could sharpen your own vision or bring an added dimension to your present dream.

The soccer coach had a vision to win the trophy.

Transvisioning took place.

Each player embraced the same vision—to win the trophy!

Guidelines and Principles

"We are not a freak of nature or a random occurrence in outer space as the agnostics and atheists would have you believe. God created us; we are spiritual beings and He meant for us to live lives of significance; there is a reason and purpose why we are here. We have a unique contribution to make while we are alive."
(Mark Orr)

God created us for a purpose. It was planned before you were conceived! Knowing this will give you a sense of meaningful, worthwhile, rewarding activity in God's great strategic plan for eternity—"...a special, unique purpose to fit that unique creation—you! There is no duplicate! You need to be 'you' and discover that *purpose and call* that God intended for you".

Envisioning comes from the heart. It is personal and unique. It may even sound unreasonable. It should be *radical and compelling*.

Envisioning points to a future state that does not yet exist. When a leader knows God's unique purpose he can guide people from the present into the desired envisioned future.

A leader with a clear vision gives to the people a true sense of destiny. We exist for God and to serve His kingdom. Vision inspires and reveals that we can be useful to God within our own sphere of influence. It eliminates mediocrity.

Communicate and transfer the vision (transvisioning) with optimism and coach others to "possess" it too. Articulate clearly. Make the vision easily understood and meaningful to others.

Be in tune with godly values, culture, environment and changing needs.

Provide continuity for your people. Do not allow setbacks and circumstances to hinder you from accomplishing what needs to be done.

> True vision generates "staying power" to get through the valley. It motivates and aids in seeing the situation from God's perspective and to keep going in spite of the difficulties, set-backs and obstacles.

Focus on the call of God and what lies ahead. Listen to the voice of God deep within your being. It will keep you on track.

Keep it fine-tuned with foresight, hindsight, world view, peripheral and depth perception, with revision and evaluation as necessary.

Ensure that your vision is fulfilled and characterized by integrity.

Address the questions:
• "What are we trying to do for whom?
• Is it producing fruit?"

The vision must "sprout", grow and reproduce before it can be realized. Implement and adjust the purpose, objectives, and goals to make it happen! Be sure you are growing new leaders of vision and purpose as you continue on life's journey.

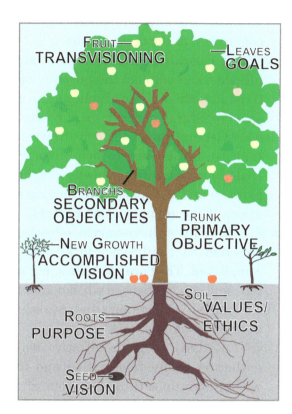

Defining Some Common Terms

VISION: An image of a need that must be met and how it can be met.

VALUES: Principles based on God's Word and His perspective regarding His purpose, morals, character, integrity and ethics that an organization chooses to maintain.

PURPOSE: The reason a person or organization exists. "Why am I here?" "Why does this ministry exist?"

OBJECTIVE: It answers the question, "How are we going to accomplish our purpose?" This involves deciding in advance what will be accomplished in a given period of time and the strategy to do so.

GOALS: "How do we accomplish our objective?" Goals are clear, short range, immediate, measurable, realistic, necessary and attainable tasks that must be completed in order to fulfill the objective.

MISSION STATEMENT: Reveals the reason for the organization's existence; what should and should not be done; the objectives and goals and how they will be met; the "ethos" and values (character, spirit, philosophy, conviction) of the organization.

STRATEGY: Overall plan or course of action needed to accomplish the purpose, objectives, implementation of policies and decisions regarding general use of resources.

POLICIES: General guidelines, driven by values, that are established to help accomplish goals, objectives and the purpose of the organization. They apply to reoccurring situations. They are guides not masters!

PROCEDURES: Lists of necessary step-by-step instructions that outline how tasks will be accomplished. They are guidelines, not masters, and can be changed when necessary.

GROUP PLANNING: Planning that involves the people who do the work.

BRAINSTORMING: It is an effective way of gathering useful information and ideas within a group setting. Everyone should be given an opportunity to participate, all ideas are accepted without evaluation or criticism, and ideas should be displayed where everyone can see them. When it comes time for evaluation check the ideas against the vision, purpose, mission statement, objectives, goals, and constitution of the organization. Modify or eliminate those that violate the values, morals, ethics and scriptural principles. Then ACT!

Nehemiah had a Vision

Nehemiah, the persistent architect, listened to the reports of the despairing situation in Jerusalem. He personally investigated the situation and determined the need. He sought the will of God. Unknown to others, God was creating a vision in his heart and a purpose to pursue. He articulated clearly the vision. He transmitted the vision to others. Objectives were formed. Clear and God-appointed plans were developed. Goals were set. He organized a strong team, delegated and set a good example. The tasks of building the wall were initiated and taken to completion.

They remained focused on the task. His deep-rooted commitment to the vision and God's calling was essential to withstand the opposition. The vision became a reality! The wall was built! He remained in touch with the situation until the dream was a reality–a great example of a VISIONARY MANAGERIAL LEADER! His vision was realistic, credible, and attractive to others for they saw a bad situation which could become better! "To everything there is a season. A time for every purpose under heaven" (Eccl. 3:1,2, NKJV).

Did Jesus Christ have a Vision?

Jesus was able to create, articulate and communicate a compelling vision; to change what people talk about and dream of; to make his followers transcend self-interest; to enable us to see ourselves and our world in a new way; to provide prophetic insight into the very heart of things; and to bring about the highest order of change.

Follow Him! That's living! That's serving! Jesus had a passionate purpose He was willing to die for "…to seek and to save that which was lost" (Luke 19:10). His mission was the cross. His vision was the salvation of all who would come. He kept on-purpose. He uncomplicated life and theological issues. Jesus referred to the vision when He prayed to His Father (John 17) and stated that He had completed the work which God the Father had given Him to do here on earth. Also when He hung on the cross and said, "It is finished." His vision of what His Father had asked Him to do here on earth had become a reality.

God's Purpose for You

Managerial leaders must be men and women of vision with special learnable skills. They unleash and harness the energy of the organization. They change the vision to reality. They make the future happen now. They are men and women who see a vision before others do. They see further than others, and their vision gives them motivation, direction and purpose.

Jesus taught His disciples (and us) to pray–"Our Father in heaven... Your will be done on earth as it is in heaven..." (Matt. 6:9-13). God uses people to accomplish His will and be part of His divine plan.

When Jesus prayed for His disciples (John 17), He included all who would believe (that includes you and me!): "...I pray also for those who will believe in me..." (v.20); "...guard them by the power of Your name..." (v.11); "...protect them from the Evil One..." (v.15); "...set them apart for holiness..." (v.19); "...that they may all be one..." (v.21-23); "...to be with Me where I am..." (v.24). God truly has a purpose for you and me. We must embrace it and make His vision our vision!

"It is easier to serve God without a vision,
    easier to work for God without a call;
because then you are not bothered by
    what God requires.
Common sense is your guide,
    veneered over with Christian sentiment.
But if once you receive a commission
    from Jesus Christ,
the memory of what God wants
    will always come like a goad;
and you will no longer be able to work for Him
    on the common sense basis".

(Oswald Chambers)

Uncle Cam's Leadership Style

(Contributed by Hilda Whealy)

Many have heard of Wycliffe Bible Translators' founder, Cameron Townsend. George Cowan wrote a tribute in honor of "Uncle Cam" as he was known. This tribute certainly reveals the vision, values and character behind this man. His vision was to get the Holy Scriptures into the utmost parts of the world.

1. He led from the front, not the rear, always out ahead of us, giving entrepreneur-type direction and decisions on the field, not from home headquarters.

2. He led by faith, not by sight; he trusted God, and he trusted God to guide and use individuals, groups and governments. He delegated authority, but reserved the right to veto.

3. He led by example, not by argument or reasoning. In fact, he often found it difficult to answer the question "Why?". He would often answer it with a story.

4. He led by suggestion not by command, but expected suggestions to be taken seriously.

5. He led openly, without secrets, resisting things that had to be kept "in confidence". But he recognized true confidentiality and kept that. He wanted meetings to be open to anyone: family, town-hall meeting atmosphere.

6. He led positively, not negatively. If he couldn't say something good, he would say nothing. He almost never "chewed us out".

7. He led by providential guidance. He walked close to God, His Word, and having committed his day to God, he interpreted unexpected circumstances, interruptions and meetings with people as divinely ordered. Opportunities, not agendas ruled.

8. He led courageously, fearlessly, calmly, doggedly. He had a fertile mind, was innovative, but single-minded in goal and direction.

9. He led by warm personal friendship rather than by rule or contract.

10. He believed everyone could do something to help, never turned down an offer to help. He drew people to be involved. He latched on to specialists and harnessed their skills.

11. He led in prayer, in turning to Scripture, in obeying Scripture (e.g. loving enemies) and in faithful witnessing under all circumstances to all levels of people.

Cameron Townsend
(1896-1982)

12. He led, excelled, in giving God the glory and giving others thanks.

13. He led by consistently emphasizing the basics and demonstrating them. He never lost sight of the Lord or of the goal of translating the Bible.

He was not perfect; he was aware of his own limitations, a "vessel of clay, that the excellency of the glory might be of God and not of man." He left an indelible imprint on many of us (outsiders comment on how much some of us act like Uncle Cam). He certainly left an imprint on the organization.

Summary

Don't get addicted to the urgent—stick with the "mission" and make a measurable and significant impact for God's glory. Stick to your purpose! A vision is of no value unless there is action! The remaining functions of managerial leadership—planning, organizing, controlling/monitoring, team building, leading and learning—are essential for the vision to become a reality.

We need to look at history. Worthwhile acts throughout history were accomplished by men and women with powerful dreams turned into reality by the ideas of the resultant vision. You see, without a cause, purpose, and ideals, you land up only with "motion," the preservation of a bureaucracy, and status quo. For exceptional performance you need to rally the team around a compelling picture of the preferred future—the vision. Often we mistake "vision" for "objectives" and "goals." Objectives and goals result from true, realistic vision. Vision is characterized by foresight, insight, optimism and hope. Vision is biblical. Managerial

Fred Smith, Yale University business student, founded Federal Express. He had noticed the problems of piggybacking parcel delivery on passenger flights. He was challenged to tackle the problem, formed a company and established one of the most efficient courier services in the world. Why did it happen? He had a vision which he turned into reality. By the way, his original plan was outlined in a paper he wrote in university—and was given a barely passing grade! The professor did not see or recognize the potential in Fred's vision.

leaders must be men and women of vision with special learnable skills that unleash and harness the energy of the organization to change that vision to reality and make the future happen now. They are men and women who see a vision before others, who see further than others, and whose vision gives them motivation, direction and purpose. Jesus was able to create, articulate and communicate a compelling vision; to change what people talk about and dream of; to make his followers transcend self-interest; to enable us to see ourselves and our world in a new way; to provide prophetic insight into the very heart of things; and to bring about the highest order of change.

May the God of our Lord Jesus Christ, the Father of glory, give you a spirit of wisdom and perception of what is revealed, to bring you to full knowledge of Him. May He enlighten the eyes of your mind so that you can SEE what hope His call holds for you, what rich glories He has promised the saints will inherit and how infinitely great is the power that He has exercised for us believers. (Eph. 1:17-19)

Assignment

1. What unique contribution has God purposed for you to give to the world? ...for the organization to give?

2. What action steps are you taking to form, sprout, grow and see your vision bear fruit?

FUNCTION # 2: PLANNING

How will we accomplish our vision and purpose?

"Plans fail for lack of counsel, but with many advisers they succeed." (Prov. 29:18, NIV; Prov. 15:22; 11:14)

"Many are the plans in a man's heart, but it is the Lord's purpose that prevails." (Prov. 19:21, NIV)

There is no more miserable human being than one in whom nothing is habitual but indecision. (William James)

"A man (or woman) without a purpose (and plan) is like a ship without a rudder (and captain)." (Thomas Carlyle)

 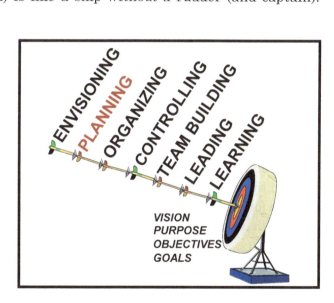

"And the things that you have heard me say in the presence of many witnesses entrust to reliable (faithful, trustworthy) men and women who will also be QUALIFIED (ABLE, COMPETENT) to teach others also." (II Tim. 2:2)

PLANNING creates the PROCESS to accomplish the strategy. It is vital to the life of the organization. If you fail to plan, you are planning to fail!

STRATEGY creates the "HOW TO" in accomplishing the vision and purpose.

VISION provides DIRECTION for our existence.

PURPOSE provides the MEANING to the mission.

VALUES provide the QUALITY to vision.

Definition of Planning

Planning is the route map that gets you to your destination.

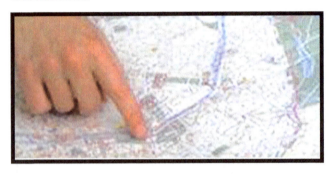

It is the process of wisely establishing, clearly articulating and effectively communicating:

a. the vision, purpose, objectives, goals, mission statement and tasks to be accomplished,

b. the methods of achieving the above,

c, and the workable and practical course of action for everyone involved. (It is thinking before doing!)

Importance of Planning

Planning is a biblical principle (Luke 14:28-33; Prov.15:22; Prov.20:18). It creates the strategy, process and means to live out our values, fulfill the vision and accomplish the purpose.

It helps us:

a. know what is the right task to be done next.

b. know why it is important enough to be done.

c. wisely use the available resources.

Clearly articulate your purpose, objectives and goals to:

a. assist in implementing clear methods and procedures.

b. help evaluate the results of the organization—its purpose and performance of the workers. People often do not strive for quality in their work when it involves church and ministry as they would in their own businesses and jobs.

c. enable wise, productive use of time. When objectives are not clear, time is wasted on tasks not relevant to the purpose.

Biblical Examples

Nehemiah effectively planned and implemented his action plan. The walls of Jerusalem were rebuilt in 52 days! A leadership classic!

Jesus warns against implementing a plan without first evaluating, analyzing and counting the cost to ensure the plan is practical, realistic and attainable (Luke 14:28-30).

Guidelines and Principles

a. Purpose, objectives and goals need to be practical, attainable and measurable.

b. Planning is "thinking" before doing.

c. Planning is a mental process. It identifies the steps to achieve our objectives but it does not get the job done. You need to act! (See Action Plan Worksheet, end of Planning Function.)

d. Planning anticipates things that are to happen.

e. Planning is a necessary activity to move from the present to the future—to change things from "the way things are" to "the way things ought to be".

f. Planning provides direction and a sense of unity for an organization. Efforts are all aimed at achieving the same objective rather than being haphazard and uncoordinated.

g. Planning is characterized by its involvement..:

1) with the future,
2) with action,
3) with and by people of action.

h. Planning is thinking of the safest and most economical way of doing your work.

i. Planning provides a clear perspective of:
   1) what is intended,
   2) how it will be accomplished,
   3) the steps for implementation.

j. A plan is a blueprint.
   1) It is used to describe how an organization expects to achieve its goals.
   2) It is used to communicate how we are going to make the vision become a reality and to fulfil the purpose.
   3) It is used to establish the strategy of how the objectives and goals will be achieved.
   4) It is used to devise a course of action that when implemented will accomplish an objective or reach a goal.

k. Envisioning is the springboard from which planning begins.

l. Planning involves gathering pertinent information, evaluating various alternatives and selecting the best one to implement an action plan effectively and efficiently.

m. Planning is a process which must be done on a continuous basis—daily, weekly, monthly, yearly. The decision not to plan is a plan in itself; but it will lead to ineffectiveness and failure. Planning makes the difference between whether we face the future with our purpose being accomplished or just face the future at random.

n. Plan, budget, organize, operate, control, evaluate, and measure them against those previous plans. Make necessary adjustments.

o. Planning includes decision-making, troubleshooting and problem-solving in every stage of the planning process.

p. Be flexible. Anticipate what may happen. Have alternate contingency plans ready.

Have extra time, money, people, materials, etc. to cope with the unexpected—when "things go wrong"!

q. Be courageous. Take wise, calculated risks, not foolish chances. Stand by your plans and decisions; admit mistakes; do not be afraid of failure. It makes you wiser! Learn and start again!

Consequences of Poor Planning

a. Unrealistic, vague or inadequate goals/objectives which lead to ill-defined methods of operation

b. Inappropriate choice of priorities,

c. Failure to implement necessary changes,

d. Lack of wise delegation,

e. Failure to train new leaders,

f. Inadequate resources to accomplish the plan,

g. Action plan is interpreted as the purpose (losing sight of why we are "doing what we are doing"),

h. Lack of evaluation and adjustment,

i. Results are difficult to measure,

j. Difficult to know when the organization is drifting from its vision and purpose,

k. People don't perform with maximum effectiveness,

l. Very little is accomplished,

m. Tendency to give up when a crisis looms.

Ultimately the vision, purpose and objectives of the organization are not accomplished.

Hindrances to Effective Planning

a. Tradition, personal feelings, status quo— what was effective 50 years ago may not be effective today. Look at today's needs and the future. Listen, understand and obey the still, small voice of God within you.

b. Fear (see 2 Tim. 1:7); inadequate evaluation; distraction; jealousy; pride; resistance

c. Faulty theology—Don't use "God told me..." or your emotions as an excuse for poor planning or not "doing". Be a tool in the hands of God whereby He can accomplish His plan through you. Accept His sovereignty, His purpose and His timing for you to fulfill the vision.

The majority see the obstacles; the few see the objectives; history records the successes of the latter, while oblivion is the reward of the former! (Alfred Armand Montapert)

Four Phases of Planning

1 visionary
2 strategic
3 tactical
4 evaluative
} ...with creative and realistic thinking

Situational Planning

Operational planning: A course of action to be used repeatedly to accomplish a specific goal (example: taking care of routine correspondence).

Program planning: A course of action for a single-use goal with a few tasks needed to accomplish the goal (example: a fund-raising event).

Project planning: A course of action for a single-use goal with many tasks and deadlines necessary to accomplish the goal (example: writing a book).

Questions to Ask

1. Who will support this program?
2. Do we have a continuing need for this program?
3. Will our organization be expected to grow financially? What is hindering financial growth?
4. Will our present organizational structure be viable and productive, and still accomplish the vision and purpose three years from now?
5. Are our present activities diverting us away from our values, vision, purpose and our organization's constitution and bylaws?
6. Do we have contingency plans developed and in place to enable the organization to respond to changing external, internal, environmental factors, emergencies or circumstances?
7. Are we developing and maintaining human resources to meet the needs efficiently and effectively?
8. Are we developing new leaders adequately and regularly?

The Planning Cycle

DECISION-MAKING

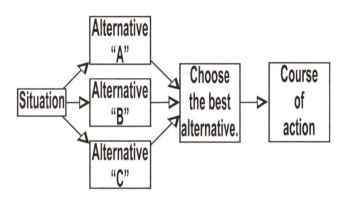

Decision–Making

Choose one alternative from a set of potentially viable options. Choose between different ways of getting a specific task accomplished. (The dogmatic approach does not evaluate alternatives.)

The wrong decision at the wrong time = disaster
The wrong decision at the right time = mistake
The right decision at the wrong time = rejection
The right decision at the right time = success.

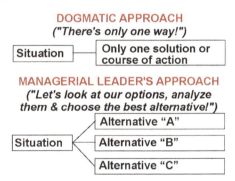

Problem-Solving

Problem solving is the process of identifying what has deviated from the present standard and how to re-establish the standard. It is essential whenever plans, strategies, goals and/or tasks are not producing the anticipated, established, effective results.

Problem-solving requires creativity and intuition. It does not always require "action"! It may require ***abandoning a particular paradigm***! It requires the discovery of the ***root cause*** of the deviation from the standard. What may ini-

PROBLEM-SOLVING

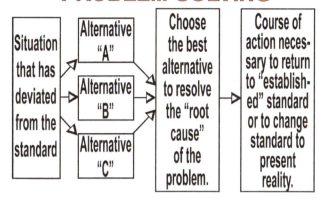

tially appear to be the cause, may not necessarily be the real root cause.

Summary

If the plan of action does not fulfill the objectives and purpose of the organization, then the plan needs to be discontinued or modified in order that the objectives and purpose can be efficiently and effectively accomplished. Wise solutions are not always the most popular. You may experience some opposition! As you trust God for wisdom and you see the good results, you will be encouraged! Take heart! Start today!

> "If we could first know where we are, and where we are going, we could better judge what to do and how to do it."
> (Abraham Lincoln)

Assignment

1. If you don't care where you are going, any road will take you somewhere—but is it where you want to be? What do you want to accomplish within one year, two years, five years?

2. Use the Decision-Making, Problem-Solving and Action Plan Worksheets (following pages) to assist you in developing, evaluating and adjusting the direction of your organization.

3. Do you have a situation such as illustrated by the story ("Belling the Cat") at the end of this section? Explain your answer.

Decision-Making Worksheet

9. Evaluation and adjustment
   a. Date of Evaluation: _____
   b. Evaluation Report: _____
   c. Evaluated by:_____
   d. Recommendations to improve action plan: _____

8. Implementation of the Action Plan:
   _____
   _____
   _____

7. Action Plan:
   a. What needs to be done?_____
   b. Why does it need to be done?_____
   c. How should it be done? _____
   d. When should it be done?_____
   e. Where should it be done? _____
   f. Who should do it? _____

external factors:
technological, political/legal,
economic, international,
sociocultural, suppliers,
customers, competitors,
unions, regulators, partners,
etc.
internal factors: individual,
task and team needs

6. Determine the **best alternative**: _____
   _____
   _____
   _____

5. Evaluate and analyze all alternatives:
   a. Advantages: _____ b. Disadvantages: _____
   c. Risks:_____ d. Obstacles:_____
   e. Information affecting the situation:____
   f. Resources and people required:_____

4. "Brainstorm" to determine possible alternatives:_____
   _____
   _____
   _____

3. Gather facts and pertinent information:_____
   _____
   _____
   _____

2. Review how a decision will affect your
   (a) values _____ (b) purpose _____
   (c) objectives _____ (d) goals_____
   (e) standards: _____

1. State situation requiring a decision: _____
   _____
   _____

Problem-Solving Worksheet

9. Evaluation and adjustment
   a. Date of Evaluation: _____
   b. Evaluation Report: _____
   c. Evaluated by: _____
   d. Recommendations to improve action plan: _____

8. Implementation of the Action Plan:

   _____
   _____
   _____

7. Action Plan:
   a. What needs to be done? _____
   b. Why does it need to be done? _____
   c. How should it be done? _____
   d. When should it be done? _____
   e. Where should it be done? _____
   f. Who should do it? _____

external factors:
technological, political/legal,
economic, international,
sociocultural, suppliers,
customers, competitors,
unions, regulators, partners,
etc.
internal factors: individual,
task and team needs

6. Choose the **best** alternative that resolves the real ROOT cause of the problem

   _____
   _____

5. Evaluate and analyze all alternatives:
   a. Advantages: _____ b. Disadvantages: _____
   c. Risks: _____ d. Obstacles: _____
   e. Information affecting the situation: _____
   f. Resources and people required: _____

4. "Brainstorm" to determine possible alternatives that resolve the root cause:

   _____
   _____
   _____

3. Gather facts and pertinent information
   (a) What is affected by the deviation? _____
   (b) To what extent does it affect the organization, values, team, goals, standards, the accomplishment
       of the purpose and objectives _____

2. Review and determine how the current problem affects your
   (a) values _____ (b) purpose _____
   (c) objectives _____ (d) goals _____
   (e) standards: _____

1. State situation requiring a decision (What is wrong? What is the REAL ROOT problem?) ___
   (a) What is affected? _____ (b) Why does it occur? _____
   (c) How does it occur? _____ (d) When does it occur? _____
   (e) Where does it occur? _____ (f) Is there someone responsible for the problem? _____
   (g) Are there inadequate resources creating a problem? _____

THE ACTION PLAN WORK PROCESS

OUR ORGANIZATION: _____
(Church, Ministry, Business, Government, Personal, etc.)

DATE OF THE PLAN: _____

EVALUATION DATE FOR VISIONARY PLANNING: _____

EVALUATION DATE FOR STRATEGIC PLANNING: _____

EVALUATION DATE FOR TACTICAL PLANNING: _____

I. VISIONARY PLANNING
Values, purpose/mandate, mission statement & identity based on the desire to MEET A NEED (social, economic, religious, etc.).

1. Need/Issue:
(What social, religious, etc. need exists?)

2. Assumptions:
(Why does this need exist? Should there be a paradigm shift?)

3. Our Core Values:
(What do we stand for? What characteristics must our organization exemplify?)

6. The Benefits:
(How will people benefit by what we do?)

5. Our Purpose/Mandate:
(Why are we here? How will we meet the need?)

4. Our Vision/Dream:
(What do we want to see happen?)

7. Our Mission Statement:
(What is our organization's purpose– its boundaries, objectives, philosophy of ministry or business?)

8. Identity:
(What is the unique distinctiveness for which people should know us?)

II. STRATEGIC PLANNING
LONG-RANGE, broad-spectrum objectives and goals.

11. Our Weaknesses:
(What are our weaknesses? How do we buttress them?)

10. Our Strengths:
(What are our strengths & level of competence? How do we build on them?)

9. Our Objectives:
(How will we accomplish our purpose?)

12. Environmental Factors: (What factors, opportunities, constraints influence how we meet the need?)
(_External_: technological, economic, political/legal, socio-cultural, international, environment, suppliers, customers, competitors, unions, regulators, partners, etc.; _Internal_: task, team or individual needs, personnel, resources)

13. Obstacles:
(What obstacles/barriers do we need to overcome? How will we overcome them?)

15. Standards:
(What conditions must be met to accomplish effectively & efficiently the goals & objectives?)

14. Financial Plan:
(What will it cost to accomplish our purpose & objectives? What resources do we have & still need? How will we get the remainder?)

16. Strategy/Course of Action:
(What course of action should be taken? What needs to be done? When? Where? Why? How? Who?)

17. Results (the fruit):
(What results need to be evident?)

Be sure to follow the arrows!

III. TACTICAL PLANNING

Establishment of standards, SHORT-RANGE goals, activities & tasks to accomplish the objectives.

20. Personnel:
(Who is responsible, "able"/competent, qualified to do the task? Who is able to assist?)

19. Activities/Tasks:
(What activities & tasks must be accomplished in order to fulfill the objectives & goals?)

18. Our Goals:
(What goals are necessary to fulfill the purpose & objectives?)

21. Resources:
(What specific resources do we need?)

22. Annual Budget:
(What will it cost to accomplish our activities & tasks? Do we have the money? If not, how will we get more?)

23. Contingencies/Adjustments:
(What alternatives do we have ready if we have an unexpected situation?)

NOTE: Evaluation & adjustment is done often in tactical planning, less frequently in strategic planning, only periodic in visionary planning. However, do not fail to do this in each area!

24. Implementation:
(When do we begin and complete each step of our action plan?)

IV. EVALUATION & ADJUSTMENT

Accountability of the plan

25. Evaluation:
(Who will evaluate the overall action plan? When? How do we know if we have accomplished our purpose, objectives and goals?)

26. Adjustment:
(If the plan does not fulfill the purpose & vision, be flexible & wise in making necessary changes.)

	CURRENT FACTS	REASONS	POSSIBLE ALTERNATIVES	ADJUSTING THE PLAN
WHAT?	What is being done now?	Why is it done?	What could be done differently?	What should be done?
HOW?	How is it done?	Why is it done this way?	How could it be done differently?	How should it be done?
WHEN?	When is it done?	Why is it done at this time?	When could it be done differently?	When should it be done?
WHERE?	Where is it done?	Why is it done at this place?	Where could it be done differently?	Where should it be done?
WHO?	Who does it?	Why is it done by this person?	Who else could do it?	Who should do it?

Planning requires realistic thinking. The principle of the following story reveals that it is possible to plan great projects but if they are beyond the capability of the people or the resources for the purpose to be accomplished, *the idea becomes a joke or nightmare*. There is more to leading and planning than making great plans and setting up interesting organizations. You must "bell the cat"!

Once upon a time there was an old lady who lived alone in an old house on the edge of a village. The house provided shelter for her as well as for the many mice that shared it with her. But the mice were at times unhappy—and frightened—for the old lady kept a large cat as company for herself. Life became unbearable for the mice. Their freedom of movement was hampered and endangered by the silent stalking of the ever-present cat. Individuals and families tried many ideas to ensure survival, but eventually the situation became critical for the whole colony. As they gathered for their annual conference, there was a sense of urgency upon the whiskered face of each mouse. The first order of business called for suggestions and recommendations as to how they might cope with this menace that was stalking them continually. Many proposals were submitted but were rejected for one reason or another. The situation had reached a desperate state. Finally a little old mouse stood up, and it was obvious from his manner that he came from the countryside. He addressed the conference as follows: "Brothers and sisters, I have listened to your problem and to the many solutions that have been proposed without success. I have an idea I would like to present for your consideration. As you see, I come from the country. Recently the man where I live bought a very interesting and effective early-warning system for his cows. He hung the device around the neck of one of the cows and as she moves around he can tell where the whole herd is. It is a simple but ingenious device. I heard them call it by a secret code name known as "bell." I would like to make a resolution to the effect that you obtain such a device and hang it around the neck of this pesky cat. I am certain that this would bring peace to your community and many lives would be saved." As he sat down a murmur swept through the building. Then with one accord all the mice shouted, "Amen, brother... so be it!" The resolution was passed unanimously and there was great joy. The chairman pronounced the benediction and the mice started to file out of the great hall. But an elderly mouse who had been sitting in deep thought called out, "But before we all part, *who will bell the cat?*" There was a moment of noisy stirring, then a deep hush fell on all present. Then one by one the mice left in silence and as far as I know, to this day that cat has never been belled!
(Source unknown)

FUNCTION #3: ORGANIZING

As we study this function, we must remember that a managerial leader looks "outside his box".

"A leader never says, "That's not my job." If you expect a team to pitch in when something unusual comes up you had better be ready to show them you're ready to pitch in when asked (needed). When people refuse to do anything that is not in their job description, you can be sure you've got a company (business, church, or ministry) in serious trouble. An (authentic) leader has an immense interest in all aspects of company (organization, ministry, church) operations. He is curious about what other departments are doing and why. He asks questions, tries to be helpful–without making a pest of himself. He loves people and is sensitive to their unique personalities and needs."

"God is not the author of confusion but of peace." (I Cor. 14:33)

"Do all things *decently* and *in order*." (I Cor. 14:40)

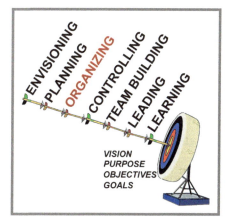

"*And the things that you have heard me say in the presence of many witnesses entrust to reliable (faithful, trustworthy) men and women who will also be QUALIFIED (ABLE, COMPETENT) to teach others also.*" (II Tim. 2:2)

Organizing Defined

It is the process of systematically arranging resources (human, financial, etc.), and coordinating activities in such a manner that each person contributes to the accomplishment of the vision, purpose, objectives and goals and feels fulfilled in the process.

Webster's Dictionary defines organization as "an association or society of people working together to some end."

"Organization" refers to a group of people united together to accomplish a common purpose. It is the systematic arrangement of duties, procedures and work habits to accomplish the purpose of the group. It's the framework that structures its activities and procedures. It delineates the lines of authority, responsibility and accountability. This activity must be evaluated continually to determine whether the end result is accomplishing the vision and purpose of the organization and its respective departments.

Balance the formal (official plans, policies and directives) and informal (staffing concerns) organizational structure so that the vision and purpose are maintained and that people are well-suited, fulfilled and at ease in their roles.

When discussing an organization, we talk about a complex social system with dynamic organizational designs; yet such designs are different for different organizations. Why?

There are different:
- visions
- environments
- strategies
- opportunities
- objectives
- products
- constraints
- resources

Tangible Components

Work: distributed and delegated among the team members in parcels of tasks

Employees: equipped, trained to use their talents and skills

Relationships: create good communication, harmony, positive morale; reduce stress and conflict

Environment: adequate working facilities

Authority: shared at every level of the delegation process; non-autocratic, people-sensitive, respected, reasonable and compassionate.

Accountability: for expected, planned results

Delegation: work divided fairly, wisely; done efficiently with empowerment and training

Team building: trained leadership at every level

Time management: time is used wisely and efficiently so that the organization effectively accomplishes its vision and purpose.

Elements of Organization

Short-term and long-term objectives: Keep on course with a clear focus. Determine what tasks need to be done. Each task fits with changing circumstances and future. All activities and efforts need to be synchronized in an orderly, logical manner. Flexibility is important. Standards are the criteria by which results will be evaluated.

Staff relationships: Focus on job satisfaction and pride in a job well done. Ensure harmony among workers. Skilled organizers motivate the followers to accomplish necessary tasks and to achieve the common purpose of the group and organization.

Staff responsibilities: Job descriptions clarify expectations, activities, organizational relationships and accountability, details of a person's limits or parameters of authority and his role within the organization. One person accountable to only one supervisor. The more complex the work, the fewer employees a manager can supervise. You give responsibility, training, empowerment and the right measure of authority to other people and receive back accountability and obligation in return (true delegation).

"The best leader is the one who has sense enough to pick good men to do what he wants done, and sense enough not to meddle with them while they do it!" (Theodore Roosevelt)

Why Organize?

It provides adequate accountability whereby everyone knows what  tasks they are responsible for and what authority they have. No one individual has complete control; each individual accounts to someone.

Effective organizing produces synergism.
Synergism is the simultaneous action of separate but related parts to produce a sum greater than that of its separate components.

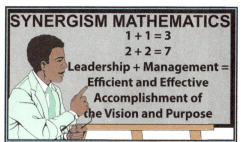

Organizing enables effective evaluation of what is being accomplished and what still needs to be accomplished.

When effective, efficient organization is *not* practised, autocratic "leadership" develops and destroys.

If no one knows what anyone else is doing, chaos, confusion and eventually anarchy result.

Skills and tools that assist in organizing the team include: time management, delegation, job descriptions and organizational charts.

Time Management

Effective managerial leaders are good stewards of their time and organize themselves well. Eccl. 3:1-11. There is a time for everything. Know yourself; know your time. Seize the moment (i.e. the book of Esther in the Holy Scriptures).

Replace less important tasks with more important ones that will move you closer to the fulfillment of your personal and organizational objectives, purpose and vision. Prioritize!
Poor time management=stress=poor productivity

10 key habits to develop in your life

1. Develop a time management philosophy and policy.

2. Get rid of the backlog.

3. Schedule your activities.

4. Organize yourself and your office.

5. Control the information/ paperwork explosion.

6. Control yourself.

7. Don't let others steal your time.

8. Delegate for good results.

9. Avoid the meeting trap.

10. Help employees manage their time.

What is stealing your time?

Responsibility

Responsibility is biblical (Luke 9:62; Eccl.9:10; Jam.4:17; etc.). Responsibility is an obligation, a duty or a commission that one receives, accepts and accounts for its accomplishment. Obligation is the guarantee, covenant, or commitment that a person will fulfill his responsibility.

Responsibility can be imposed, invited, volunteered, or created. Regardless of how the responsibility is acquired, one is obligated to be accountable and to fulfill the task.

Responsibility always carries accountability with it.

Lines of responsibility are two-directional. The higher level is responsible for the lower level; the lower level is accountable to the higher level.

Authority

Authority is the right and the power to influence, to give command, to be obeyed, to receive accountability and to perform.

Authority is in a position (such as job title, badges of rank, appointment, etc.), not in a person except where he/she has authority based on earned credentials, knowledge and influence. Authority is taught in the Holy Scriptures. (Matt.7:29; Matt.8:7-9; I Cor.9:16; Mark 1:27; etc.)

Authority can be created, received, and delegated. It can be used wisely or abused. It can be misinterpreted. It cannot be transferred from one responsibility to another. It remains with the position and the job description for that particular position.

The greater the responsibility, the more authority we must assign to empower that responsibility.

Sources of Authority

The sources of authority are God, other people and oneself. Authority may be given or, in some cases, created positionally by oneself. Leaders can use their authority—autocratically, democratically, passively or even by wrongful force. (Remember the parable of Bramble Leadership, Judges 9:7-15.)

Might this be your photo?

Caution: Do not take authority that does not rightfully belong to your position!

Elements of Authority

a. Responsibility – The amount of authority must be proportional to the amount of responsibility. He who gives authority imposes responsibility. He who accepts authority must also accept responsibility.

b. Backing – Leaders need the backing of their superiors; they give their support to their subordinates. The superiors must be trustworthy.

c. Confidence – It is gained when one knows:
   1) what his authority and responsibilities are.
   2) how much authority he has, and that the backing from higher authority can be counted on.

d. Influence – Influence is affecting another so that a change of behavior or attitude results. Use your authority to influence your subordinates to accomplish the organization's purpose.

e. Consequences – The leader has the authority to enforce the consequences of behavior (the "or-else factor") or to reward for a job well-done.

f. Submission – is an attitude in which one accepts and respects the authority of another without fear, humiliation, or put-down.

g. Amount of authority – should be in proportion to the amount of responsibility, influence, and accountability given.

Empowerment

Empowerment involves the equipping and the provision of sufficient authority, training, resources (personnel, financial, equipment, facilities, etc.), conditions, encouragement and motivation to fulfill the delegated responsibilities efficiently and effectively.

Empowerment involves adequate backing and support to those who receive the authority and delegated responsibilities.

Accountability

It is the process in which a person reports the details of the accomplishment of his work to the person to whom he is accountable.

The subordinate incurs an obligation to carry out a responsible job or function delegated to him.

It enables the managerial leader to determine how the departments and subordinates are performing.

It requires the acceptance of the consequences for failing to fulfill a responsibility.

It must include positive reporting, not just when things go wrong.

It is not only a function of structure; it is also a function of relationships, allowing mutually beneficial and healthy scrutiny to enable everyone to become more effective and efficient.

It is not to be feared. Avoid the idea that it is not "Christian" to hold people accountable for their work. Often the excuse is "After all, we are brothers in Christ. Don't you trust me?" Wrong, the issue is not trust, but rather accountability!

He who accepts authority and responsibility must give accountability and obligation in return.

Delegation

Delegation is the process that involves as many people as possible in decision-making, directing the work, and doing the work. You cannot and must not do all the work yourself!

Delegation is the exchange of a certain amount of authority, responsibility, and empowerment (including training and resources) for an equal amount of obligation and accountability in return.

Principles and Guidelines of Delegation

1. When a leader delegates, he spreads and enlarges his influence, responsibility, and authority beyond himself, accomplishing much more than what he could ever do himself!

2. A leader does not lose his own authority when he delegates and gives authority to someone else.

3. A person who delegates a task or responsibility must have the authority to do so.

4. A good leader gives credit where credit is due and will accept his own share of blame for failure.

5. A subordinate should be accountable to only one individual, unless performing another separate role in a different department.

6. A person may do the task differently but equally as well as someone else. "Different" does not mean it is wrong!

7. Appropriate delegation depends on the task and its requirements as well as the people involved. Delegate the right responsibility to the right person based on character and abilities. Select people carefully; ensure proper training for the job. Don't show favoritism!

8. Sometimes the task needs to be divided into several smaller ones so that several people, who have the ability and time, can accomplish the bigger task that no one is able to do alone.

9. No one should be expected to do more than he or she is capable of accomplishing. A person who has been given too much to do or more than he is capable of accomplishing may become discouraged, lose motivation, lose interest and confidence in himself and the organization, and eventually may quit.

10. Rotate responsibilities so that different people will learn different responsibilities.

11. Know when to replace someone or to give him authority and responsibility which better fits his abilities.

12. Your goal is to accomplish the purpose and vision effectively and efficiently, as well as to provide the environment in which the individual can develop his abilities and feel fulfilled.

Jesus made truth, not position, the foundation of His authority. He made decisions because He was, and is, the truth. Authority from the biblical perspective continues to be based in truth and righteousness, not natural ability, wealth, or position. ...Our relationships with each other must always override our status.

Delegation Process

1. Seek God's wisdom (James 1:5). Unwise delegation can be as damaging as a lack of delegation.

2. Accurately and precisely describe the responsibility which needs to be fulfilled and accomplished.

3. Determine the parameters of authority that will be needed to fulfill the responsibility.

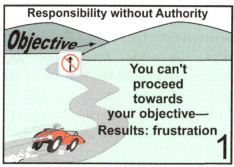

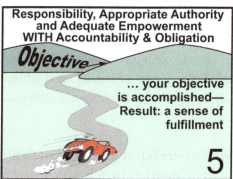

4. Determine the possible difficulties or problems.

5. Establish the checkpoints to monitor.

6. Select the right person for the responsibility.

7. Prepare a clear, precise written description of the authority and responsibility that will be given, the limitations (parameters) of that authority, and the procedure for accountability.

8. Discuss the situation with the individual to ensure that he understands the responsibility.

9. Ensure adequate training and support for the task.

10. Evaluate the results and adjust if necessary.

Delegation in the Scriptures

The classic example of delegation is recorded in Exodus 18:19-23. Moses was doing everything himself.

Jethro, his father-in-law, is one of the first management consultants we read about in Scripture! He found Moses trying to deal with everything himself and Jethro sharply reprimands him. He convincingly showed Moses that he was hurting the people by his faulty leadership—he did not delegate! He was too busy to train others! He told Moses to choose men to help lead the people—leaders of 10, 50, 100, and 1000.

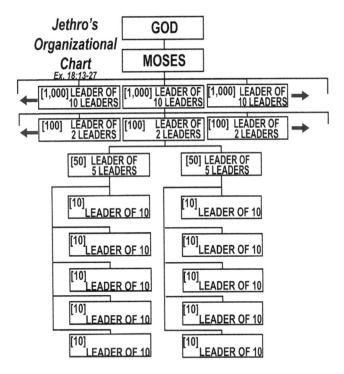

God told Moses to delegate even more responsibilities and instructed him to reduce his direct team to 70 men!

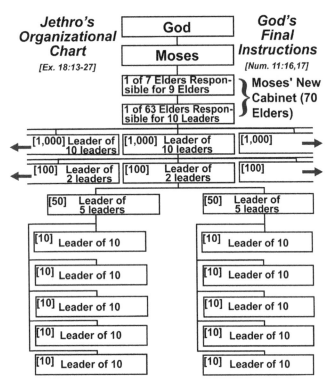

Historical approximation data indicates there were 630,000 men at that time in Israel. Moses would have 630 leaders accounting to him! God

indicated that Jethro's advice needed further modifications! God had Moses choose 70 men to help relieve the burden further (possibly 63 of the 70 men were to lead the leaders of 1000 and the remaining 7 men were to lead the 63 men). It would be reasonable to conclude that Moses' Inner Cabinet consisted of only 7 men.

Problems in Delegation

Unauthorized Delegation: A person may not have the authority and responsibility to delegate a particular responsibility, or delegate to untrained or incompetent individuals.

Extreme Delegation: A person may delegate nothing OR he may delegate too much or everything. A person who does not delegate is not really leading!

Rejected Obligation and Accountability: The one who receives the delegated responsibilities and authority chooses not to be accountable. Bad!

Supervision

Delegated authority and responsibility as well as the boundaries and limits (parameters) must be clearly stated.

Obligation and accountability directly correspond to the amount of authority and responsibility given.

We cannot excuse those who do not fulfill their responsibilities and obligations; nor can we demand more than what they have been assigned to do.

Types of supervision, job descriptions, organizational charts, delegation worksheets are tools to be used for more effective and efficient accomplishment of the vision and purpose of the organization.

General Supervision gives the individual the freedom to do many things his own way and the

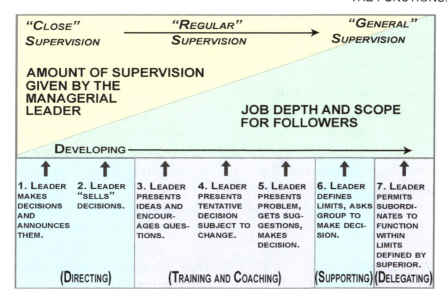

"CLOSE" SUPERVISION	"REGULAR" SUPERVISION →				"GENERAL" SUPERVISION	
AMOUNT OF SUPERVISION GIVEN BY THE MANAGERIAL LEADER				JOB DEPTH AND SCOPE FOR FOLLOWERS		
DEVELOPING →						
1. LEADER MAKES DECISIONS AND ANNOUNCES THEM.	2. LEADER "SELLS" DECISIONS.	3. LEADER PRESENTS IDEAS AND ENCOURAGES QUESTIONS.	4. LEADER PRESENTS TENTATIVE DECISION SUBJECT TO CHANGE.	5. LEADER PRESENTS PROBLEM, GETS SUGGESTIONS, MAKES DECISION.	6. LEADER DEFINES LIMITS, ASKS GROUP TO MAKE DECISION.	7. LEADER PERMITS SUBORDINATES TO FUNCTION WITHIN LIMITS DEFINED BY SUPERIOR.
(DIRECTING)		(TRAINING AND COACHING)			(SUPPORTING)	(DELEGATING)

supervisor checks only occasionally.

Regular Supervision involves closer supervision and the supervisor checks regularly on the progress made.

Close Supervision involves constant supervision in which little freedom is given to perform certain tasks. This type of supervision is necessary sometimes for new or immature employees; ideally it should never be permanent.

Feedback may include such methods as written or oral reports, staff meetings, etc. Controlled feedback involves giving specific information from the workplace. Uncontrolled (informal, unsolicited, unstructured) feedback is spontaneous, unpredictable, and usually from outside of the organization or department. Listen to it because it can help you and your organization to keep an impartial perspective on the condition of your organization and how well it is accomplishing its purpose and objectives.

Job Descriptions

Job descriptions are written outlines of what an organization expects from each person– his particular function, role, responsibilities and to whom he is accountable.

They show how the specific role fits into the or-

ganization to achieve its overall purpose and specific objectives.

They specify who should fulfill the role.

They guide the individual to fulfill the objectives of the position.

They permit enough flexibility to be creative in the methods of performing the duties.

They provide essential information for the employer and employee in order for them to know what is expected of each other.

Job descriptions indicate the boundaries, limitations, parameters and the extent of the delegated authority.

A job description helps us know what our tasks are and why we are in the organization. A job description helps our boss to know what we are doing. It helps us to know what he expects of us, and it lets people around us know what we are doing. Likewise, we know why their jobs exist.

It is my absolute conviction that all of us in Christian work should have job descriptions and those job descriptions should be living, dynamic tools like the organizational structure (clarified by organizational charts).

The best job descriptions are specific, definite, and measurable. They have teeth; they are binding; they are clear.

However, they are not legal documents. But a leader also sees beyond his "box". He likes people and is sensitive to their needs and "unique" personalities.

Job Description Worksheet

Job description for the position of _____
Effective date: _____
Revised date: _____
My name: _____
Purpose of my organization: _____
Primary objective of my organization: _____
Organizational chart with my respective position highlighted (attach to job description):
Primary objective of my position: _____
I am accountable to: _____

Details of my responsibility (responsible for what and for whom): _____
1. _____
2. _____
3. _____
etc.

Parameters (boundary/limits) of my authority:
_____
Special requirements, education, experience:
_____
Future training programs: _____

I have read and do understand the above job description. I willingly accept the authority and responsibility of this position. Furthermore, I realize that I am accountable to (name)_____ who will hold me responsible for the proper exercise of authority and fulfillment of this job description.

Date: _____
My signature: _____
My leader's signature: _____

Organizational Charts

Organizational charts are diagrams comprised of rectangles and lines to represent how an organization is structured.

They help to visualize the formal organization, the activities to be performed and by whom.

They show the work groupings, their activities and their relationships.

They could be called pictures, blueprints, or maps of the organization's structure.

They are used to identify and show the orderly relationship regarding communication, authority, responsibility, and accountability of each position.

They show how each position relates to the other positions to fulfill the purpose and objectives.

They show how people plan to work together to accomplish the purpose and objectives.

They are guideposts (therefore changeable!) to keep the organization on track.

They visualize how the constitution, bylaws, and lines of authority and responsibility of the organization all come together so that everyone can function synergistically as a whole unit.

Principles in Preparation

Clearly define and write out the purpose, primary and secondary objectives of the organization.

Determine the relationship of each position in the organization.

1. Organizational charts use only rectangles (single- or double-lined) and lines (solid and broken, vertical and horizontal).

2. A single-lined rectangle represents a position occupied by one individual. A double-lined rectangle represents a position occupied by a group of people.

| INDIVIDUAL |
| GROUP |

3. All rectangles are the same size to indicate each job is of equal importance (but differ in authority and responsibility). Each person holding the position is just as significant, whether the president or the janitor.

4. A solid vertical line joining two rectangles indicates the formal line of responsibility, accountability, and communication. A horizontal line (side-to-side) indicates communication only.

5. The top rectangle represents the vision and purpose (Why are we here? What are we here to accomplish?). The next level of rectangles represents the primary objective and the next level the secondary objectives, and so on.

6. Each rectangle represents a degree of authority. The top rectangle represents the first level of authority; the next row of rectangles represents the second level of authority, etc. The first level has the most authority and responsibility; the second level has less authority and responsibility, etc.

7. All lines should be drawn vertically or horizontally, not diagonally, in order to produce a neat, professional appearance.

8. A line joining the bottom of one rectangle to the top of another rectangle indicates the line of responsibility. For example, "Who is responsible for whom?" and the line of accountability "Who is accountable to whom?"

It assumes the necessary communication.

9. A solid line going from the side of a rectangle to the side of another indicates a frequently used line of communication only. A broken line represents lesser-used lines of communication (such as consultants, accountants, advisors, etc.).

10. A line should not be drawn from the bottom or top of one rectangle to the side of another.

11. Formal lines of communication are indicated by:

   • *Lines of responsibility*–a subordinate and supervisor should communicate; it's implicit!

   • *Common superior*–if two people are on the same level of authority and account to the same supervisor, there is a line of communication between them (but there is not a responsibility/accountability relationship). (See line b-c.)

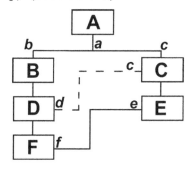

   • *Different superiors*–if two people must communicate on a regular basis as part of their jobs and if they are not at the same level of authority or have different superiors, a line of communication (side to side of the rectangles) needs to be drawn. A solid line indicates frequent communication; a broken line represents special but infrequent communication.

Formal Lines of Communication are represented by line a-b (between box A and box B) and line a-c (between box A and box C).

Line b-c is a formal line of communication between box B and box C (solid horizontal line), but there is not a responsibility/accountability relationship. A special line of communication (line e-f) is between box E and box F (because they have different superiors). Line c-d (the broken line) indicates a special but seldom used line of communication.

12. Only one line comes out of the side of a rectangle.

13. To look balanced and professional, draw all lines from the centre of the sides of the rectangles.

14. Keep the charts as simple, uncomplicated, and balanced as possible, so that it gives a sense of unity and organization. (In larger organizations, it may be necessary to divide the large chart into smaller sections, by departments, or other logical divisions.)

15. To indicate a different relationship from the rest of the positions, a rectangle can be drawn to the side. This is used in such cases as a Vice-President whose sole role is to become Acting President if the President cannot perform his responsibilities or in the case of a special assistant to the CEO.

Types of Organizational Charts

Structural Chart: It is the basic chart upon which the other charts are built. It indicates the organization's activities by department, section, units, etc. It indicates how the various activities are related and the span of control (the number of people responsible to one person). It indicates the levels of authority, lines of responsibility and communication.

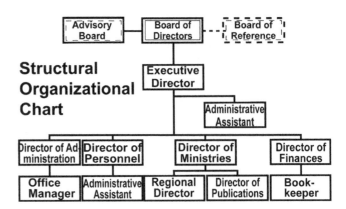

Positional Chart: It is a structural chart plus the names of the people responsible for the activities added.

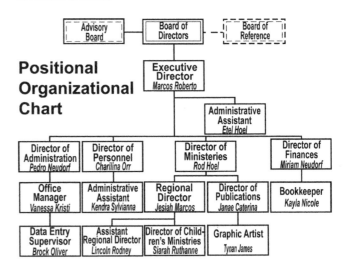

Functional Chart: It is a structural chart plus each rectangle containing a mini-job description, outlining the objectives of the position and what each unit or individual does.

Positional-Functional Chart: It combines the features of the positional and the functional charts.

Pictorial Positional Chart: It is a positional chart with a photo of each person filling the positions. It is especially useful when there are many positions in a large organization. All photos must be the same size and all in color or all in black/white (not mixed).

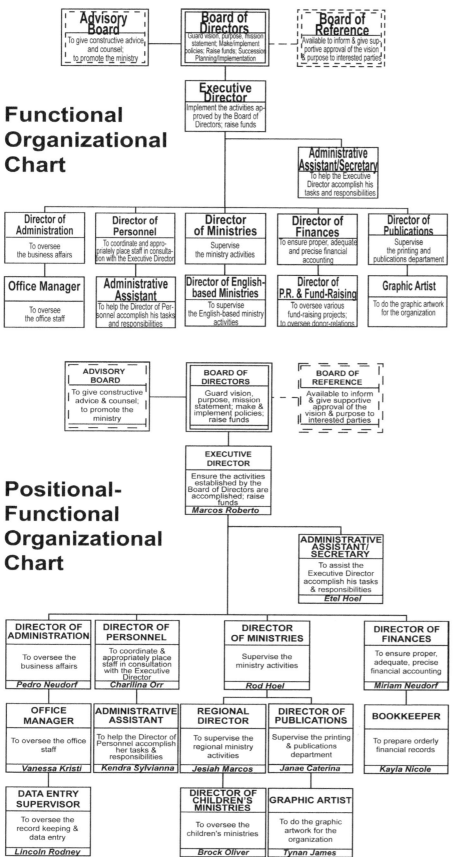

Functional Organizational Chart

Positional-Functional Organizational Chart

Note: The Board of Directors delegates.

The Advisory Board gives advice and counsel.

The Board of Reference recommends the organization and its vision to others.

Pictorial Positional Organizational Chart

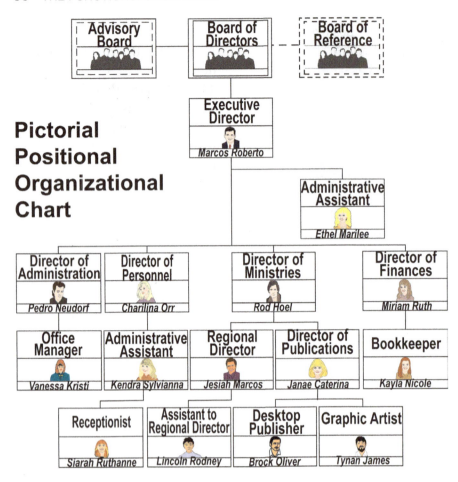

Summary

The act of effectively and efficiently organizing produces a synergism that enables an organization to attain its vision and purpose. The managerial leader seeks for this synergism within the organization.

I have good people working for me! I don't want to meddle in their work!

The best executive is one who has sense enough to pick good men to do what he wants done, and sense enough not to meddle with them while they do it! [Theodore Roosevelt]

Assignment

1. Prepare an organizational chart for your department/organization and a job description for yourself and your subordinates. Discuss the chart and corresponding job descriptions with each subordinate. Resolve any discrepancies and conflicting perceptions.

2. Evaluate your delegation procedures. Do you delegate all that you should? What can you do better?

3. What are the ten key time management habits to put into practice in your life?

FUNCTION # 4: CONTROLLING and MONITORING

Jesus, "the Lord of the Church, the Head of the Body… has not abdicated His leadership role simply because He changed addresses. He is still in control. Through His executive officer, the Holy Spirit, He constantly checks the program of His church and takes corrective action when necessary … checks must be made to determine if we're on target. Corrective action, taken quickly when necessary, can spell the difference between success and failure in any program. Model leadership maintains (reasonable) control" (Eph. 4:15;5:23)

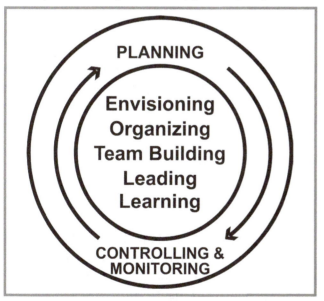

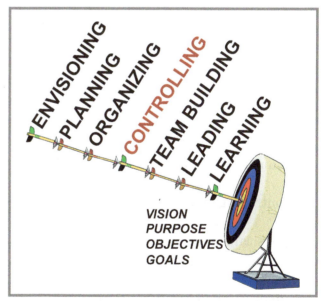

"And the things that you have heard me say in the presence of many witnesses entrust to reliable (faithful, trustworthy) men and women who will also be QUALIFIED (ABLE, COMPETENT) to teach others also." (II Tim. 2:2)

Controlling and monitoring involves setting standards including necessary, enforceable, evaluating and adjusting activities for efficiency and effectiveness in goal attainment. It includes necessary, enforceable controls governed by standards.

The process guides the work of the team. It detects and corrects significant variations in the results obtained from the planned activities and small problems and mistakes before they become big and critical.

Monitoring is like using a compass to keep you on track and to direct you to your destination.

As a pilot, I am alive today because I obeyed the strict controls in aviation!

Controlling should be a positive, productive process. "Controlling" often has a negative connotation because people have seen those who misuse and abuse "controlling" procedures to dominate, to build their own little kingdoms, and instill fear, etc. (wrong use!).

The process enables values and standards to remain consistent while adjusting to a changing environment. It creates better accountability.

The controlling and monitoring process ensures that:
 a) physical resources are well maintained;
 b) equipment is appropriately designed for the task need;
 c) quality and quantity controls maintain the excellency of the standards.
 d) the right people work at the right activities and their performance is evaluated.

Principles and Guidelines

The monitoring system should be integrated into every level of the organization and coordinated with each area.

An effective leader needs to be objective in evaluating the real picture For example, are you pushing productivity too hard to the extent that the people are discouraged, etc.? Are reports being exaggerated to meet the demands, etc.?

Ensure accuracy and encourage honest, accurate, truthful reporting.

Be flexible in evaluation and change. Adapt to the changes in procedures and the action plan.

Focus on the areas with the greatest potential to deviate or stray from the normal as well as the areas most critical if something deviates from the normal.

The controlling process should be economical in time and cost. It should be workable and practical. It should be focused primarily on long-range operations and secondarily on the short-range operations. Be realistic.

The monitoring system must be understood and accepted by everyone. It needs to be in balance with the operations and procedures. Excessive monitoring can give the perception that monitoring, not the vision, is the goal!

Ensure the controls have realistic and practical standards for the activities and tasks. They should suit the situation.

Controlling will only be beneficial and successful if implemented by persons who have a good working "hands-on" knowledge of leadership principles and management skills. In the wrong hands, controlling and monitoring will lead to abuse, chaos, anarchy, and break-up of the organization.

Necessary tools for controlling and monitoring your organization are: budget, financial statements (including break-even analysis, ratio analysis), human resource analysis (see team building sheet), the constitution and by-laws of the organization, legal, government requirements, policies and procedures manual.

Examples

Controls are necessary in many situations (ministry, society, business); without them tragic failures (and sometimes even death) occur.

a) As a pilot for many years, I would make a flight

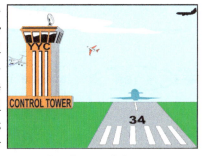

plan in cooperation with air traffic control personnel in order to meet the standards and procedures that would bring my passengers and me to the desired destination. At the destination the control tower led me into the strictly controlled pattern around the airport that controlled the many landings and take-offs. Controls were used for our safety.

b) Lab technologists use "controls" and "standards" to monitor the sta-

bility of their solutions and chemicals, etc. and to monitor their procedures to ensure accuracy of results. If there were no controls or standards to monitor their work, patients could die!

c) Sports use controlling and monitoring rules.

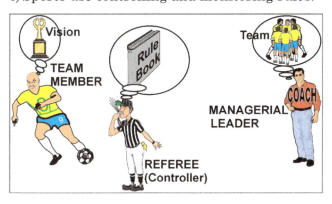

Excessive Monitoring

When monitoring becomes out of control and is dominated by a few "power-hungry" people, monitoring becomes negative controlling. Too often potential leaders and managers are very capable of having positions of authority in their organizations but the present "leaders" are unwilling to relinquish the "controls" to the younger people. In this type of situation, mutual trust and confidence are lacking. The "leaders" believe that no one else can do the job or that mistakes will occur or…the list of excuses is endless! Finding a solution using discussion and interaction is extremely difficult with these controlling leaders (and often cannot take place). After much prayer, if discussion is futile, the potential leaders may need to start their own organizations in order to accomplish the vision or work with another organization which would allow their leadership skills, gifts and talents to be used in a positive manner.

Analysis Worksheet

1. Purpose of the organization: _____
2. Objective: _____
3. Goal(s): _____
4. Desired results: _____
5. Standards necessary to measure the desired result: _____
6. What is happening presently? _____
7. How does our actual performance compare with the standard? _____
8. Evaluation and analysis: _____
   a) Are we within the limits? If "yes", should we adjust our procedures to attempt to improve our effectiveness and efficiency, or should we maintain our present procedures? If "no", what are the deviations from the standards? _____
   b) What are the *root causes* of the deviation?___
   c) What basic functions are weak and create an environment for deviations from the standards?_____
   d) What corrective action do we need to take to improve the implementation of our weakest functions? _____

Controlling and Monitoring Process

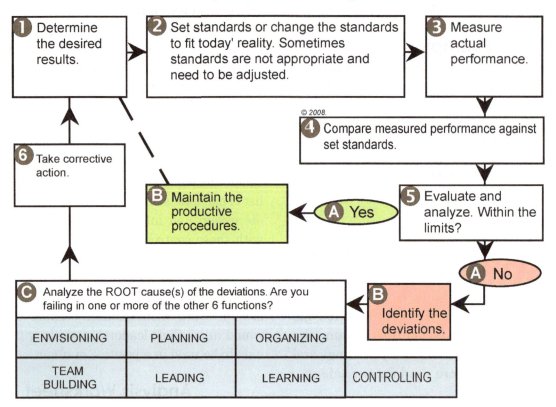

e) What corrective action needs to be taken so that we can maintain our standards?

f) How will we begin to take action?

g) When will we begin to take action?

h) When will we evaluate this corrective action?

i) Who will oversee the corrective action?

j) Who will oversee the evaluation of this action?

Summary

To reach our objectives and fulfill our purpose we need to wisely implement effective and practical controls and standards to ensure that we remain true to our values, vision and purpose. We continually need to evaluate and update our standards and procedures.

Assignment

1. Begin the planning, controlling and monitoring process in your life, ministry, and organization.

2. Why are controls and monitoring important in your organization?

3. What is hindering the controlling process from being effective and efficient?

4. What steps will you implement to improve the effectiveness of your organization?

Old Paradigm

New Paradigm

FUNCTION # 5
TEAM BUILDING

"…stand fast in one spirit, with one mind, striving together (as a team) for the faith of the gospel."
(Phil. 1:27b)

"In things essential, unity;
In things non-essential, liberty;
And in all things, charity (compassion, love)."
(Evangelical Church Alliance).

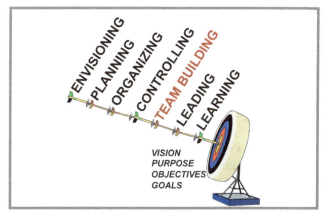

"And the things that you have heard me say in the presence of many witnesses entrust to reliable (faithful, trustworthy) men and women who will also be QUALIFIED (ABLE, COMPETENT) to teach others also." (II Tim. 2:2)

Defining "Teamwork"

Teamwork is the ability to work together toward a common vision. The ability to direct individual accomplishments toward organizational objectives. It is the fuel that allows common people to attain uncommon results.

"Teamwork divides the task and doubles the success."

...it is increasingly evident that groups enjoy their greatest success when they become more productive units called teams.

"Now this is the law of the jungle,
It's as old and as true as the sky.
And the wolf that shall keep it may prosper
As the creeper that girdles the tree trunk;
The truth runneth forward and back.
For the strength of the pack is the wolf,
And the strength of the wolf is the pack".

(R. Kipling)

"A strong leader knows that if he develops his associates, he will be even stronger."

People are the team's most important resource! All else are aids to help these people become productive, efficient, and effective as they work together to see the vision realized, the purpose fulfilled, and the objectives and goals reached, as well as feeling fulfilled and being successful in the process.

TEAMWORK: Coming together is a beginning... keeping together is progress ...working together is a success. (John Maxwell)

When establishing and developing teams, a leader needs to understand the basic nature and traits of individuals.

The Nature of Man

What is man? (Ps.8:4,5; Heb.2:6-8; Gen.1:27, 31)

Created in God's Image

Human beings are a very special creation. "And God saw that it was very good" (Gen. 1:31). When we work with people we are working with persons who are very precious in the sight of God.

Created with Basic Needs

You must understand and work in harmony with the basic human needs. The list of five basic needs originated with Maslow; however he omitted the spiritual needs of each human being.

Meeting man's basic needs is crucial in motivation.

5. SELF-ACTUALIZATION: realize one's potential; feel fulfilled; personal satisfaction

4. ESTEEM: self-esteem; respect from others & self; achievement; recognition

3. BELONGINGNESS & LOVE: love, affection; feeling of belonging; human contact; social interaction; acceptance

2. SECURITY: protection; safety; freedom from chaos, fear or threat

1. SPIRITUAL* & PHYSICAL: relationship with God through Jesus Christ*; air, water, food, shelter, health, etc. (* added by author)

Created to Have Dominion

Although it is natural for man to desire leadership positions and to dominate creation, the skills and art of leadership must be learned! (Gen.1:26; Heb.2:6-8; I Tim.3:1)

Slow to Change

It is true some things must not change such as Biblical values, but many other components must change such as the strategy ("how-to") to get things done, etc.

Created to be a Doer, Called of God

Man's work is important to God; He evaluates all work—His own, yours, mine, the Church's, your business, ministry, etc. (1 Thess. 5:24)

In God's plan, there is no distinction between "secular jobs" and "full-time ministry" for the Christian.

Each legitimate vocation is acceptable to God when it is done as service to Him and in obedience to His calling. Discover your talents and His purpose for you. Use them!

Recognize your activity as God's work. Responsibly do it His way. Believe He can bring satisfaction, fulfillment, and God-honouring results.

Combine or integrate your work and your spiritual life into one meaningful whole lifestyle. You are participating in the highest and most noble work–God's work.

Focus on God's priorities. Eliminate "clutter" and distractions to fulfilling His call.

Created with a Unique Blend of Strengths and Weaknesses

Each person thinks, analyzes, and responds differently, due to unique personalities.

It has been proven scientifically that the brain has a creative side and a judicial side. One side dominates the other at any one time. Those who are more managerial in their approach tend to use the judicial, analytical left side of their brain; those who are leadership-oriented tend to use the creative, innovative, intuitive right side of their brain.

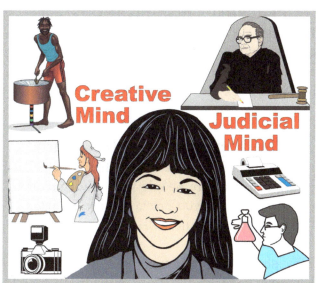

We need to grow in the area of our gifts.

Each person has strengths and weaknesses. A strength gives you confidence and from that platform of strength you can deal with your weak points. One major way to buttress your weak points is to delegate tasks in which you are weak!

When a leader delegates tasks to someone else who is stronger in a particular area, both persons become stronger! Each will be more effective in situations and surroundings that build on their strengths. *This is synergism in action*!

Basic Tendencies and Styles

To help you work with people, it is good to know something about their unique personalities. However, in addition to reviewing the four basic personality traits below, we need to understand that human behavior falls generally into two broad categories: extroverts and introverts.

"*Extroverts*" tend to be sociable, and choose to interact with others, especially in group settings. "*Introverts*" prefer one-on-one interaction rather than group settings. Both extroverts, introverts, and the following four traits, are ALL needed on a well-balanced team.

Doers

Strength: They tackle difficult tasks. They are motivated by challenges, vision, and the results of their envisioning. They tend to lead forcefully and persistently.

Weakness: They can be insensitive, impatient, inflexible. When under tension or pressure they can become autocratic.

Doers are needed when there is a difficult, challenging task to be accomplished!

Influencers

Strength: They get things done by influencing others with their articulate, verbal skills. They are motivated by recognition (the desire to be recognized for what they are doing).

Weakness: They tend to be impulsive. They lack the ability to follow through. They have too much optimism without reality and objectivity.

Relators
Strength: They like appreciation for what they do. They implement plans that have to do with people. They lead through relationships.
Weakness: They are non-initiators and resist change. They need a secure environment. Under tension or pressure they often acquiesce– a "yes" is said, but they don't mean it.

Thinkers
Strength: They are motivated by being "right". They insist on quality. They criticize on the basis of deep thought, objectivity and documented facts. They lead through structure and methodology. They search for the "right" plan.
Weakness: Under tension and pressure they avoid appearing. They retreat and are not to be found!

The Nature of the Church
The true CHURCH is a "LIVING BODY" made up of many members (I Cor.12:12-27).

Each member has a specific role to play within that body (I Cor.7:7; I Cor.12:4-31). Leadership discovers and empowers that role!

The Church must look after itself so that it can be healthy, grow, and perform the ministries for which it was created (Acts 6:1-7)–to bear fruit.

God evaluates the Church (Rev.2:3); the world evaluates it also (I Peter 2:12).

Unfortunately the world often sees the Church as having the largest registered membership, more facilities and material resources than any other one organization, well-paid ministries, ministers and missionaries–but very inadequate and inefficient stewardship!

The world often sees the Church as the least effective in its performance, exhibiting low productivity, low quality, and unfinished products, etc.

Churches are often "meeting oriented" and generally lack "specific" objectives for itself and individual believers. Mediocrity reigns!

More money and emphasis is placed on property, church buildings and program development than into "people" development. How tragic!

The focus is often on "activities" and entertainment, rather than "accomplishment". The Church has developed "actors" and "spectators" rather than fulfilled, successful "doing" participants.

There is a lack of proper delegation. Many churches operate as a "one-man" organization with a benevolent dictator–or ruthless master!

Three-fold problem facing the Church
  1. Many idle "members"
  2. Unclear objectives and priorities
  3. Ineffective mobilizing, energizing, training and empowering of the potential

Jesus and His Team
How did He select His team? He prayed (Luke 6:12,13) then He selected those who were willing to sacrifice, learn, follow, be loyal to Him, complete the work, be responsible and accountable.

The Importance of the Team
Leaders look for people better than themselves!
   "When you hire people who are smarter than you are, you prove you are smarter than they are". (R.H. Grant)

Why should we function together as a team? Why can't we all function individually? God's design is that we should function together as a team; more can be accomplished than if we worked individually.

The absence of teamwork in any department will limit the organization's effectiveness and can eventually destroy a church, ministry, or business.

People need to participate as "stakeholders". Their input matters. They will be better at decision-making, problem-solving and at using their skills.

"... with one mind striving together for the faith of the gospel." (Phil. 1:27b)

The Attributes of a Good Team
• Interdependence—less "power" struggles

• Ownership—buying into the vision, purpose, objectives, etc.

• Contribution—unique skills, talents, abilities, gifts, knowledge, ideas, resources

• Trust—can express ideas, opinions and feelings without feeling threatened

• Communication—clear, accurate; avoid malicious gossip and wrong perceptions; show you care.
  "An eye can threaten like a loaded and leveled gun; or can insult like hissing and kicking; or in its altered mood by beams

of kindness, make the heart dance with joy." (Ralph Waldo Emerson)

• Development—improve skills, abilities and how to put them to good use

• Interaction—environment for creative, new ideas with positive conflict resolution

• Decision-making—team participation helps the leader come to a final decision for which he will be responsible with the team

• Evaluation—recognition, constructive analysis

• Role dynamics—a clear and consistent understanding of our roles in the team generates a high level of cohesion and productivity, reducing ambiguity and conflict in functions and communications

• Cohesiveness—motivates team members to remain together. Highly cohesive teams pull together, enjoy being together, perform well together and are not looking for opportunities to get out of the team. Teamwork and productivity go hand-in-hand.

The Team Leader
• The team leader exemplifies godly character (integrity, honesty, ethics) for all to follow.
• He carefully selects team members.
• He coordinates the team's activity.
• He encourages vision and goal ownership.
• He oversees, communicates and encourages.
• He ensures adequate training.
• He trusts, supports and resolves conflicts.
• He is a self-starter.
• He plans, organizes, motivates and informs.
• He monitors, replaces or transfers personnel who do not fit with the team.
• He takes responsibility for both good and bad results.

- He demonstrates competence and wisdom.

Selecting a Team Leader

Look for:
- Purpose (for himself and the team)—He must be able to define clearly what the team should be doing, its focus and goals.
- People-oriented—He needs a heart for people. Research has shown that 85 percent of leadership failure is due to a lack of ability to work with people! Matt.20:25
  We must serve people by showing:
      empathy, loyalty, friendliness, kindness social manners, good "PR" (public relations), expressing one's viewpoints respectfully so that others can accept or consider what is said, being tactful

- Character and integrity—authentic, whose walk follows his/her talk; exemplary

- Value system based on the Holy Scriptures

- Goals (beware of possible hidden agendas)

- Reasonable measure of intelligence that is sharpened and complemented by additional and challenging studies.

- Honorable, ethical work habits

- Ability to adjust and maintain proper balance. He keeps calm when chaos is all around him.

- Overall personality—
  Is it dominant? detached? calm? rational? generous? dependent? warmhearted? selfless? energetic? enthusiastic? sense of humor?, etc.

- Experience and expertise in:
  - group problem-solving,
  - conducting effective meetings,
  - presenting good ideas in an influential manner,
  - pulling the team together, keeping it on track and focused on the overall purpose.
- Acceptance of responsibility—A leader must accept the responsibility of the group regardless of its success or failure. If he is not willing to accept the responsibility of the group, then he should not accept the position of leadership.

The one who leads the band must face the music!

Selecting a Team Member

Team effectiveness and success depends on individual members who share knowledge and experience (ability and skill); commitment to the purpose and objectives; open communication with both the leader and the team; trust and cooperation.

Select someone who has the following abilities, skills and experience.
- He understands the organization's purpose and vision.
- He has training in the particular area in question and is willing to have further training. He has the gifts and abilities for the task and keeps a commitment.
- He works well with others. He listens and respects fellow teammates.
- He works hard. He can expose and solve problems creatively.
- He can take initiative and creatively make decisions.
- He speaks up with wisdom and kindness when the team heads in the wrong direction. He demonstrates suitable discussion skills.
  - He gives reasons for his own opinion.

- He listens to the reasons behind other's opinions. He pays attention to body language and feedback.
- He collects ideas to find areas of agreement.

Do not try to force a person into a mould that God never intended him or her to fill. Disaster will result! We must recognize that character, personality, skills and personal experience mold each person into a unique individual. This means you must carefully place that person in the appropriate position where he/she fits well and feels fulfilled.

Never try to teach a pig to sing! It wastes your time and it annoys the pig! (Paul Dickson)

Growing a Cohesive Team

"The three circles suggest that the task, individual, and team needs are always interacting upon each other. The circles overlap but they do not sit on top of each other... there is always some degree of "tension" between them. Many of an individual's needs, such as the need to achieve and the social need for human companionship, are met in part by participating in working groups... the circle must always

be seen in relation to the other two. As a leader you need to be constantly aware of what is happening in your group in terms of the three circles". The managerial team leader is accountable for the three areas to work together harmoniously:

- to achieve the common *task*
- to work well as a *team*
- to respect and develop its *individual* members

Team Building Process

1. Define the purpose, strategy, etc.
2. Appoint an accepted leader.
3. Delegate.
4. Build on the strengths of individual team members. Each team member has strengths. Each team member has weaknesses. Each is more effective in some situations and less effective in others. Leadership potential and personal effectiveness is determined by matching strengths and skills against specific situations. The application of "learned" skills turns the potential into active performance. Buttress the individual's weaknesses. Do these factors blend and overlap sufficiently to be balanced?
5. Activate the process with careful evaluation. Use the 20 Characteristics of an Effective Team as a guide so that positive synergism, change and productivity results. This enables the vision and purpose to be accomplished. See where you are weak or failing and needing to give serious attention.

1 John 17:21; Eph.4:1-6 Phil.3:12(b)-14;Heb.12:1 I Cor.9:24

Common Vision & Purpose

Provides FOCUS for cooperation

2 Is.1:18;Proverbs; Jam.1:19;Gn.11:1-9

Good Communication

Provides OPENNESS for cooperation

3 Exod.18:17,18 Num.27:15-23 Acts.16:9,10

Accepted Leadership

Provides AUTHORITY for cooperation

4 I Kings. 5; Neh. 3; Eph.4:7-13;I Cor.12

Appropriate Division of Labor [Delegation]
Provides INTERDEPENDENCE for cooperation

5 I Cor.14:40; Tit.1:5 Acts.6:1-7

Organization

Provides STRUCTURE for cooperation

20 Gen.6:5-7;Exod.32:14 Jonah 3:10 I Sam.15:11-26

Adjusting the Action Plan
Provides NECESSARY CHANGE for success

6 Job 19:4; Prov.9:12 Gal.6:5; Ezek.33:6

Responsibility

Provides CREATED OBLIGATION for cooperation

19 Gen.1:31;Matt.25:14-30 Luke19:12-28; Rev.2,3 1 Cor.3:6-15;Matt.3:17

Evaluation of Performance

Provides REALISTIC ANALYSIS for success

Characteristics of an Effective Team that produces Synergism, Change and Productivity

7 Acts.6:1-6;15:36-40 Neh.; Josh.6; Jud.7:16-22; Prov.15:22

Accepted Plan

Provides the PROCESS for cooperation

18 I Cor.9:18-27;Nehemiah

Controlling Performance

Provides the STANDARD for success

8 Nehemiah; Esther (esp.4:15-17)

Commitment

Provides STAMINA for cooperation

17 Matt.12:36;18:23 Luke 16:2; Rom.14:12 I Pet.4:5

Accountability

Provides the DISCIPLINE for success

A team is a group of people who must cooperate to succeed in the achievement of exceptional results ... and do! As a result, each team member is rewarded with a sense of fulfillment.

9 Heb.13:17; Exod.14; Luke.5:4-7; Mk.4:35-41

Trust

Provides CONFIDENCE for cooperation

16 Phil.2:13;3:14;4:13 Matt.28:19,20 Acts.1:10-26 Jam.1:22-26

Action

Provides the OUTCOME for success

10 Acts.6:1-6; Prov.24:5,6; Neh.1:11-7:3

Effective Decision-Making & Problem-Solving

Provides STABILITY for cooperation

15 II Tim.2:2,15;Tit.1:5; Prov.4:13;22:6;Deut.6:7

Training

Provides the SKILLS for success

14 Josh.1:8,9;Nehemiah Matt.4:19;Mark10:29,30

Motivation

Provides the MORALE for success

13 John 20:19-29; John 21 II Tim.4:9-22; I Sam.19; I Sam.20; I John3:17-19

Solid Relationships
Provides COHESIVENESS for success

12 John13-15;Matt.13:1-23 John11;Luke10:1-24

Formal & Informal Interaction

Provides UNITY for success

11 Luke11:1; Ps.1; 2 Tim.2:15; 2 Cor.1:11

Prayer & Bible Study

Provides SPIRITUAL STRENGTH for success

Belbin Team Analysis Tool

The following was contributed by Mark Orr.

The Belbin Team Analysis tool is developed by Dr. Meredith Belbin. His full materials and assessments can be obtained at http://www.belbin.com By working as a team, we know that we can accomplish so much more than working individually. But teams require the right combination of team members, and a good team leader. I have found the Belbin Team Analysis to be a very simple yet powerful tool to help you analyze your existing team, or use it as a roadmap to build a new team. This short introduction to the Belbin tool is only to stimulate your thinking, and show you that there can be structure and meaning to how you construct your teams.

Here is how it works: A simple questionnaire tool is provided for each person you are assessing. When analyzing your team, place their names next to the roles that represent their primary and secondary strengths. You will then see your team mapped and team issues will begin to be evident

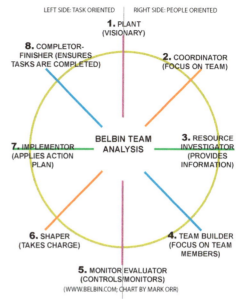

to you. Once completed, the person's primary and secondary team roles are determined, as well as the person's particular weak roles. (Applying this tool requires a little training, so it is not included in this book. However, with some wise judgement you can do well at placing your team members without the tool). These results are plotted on a circular graph, and a team's gaps, strengths and

---

1. THE PLANT   *opposite to*   5. THE MONITOR EVALUATOR

This person is the source of ideas, dreams, and creativity. They are excellent at generating many new ideas, but very poor at evaluating and choosing the best ideas.

This person evaluates ideas, often pointing out all the reasons why an idea won't work.

Comment: Plants and Monitor Evaluators are on opposite ends of the same axis. Although there may be conflicts between them, they need each other. Without a Plant, teams stagnate. Without a Monitor-Evaluator, teams go in far too many directions, without focus.

---

2. THE COORDINATOR: *opposite to*   6. THE SHAPER

The Coordinator is someone whose main focus is the team itself, ensuring that each member is fulfilling their maximum potential, is serving in the right job or role on the team, and that the team is experiencing the synergy that good teams should produce. In an ideal world, Coordinators would be the team leaders. Shapers and Coordinators are all about control, and are placed on opposite ends of the control axis. However, their styles of leadership are very different, and serve the team at different times and places in the life of a team.

The Shaper on the team is a natural leader who likes taking charge and giving orders. They can make quick decisions and get a job done. They may make good team leaders in emergency or crisis situations. Shapers, however, tend to pay little attention to the health of the team or whom they may hurt in the process.

3. THE RESOURCE INVESTIGATOR *opposite to*   7. THE IMPLEMENTOR

A Resource Investigator is not afraid to cross lines (organizational, denominational, national) to find the resources, funds, information, or materials that are needed for the team. They are the ones you ask questions such as "Do you know where to find..." They are the networkers of the team.

This person is on the opposite end of the axis from Resource Investigators. They are concerned with applying the resources and ideas and putting the plan to work.

4. THE TEAM BUILDER *opposite to*   8. THE COMPLETER-FINISHER

Every team needs a Team Builder. These are not the team leaders, but rather those who are concerned with the feelings, health, and emotions of team members and the 'air' around the team. They love parties and celebrations and want to make sure no one is getting hurt.

Opposite team builders are Completer Finishers, who are very task oriented and want to make sure the project gets finished, down to its final last detail. They help keep a team goal-focused and always remind the team about the task at hand.

weaknesses can be analyzed. Example: #1 is opposite to #5. Effective teams have members (not necessarily eight people) who are strong in at least one of the eight roles. These roles are:
There is much more than can be discussed about teams and the Belbin assessment system. In this space, I will just mention a few notes:

- Everyone has primary and secondary team role strengths. If you find yourself on a team where your primary role is well represented by others, it may be natural for you to serve rather in your secondary strength.

- One person can fill several roles. For example, in a small team of four people, all eight roles could be covered through primary and secondary role strengths in each person.

- A team leader can come from any role. However, the team leader must recognize the importance of having a Coordinator on the team, and of delegating significant team leadership responsibility to this person.

- Team assessment asks three basic questions:
  - Does my team have too many people trying to fulfil one or two roles?

  - Does my team have gaps, that is, roles that are not filled by anyone?
  - Am I loading a person with expectations to fulfil a role that he or she is not suited to fulfil? Are they serving in the wrong role or job?

- If you ask yourself the above questions, that is often enough to uncover the real reasons for team discord and ineffectiveness.

Motivation

Motivation is the inner desire of the worker to accomplish a particular task or goal. People follow a managerial leader who gives them compelling reasons to reach an objective.

An effective leader ignites imagination and communicates passion.

To motivate means to impel and incite that which is within the individual, rather than without or exterior (the exterior is very temporary), and that which incites him to motion. Motivation involves any idea, need and emotion that prompts someone to an action. Action is the end result of motivation. "As he thinks in his heart, so is he" (Prov. 23:7).

The reality of the vision embodied deep within one's soul will motivate a person to accomplish the vision and purpose in spite of hardships and difficulties. This is why a leader must know how to transvision (to transfer that vision to the team members in such a way that they embrace it as their own).

Managerial leaders cannot lead unless subordinates are motivated from within to follow and excel.

The five basic levels of needs, beginning with the spiritual and physical elements, should be addressed in order to motivate an individual. (See Maslow's Hierarchy of Needs, pg.92)

God chooses a person on the basis of what he is to become. Increase motivation by taking others with you, and letting them watch you fulfill certain tasks. Create a need through exposure to reality.

Creating an Environment for Motivation

Recognize the problem of overcoming initial inertia. Capture the person's potential.

Believe God can make each person significant. There are no unimportant people in God's creation!

Intensify interpersonal relationships. Know each person well.

Dissolve emotional blocks such as: fear, insecurity, worry, anxiety, depression, anger, pride, arrogance.

Create trust and loyalty.

Expose people to reality. This creates a need they will want to meet. Expose and address major problems before followers raise them as obstacles or barriers.

Delegate. Feed and develop responsibility through delegation. Call for commitment.

Show them how through personal interaction, formal and informal training. Ensure they know what is expected.

Publicly reward good performance and privately correct poor performance. Take notice of the person who is doing something helpful for the team.

Be sensitive to emotional blocks and choose the best way to overcome such blocks.

Communicate the purpose, vision, objectives and goals clearly and concisely. You must ask yourself, "What am I producing?" Encourage feedback. It doesn't mean automatic agreement but you try to understand each other's concerns.

Be enthusiastic. It becomes contagious!

Demonstrate unconditional love.

Pray that they will respond.

Evaluate and change.

Leaders know very well that *"destroying capable men and women simply because they fought and lost can result in many good people being thrown out and into the hands of a competing company"* (business, organization, church or ministry).

Self-starters

Self-starters are motivated people who have the inner drive to get moving.

To develop a motivated self-starter, develop four essential qualities:

1. high energy output,
2. commitment,
3. creativity,
4. resourcefulness (the ability to demonstrate an extra resource that is drawn upon when the going gets tough, the challenge is great, and the stakes are high.)

Those who are *unmotivated* will stop in their tracks whenever they face a hurdle or barrier.

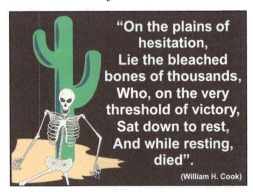

"On the plains of hesitation,
Lie the bleached bones of thousands,
Who, on the very threshold of victory,
Sat down to rest,
And while resting, died".

(William H. Cook)

Gangel's Five Principles of Motivation

1. Motivation depends on mutually accepted goals.
2. Motivation is unleashed, not superimposed.
3. Motivation builds on the basis of need fulfillment.
4. Motivation tends to follow positive ministry satisfaction.
5. Motivation relates dynamically to leadership style.

A leader who appears often before his teammates can transmit enthusiasm, sincerity, and zeal in his team. This can help him and the team go through very difficult times. He shows his identification with the team and the vision to be achieved.

Stress Management

Stress is the wear-and-tear on the body as a result of the demands and challenges of life.

When coping with stress, do you sometimes feel like you are sliding down a slippery slope?

Sources of Stress:

• Family, relatives, friends
• Social/community interaction
• Work Environment
• Change
• Decision-making
• Commuting
• Phobias
• Physical ailments, disease and pain
• Environment (chemicals, etc.)
• Lack of implementation of managerial leadership principles

Stress can be minimized when:

• authentic leadership principles and management skills are implemented,
• effective evaluation and adjustment takes place,
• training and development of each person on the team becomes habitual.

Conflict and Negotiation

The majority of human conflicts are leadership issues. An effective managerial leader should not be quick to intervene in a conflict between two individuals, unless it is a very serious conflict. If he is too quick, he may be the one whose respect is lost forever with the conflicting persons.

Do not allow conflict to "smolder"! The managerial leader should attempt a win/win outcome in any conflict so that no one feels like he was taken advantage of, or manipulated, or "got the short end of the stick".

Remember to separate the person from the problem. *Be hard on the problem; soft (compassionate) on the person.*

Be prepared to walk away when you detect a belligerent attitude of absolutely no compromise or negotiating will.

Leaders work with people and managers work with things. Managerial leaders need people-skills with versatility. This enables them to assist in conflict resolution and negotiations.

Versatility: "The ability to adjust your behavior as a leader to meet the changing needs of your team members and of the situation".

Sources of Conflict
- Goal incompatibility,
- Overly structured relationships,
- Limited resources,
- Communication distortions,
- Individual differences,
- Ignoring information,
- Distorted judgment,
- Inconsistency,
- Emotions,
- Screening out the communications.

Sometimes it is necessary to bring in outsiders to "shake things up" (for example, a management consultant who will stir up the stagnant unit, its "leadership", or the whole organization and who can add a fresh perspective in the process)—get this course into your organization!

Overcoming Communication Barriers
- Clarify.
- Understand the true purpose of each communication.
- Regulate information flow.
- Encourage feedback.
- Simplify the language.
- Be an active listener.
- Constrain emotions and keep rational.
- Use face-to-face communication.
- Support your ideas with information, photos and truthful data.

Effective Communication
Effective communication is "the act of exchanging information between individuals by a common system of signs, symbols, or behavior. The key to effective communication involves using commonly understood language to communicate ideas".

It is the transferring of information and the understanding of its meaning.

It involves the art of:
- seeing the other person's point of view,
- sensing and understanding how things feel to the other person,
- using stories, illustrations, graphics, etc. to clarify concepts and ideas,
- listening (Seek not only to be understood, but to understand—be a good listener!).

Effective communication involves accurately interpreting non-verbal communication (for example: body language, vocal tone, etc.) to understand what the other person is feeling.

Intuition
"What about intuition? How does that fit into such a "rational process"? Intuition, "the sixth sense," is the ability to perceive things or come to conclusions without appearing to work through a conscious reasoning process. ...Intuition

is the ability to very rapidly process large amounts of information, integrating current data with past experiences and impressions stored in our subconscious mind. With proper stimulation, these pieces of information can surface as thoughts and judgments... pray about and work on this decision until the two elements (reason and intuition) are in congruence".

Intuition is important, not only in making decisions, etc. but also in effective communication. It helps a person to "read" the other person (his feelings, thoughts and reactions).

Perpetually Redefine Quality

View the past as experience, not impediment. Pursuing excellence is more than just solving problems. Realize that when things are going well it is time to improve and do better! Emphasize that excellence begins in the boardroom and must filter throughout the organization.

> "Excellence is dedication to a job that's hard to do,
> Going the extra mile and always trying to follow through.
> Excellence is communication, sharing everything you know,
> And learning how to listen so your expertise will grow.
> Excellence is appreciation of the talent that you see,
> Acknowledging a job well done inspires success and loyalty.
> Excellence is aspiration with a higher goal in mind,
> To trust in God and reach for things of a more rewarding kind".

The subtle art of leadership is apparent when you observe the leader sharing and teaching responsibility to subordinates, who themselves, are individually and collectively coming up with answers, solving problems, and making good decisions. Obviously when this is happening the leader has been able to get them to pull together; they have bought into that special, unique, and exciting vision.

- Do unto your boss as you would have your subordinates do unto you! Do unto your subordinates as you would want your boss to do to you!
- Be sure to cooperate sideways.
- Respect the chain of command from the top down and the bottom up.

Conducting Productive Meetings

A meeting leader or chairman must be a facilitator.

- He opens the meeting.
- He reviews the agenda.
- He designates a "minutes" or note-taking person.
- He moves on time through each agenda item.
- He evaluates prior actions taken.
- He encourages discussion that leads to decisions, avoiding one person's power and authority from stifling the ideas and contributions of other team members.
- He gathers ideas for the next meeting.
- He makes sure that the actions (and their deadlines) to be taken are delegated to the right person for implementation and follow through.
- He keeps the meeting from handling too much in the allotted time. He narrows the focus.
- He doesn't let the meeting flounder or wander off the intended path or agenda.
- He avoids distraction.
- He closes the meeting on time.

Boards and Executives

Why are some organizations ineffective? Why do some fail? Why are there so many struggles, conflicts, and stress in such organizations?

A main cause is ineffective Boards and Executives.

- The board does not trust the CEO, executive officers, and staff to function properly. As a result it meddles with daily operations. The line between board function and the staff management team is constantly violated.
- The board "rubber stamps" everything the CEO and staff do.
- The board is aloof and out of touch with the organization, its work, and its struggles.
- The chairperson, president, or another member of the board is given authority beyond his/her responsibility and job description.
- The board restricts the CEO to the point that he/she cannot fulfill his assigned responsibilities.
- The board unfairly criticizes the CEO's personality, character and how he does things.
- The CEO or a member of the board lacks values, godly character, or people skills.
- The board does not establish, understand, or protect the organization's values, vision, mission statement and policies. It fails to stay on the cutting edge.
- The board does not evaluate on a regular basis the direction and effectiveness of the organization, its changing environment, the economic and political situation of the country, and the needs of the people for whom it serves, etc.
- The board does not understand its own role, the roles of the executive, CEO, staff, etc.
- The board confuses policies with "rules" and "procedures" and restricts the CEO and staff from functioning in line with the policies based on the values of the organization.
- The board sincerely believes it is being effective but in reality the organization may be in the final stages of its life-span.

Relationships in the Organization

There are diverse organizational structures and differently perceived roles. The following is a general structure to use as a guideline.

BOARD INEFFECTIVENESS

Purpose of the Board

"In the multitude of counsellors there is safety" (Prov 11:14b KJV). The Board of Directors' role is to be the trustee of the values-based vision. Its governance must not lose sight of this! All that the board does must be directly related to the accomplishment of the vision.

A sound, effective value system is the basis for the vision, the establishment of governing and general policies that ensure obedience to the **mission statement** all throughout the organization.

POSITIONS	RESPONSIBILITIES
Board President	Responsible for the integrity of the board
Board Vice-President	Responsible for the integrity of the board when the President is unable to fulfill his responsibilities
Board Chairperson	Responsible for the integrity of the board meeting process
Board Secretary	Responsible for the integrity of the board documents
Board Treasurer	Responsible for the integrity of the financial policies, records, and audits
Board Unit	Responsible for the integrity of the values, vision, purpose, mission statement and evaluation process
CEO	Responsible for the integrity of the organization's activities; the implementation of the agreed-upon plans and objectives; attends all Board meetings
Executive Unit	Responsible for the integrity and oversight of the compliance to the values, policies, constitution, mission statement; for the strategic implementation and accomplishment of the objectives and goals
Staff Unit	Responsible for the integrity of the daily operations (which accomplish the goals and objectives effectively and efficiently)

Responsibilities of the Board

The Establishment of Values

A value system needs to be deeply rooted in Scripture with Jesus' values as the model. Values are general in nature—they apply at any

MODEL FOR BASIC ORGANIZATIONAL STRUCTURE

time in any circumstance with anyone.

An organization is known for its value system (what the organization believes and stands for). Setting goals, deploying staff, formulating procedures, planning, strategizing, and all other board, staff and management activity are controlled by those underlying "values".

The Establishment of General Policies

The general policies are rooted in the values. They guide the nature or direction of the organization. They ensure that the vision, purpose, objectives, and goals are accomplished effectively and efficiently. General policies need to be explicit, brief, current, literal, applicable and effective in all parts of the organization.

These essential, values-based policies are used

by the Board of Directors for long-range planning and to establish and ensure the accomplishment of the vision, the financial stability, and the integrity of the organization. These policies are used by the staff to guide them in short- and long-range planning.

The Establishment of a Mission Statement

Boards must be able to articulate clearly a mission statement for the organization. The mission is the theme and backbone of the organization and is firmly rooted in the values and vision.

The mission statement must be powerful, succinct, accurate and current. It must state the desired results. It must include the reason for the organization's existence. The organization's ethos and values need to be stated.

The Board of Directors must establish and take ownership of the mission statement and live out the mission of the organization. The Board must establish a process of evaluation of the mission and deal with necessary change.

Board Governance

When the right values, policies and vision are established, effective directors can affect many issues with less effort and less interference in the management process—yet address that which is of enduring importance.

The Board enforces finely-crafted policy-making based on what the organization believes and stands for—its values.

It communicates and delegates effectively to the CEO and his creative management team who in turn work at producing effective results. With good policies in place, the board can delegate authority to the CEO to make further choices as long as they are "within" the organization's values, policies, and vision. *This requires the board to exercise discipline to "let go" and to delegate.* It delegates authority to the CEO to make fur-

ther decisions within the parameters of the organization's values, policies, and vision. It exercises discipline to delegate authority, responsibility and empowerment to the CEO.

It develops effective board and executive relationships. *It needs a strong executive!* It is critical that the relationship between the two is healthy and the link is well established to set the stage for effective board governance with good management by the Executive Committee.

It possesses the responsibility of the organization in partnership with the CEO, the team that is doing the front-line work, and the constituency that supports it.

It empowers others but does not give them a "carte blanche" or freehand. Delegation should not dissipate into "abdication"! It can trust the staff to figure out the best way to do the job within the well-defined policy boundaries.

When policy boundaries are well defined, the board can rest easier while the staff figure out the best way to do the job within those boundaries.

It delegates without meddling. It provides spiritual leadership, insight, counsel, support, communication, harmony and encouragement to the CEO. It trains young people to become effective board members.

It serves in public and community relations, assists in fund-raising and exemplifies strong Christian character.

Remember: anyone can rule—that's easy. To govern is difficult for it means shifting from old to new paradigms. It means serious trusteeship, being big enough to embrace the farsighted view, concern over results of the endeavour, and obsessive empowering and building of people to do the job. Let's re-create our governing boards—they too must learn to lead!

Responsibilities of the CEO

Wherever I've seen a non-profit institution with a strong board that gives the right kind of leadership, it represents very hard work on the part of the CEO—not only to bring the right people onto the board but to mold them into a team and point them in the right direction. In my experience, the CEO is the conscience of the board.... The tendency of so many CEOs is to try to have a board that won't do any harm because it won't do anything. It is the wrong tendency.... It requires continuing work to find the right people and to train them. They come in knowing what you expect of them, and they have very tough expectations in terms of time and money and work and responsibility.

The CEO is the leader of the organization as a whole. He accounts to the collective board (not an individual board member). However, when the Board is not in session, he needs to account to the president of the Board.

He needs above average public relations and team building skills.

The CEO is the bridge between the board and the rest of the organization (the staff, the management process, etc.). He develops trust between the board, CEO, executive and staff.

The CEO develops the executive and operating policies that directly relate to the organization's daily operations. They are based on the general policies. They are the responsibility of the CEO and his/her staff (not the responsibility of the board). They need to be explicit, brief, current, literal, applicable and effective in all parts of the organization.

The CEO recommends appropriate policies, projects, programs, budgets, other agenda items to the board. Strong boards need strong executives.

The CEO assists the board chairperson in the preparation of the agenda for the board meetings. He oversees the establishment of operating and executive policies. He implements the general policies adopted by the board.

The CEO sees that all activity moves towards accomplishing the purpose, objectives and goals of the organization.

The CEO ensures adequate, effective delegation to and accountability from the executive officers and through the executive officers to the rest of the staff.

The CEO is a listener! When team members have personal problems, be careful to listen to them and be sympathetic BUT encourage them to resolve problems themselves. Compliment them when they do.

Can the CEO be a Board Member?
The CEO can be a board member only if all of the following criteria are met:
- if the board of directors so chooses,
- if the constitution permits, and
- if the law of the province, state, or country permits.

Caution: The board should hear the positive and the negative from the CEO, not via the grapevine. *Therefore, CEO, keep your board well informed!* A good public relations gesture is to meet informally and individually with the president, chairperson, and other board members; they will appreciate it!

> Any organization needs a strong board that is committed, energetic, and supportive. Good boards do not fall out of the sky. It takes hard work to select the right members and to work together as a team. Then it is the responsibility of the CEO to build a strong team of staff who together can accomplish the vision and purpose of the organization.

Summary

Teamwork is the collective talents of many individuals. It is essential for the vision, purpose, objectives and goals to be accomplished effectively and efficiently. Use all available resources and empower each team member to work together and to develop his or her own abilities, talents, and skills so that they become successful and fulfilled.

> Once upon a time, the animals decided they should do something meaningful to meet the problems of the New World. So they organized a school. They adopted an activity curriculum of running, climbing, swimming and flying. To make it easier to administer the curriculum, all the animals took all the subjects. The duck was excellent in swimming; in fact, better than his instructor. But he made only passing grades in flying, and was very poor in running. Since he was slow in running, he had to drop swimming and stay after school to practice running. This caused his webfeet to be badly worn, so that he was only average in swimming. But average was quite acceptable, so nobody worried about that—except the duck. The rabbit started at the top of his class in running, but developed a nervous twitch in his leg muscles because of so much

make-up work in swimming. The squirrel was excellent in climbing, but he encountered constant frustration in flying class because his teacher made him start from the ground up instead of from the tree-top down. He developed "charlie horses" from overexertion, and so only got a "C" in climbing and a "D" in running. The eagle was a problem child and was severely disciplined for being a non-conformist. In climbing classes he beat all the others to the top of the tree, but insisted on using his own way to get there.

Leaders know that they should never try to make a duck become a runner or a climber—but rather they must improve his swimming! A leader builds on the strengths and buttresses the weaknesses.

Team building is essential for the vision, purpose, objectives, and goals to be accomplished effectively and efficiently. Use all available resources. Empower each team member to work together and to develop his or her own abilities, talents, and skills so that they become successful and feel fulfilled.

Teamwork is the collective talents of many individuals.

A Story of Four People

The following story, although humorous, shows the importance of choosing the right person for the right task—expecting someone to do something which he or she is not trained or capable of doing can be devastating and damaging—boards and CEOs must understand this!

Four people in a dysfunctional team are named, EVERYBODY, SOMEBODY, ANYBODY, and NOBODY. There was an important job to be done and EVERYBODY was sure that SOMEBODY would do it. ANYBODY could have done it but NOBODY did it. SOMEBODY got angry about that, because it was EVERYBODY'S job. EVERYBODY thought ANYBODY could do it, but NOBODY realized that SOMEBODY wouldn't do it. It ended up that EVERYBODY blamed SOMEBODY when actually NOBODY accused ANYBODY. (source unknown)

Assignment

1. Of the 20 characteristics of a team, list those evident in your organization and those which are weak or absent. Develop and implement a plan to improve.

2. Ensure your organization has a Board of Directors. What are the responsibilities of each position and that of the CEO?

AN ENABLING AND EMPOWERING ORGANIZATION

ENVISIONING
PLANNING
ORGANIZING
CONTROLLING/MONITORING
TEAM BUILDING
LEADING
LEARNING

PURPOSE
VISION
OBJECTIVES

FUNCTION #6: LEADING

"...stand fast in one spirit, with one mind, striving together (as a team) for the faith of the gospel." (Phil. 1:27b)

"In things essential, unity;
In things non-essential, liberty;
And in all things, charity (love, compassion)."
(Evangelical Church Alliance).

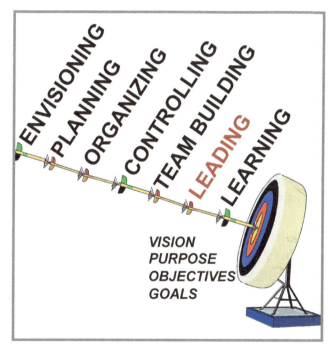

"And the things that you have heard me say in the presence of many witnesses entrust to reliable (faithful, trustworthy) men and women who will also be QUALIFIED (ABLE, COMPETENT) to teach others also." (II Tim. 2:2)

Learning godly and effective leadership isn't a simple "three-easy-steps" process; it is a complicated life-long, life-changing approach to one of managerial leadership's most critical functions, namely, *leading is serving*!

The determinative characteristics of the function of *authentic managerial "leading"* demands a very high quality of character. Leadership implies a reproductive role! All the previous topics have prepared us for this *practical* function.

Authentic leadership cannot ever be put aside! It has to be at the centre; it has to be true and good. We often forget about it, ignore it, fail to teach it and fail to follow a process whereby we prepare new leaders at every level of the organization. We focus excessively on the mechanical and technical aspects of the organization.

Attributes of an Effective Leader

Managerial leading involves using the practical, useful tools and processes for handling the down-to-earth daily operation of an organization with all its trials, problems, difficulties, *people*, budgets and challenges to bring about necessary change, increased productivity and effectiveness.

> (A leader is) "one who guides activities of others and who himself acts and performs to bring those activities about. He is capable of performing acts which will guide a group in achieving objectives. He takes the capacities of vision and faith, has the ability to be concerned and to comprehend, exercises action through effective and personal influence in the direction of an enterprise and the development of the potential into practical and/or profitable means. To accomplish this, a true leader must have a strong drive to take the initiative to act — a kind of initial stirring that causes people and an organization to use their best abilities to accomplish a desired end". (Ted Engstrom)

Task-oriented managers need to develop some leadership skills and the art of leadership is NOT a bag of tricks!

a. It is a constant stimulated awareness of leadership in all its different aspects.

b. It is an understanding of the principles, requirements and functions of leadership.

c. It is the development of one's own skills in providing the necessary functions and using the right methods for the different situations.

You have to become something. Although people are born with certain abilities that are enhanced or suppressed by their environment, leadership skills need to be learned and developed. The qualities, characteristics and skills required of a leader are determined much by the demands of the situation in which he or she is to function as a leader. These attributes have been covered all through this book.

Character is essential as well as unique personality. Integrity must be added to this. Leaders must be trustworthy and uphold high values and standards. These traits can be developed along with the learning of the functional skills. True authority is a proper blend of authority of position, authority of personality, authority of knowledge and authority of influence.

The difference between great and ordinary leaders is rarely formal intellect but rather insight.

> The great man understands the essence of a problem; the ordinary man grasps only the symptoms. The great man focuses on the relationship of events to each other; the ordinary man sees only a series of seemingly disconnected events. The great man has a vision of the future which enables him to place obstacles into perspective; the ordinary man turns pebbles in the road into boulders. (Henry Kissinger)

Leaders have "staying power"; success is simply "to last".

Challenges of Leadership

Leadership and management must complement each other. Those who are able to fulfill managerial responsibilities effectively while leading at the same time, with the respect, and loyalty of the followers are very scarce! *That is why two people often fulfill this role,* each complementing the other, one in leadership and the other in management. This *"conceptual"* yet practical approach benefits each role blending together into managerial leadership!

Leadership carries a difficult challenge–the ability to resolve those difficult problems and to go through with unpopular decisions. (See "Decision-Making" and "Problem-Solving" in "Planning".)

Leading also involves power, one of the key ingredients of leadership. Yet the danger and peril to abuse such power has been so prevalent.

Legitimate Power– power of authority that lies in the position that the managerial leader holds.

Reward Power– grants or withholds various kinds of rewards in order to get its way.

Coercive Power– can force compliance through psychological, emotional, or physical threat.

"Do as I say! Don't ask questions or make suggestions!" This is the usual philosophy of the authoritarian leader.

Expert Power– is based on knowledge, expertise and influence.

Referent Power– sets leaders apart from the non-leaders. The leader exercises this type of power by respect for and identification with others. He seeks to understand their problems. He

does not put himself up on a pedestal. He sacrifices himself. He maintains the same guidelines and policies he expects of others. He seeks to serve by leading well. Often he will use a combination of expert and referent power.

Behavior of a Leader

An individual is influenced by personality and situational factors. Organizational behavior has much to do with the actions of people– supervisors, managers, peers, and subordinates– and leaders themselves!

We categorize managerial leadership behavior into at least three categories and must expect a mixture of these in the leader's overall behavior for him to be effective.

1. *Supportive leadership* considers the needs and welfare of subordinates, as well as creating a friendly climate in the work environment or unit.

2. *Directive leadership* lets subordinates know what is expected of them and gives specific guidance. This category requires rules, procedures, and schedules to be followed, and the coordination of the work.

3. *Achievement-oriented leadership* sets challenging goals, seeks improved perfor-

mance and quality, emphasizes excellence in performance, and shows confidence that subordinates can and will live and work by high standards.

Traits and Characteristics

(See also "The Character of Leadership".)

Integrity, honesty and ethics

An authentic leader stands for and strives to maintain the consistent ordering of his lifestyle by values and goals which demonstrate moral character and principles consistent with the Holy Scriptures.

> **The 8 Deadly Sins of Modern Society**
> Policies without principles
> Wealth without work
> Pleasure without conscience
> Industry without morality
> Knowledge without character
> Science without humanity
> Worship without sacrifice.
> Christianity without godly ethics*.
> (*added by author.)

"To aspire to a position of leadership is an honourable ambition" (I Tim. 3:1). However, avoid being seduced by the so-called pragmatic efficiency of the world's materialistic system with its corporate and selfish techniques to win at any cost—even at the cost of human lives.

Intelligence and wisdom

The leader needs to have the capacity for understanding and interpreting truth, facts, and meaning in order to make meaningful and wise decisions to solve problems efficiently and effectively.

Enjoy leading

Self-confidence and enthusiasm

Followers feel secure when the leader shows good judgment, ability, and a well-balanced, wise use

of power. People feel safe and non threatened around you. It creates trust and credibility.

Open-minded and learns from mistakes

A leader needs to humbly take responsibility, be eager to learn more and to deal with new issues. Thomas Edison, said, "Don't call it a mistake; call it an education." Sometimes big mistakes are made as the leaders take on bold initiatives (not thoughtless or reckless) to create new "boxes" (paradigms). They abandoned outdated ideas.

Learn about themselves

Introspective

Leaders are able to look at themselves and see their weaknesses and work on them. Leaders are encouraged by their God-given strengths and strive to improve them.

Passionately focused on the vision and responsibilities

Compassion, feeling pain jointly

Often the only means of rescue for persons without hope, leaders need to show compassion and hope.

The Good Samaritan
(Luke 10:25-37)

Optimistic

Those who are optimistic don't always conform to the status quo. They forget the old ideas and paradigms that no longer are necessary.

Effective People Skills

The leader is available when necessary. He breaks down barriers. He is great at the art of listening and relationship building. He is effective in networking, connecting and partnering. He is a story teller.

He is tactful (having the ability to deal with others or difficult issues with resourcefulness and sensitivity).

Responsibilities of a Leader

Leaders anticipate crises. They are prepared. They have alternatives.

Leaders define the mission after much careful thought and prayer. They ensure it is operational through all the levels. They set definite action goals.

Leaders demonstrate the "discipline of abandonment". They face up to critical choices. If something is wrong or doesn't work, they can abandon it.

Leaders seek to nurture and prepare new leaders who:
1. display godly character,
2. are enemies of mediocrity,
3. take their well-fitted roles seriously,
4. think "we" rather than "I".

Leaders balance long-range plans and objectives with the short-range plans so that the view of the big picture is clear without disregarding the details. They create balance between opportunity and risk.

Leaders develop people as the primary foundational function. They are talent-developers. The organization is secondary.

Leaders delegate. They ensure people have the needed space in which to realize their potential and be accountable to achieve the desired results.

Leaders delegate but follow clear rules to be successful and productive delegators.

Delegated tasks and responsibilities need to be clearly defined. (See sections on "Job Descriptions" and "Organizational Charts" in "Function #3 Organizing".)

They need to have mutually understood goals and accepted deadlines for progress reports and the accomplishment of the task.

They need to be balanced with the right proportion of authority and empowerment. Clear accountability and reporting of the performance of the right job being done right is expected in return.

Delegated tasks and responsibilities need to be wisely and appropriately entrusted to others. Avoid the danger of delegating everything. An effective leader cannot delegate what is his own specific responsibility in which he has authority and for which he is accountable. He has the responsibility of being the "keeper" of the vision and its "protector" until sufficient "transvisioning" has occurred (when the team members understand and embrace the vision as their own vision) and new leaders have started to surface.

Leaders are accountable. They do not shun accountability. They do not settle for the good, when the excellent is possible. Mutual evaluation of follower and leader occurs.

Leaders are mentors and encourage others to be mentors so that the right connections between people happen without having to structure it formally. Leaders create opportunities for people.

Leaders seriously think through priorities. This is easy to say but hard to implement! It involves "abandoning things that may look very attractive and what people both inside and outside the organization are pushing for."

Leaders convert...
1. good intentions into effective results,
2. busyness into productivity,
3. "routine status quo" philosophy into "changing to improve" philosophy.

Leaders accept responsibility for major decision-making that could not be dealt with by others. Remember there are risks! Leaders take the time for thought and keep away from the trivial. A decision is a commitment to *action* and not "*pious intention*". When the leaders are successful at something, they run with it! This is the most effective road to self-renewal! Leaders don't brush success aside and stay problem-focused. They run with the part that is proving successful.

Leaders accept some dissent and disagreement as healthy when decisions need to be made concerning some important matters. If there is no dissent, but rather complete consensus, you can be sure nobody did his homework! "In essentials unity, in action freedom, and in all things trust." (Aristotle)

Trust requires that dissent comes out into the open, and that it be seen as honest disagreement. Often when varying opinions and ideas are shared, evaluated and merged, the resulting solution is better than any of the original ideas.

Leaders look at performance, not promise, and in the process insure that each person has:
1. a mentor to help guide him or her,
2. a teacher to develop the person's skills,
3. an evaluator to check progress,
4. an encourager to cheer the individual on (even when he stumbles and falls flat on his face).

Leaders find, motivate and maintain the right and committed people who fit the task and expectations and who can survive the heat of battle.

Leaders ensure that there are effective boards and executive committees for their organizations.

Leaders encourage personal development and modeling of effective managerial leadership. Leaders manage change. Ignoring the need for constant change is to be blind and to capitulate to the "status-quo slow-death" syndrome. People must change their attitudes, skills, expectations, perceptions and behavior.

Leaders energetically and conscientiously seek to recognize and maintain balance in dealing with the *task, individual,* and *team* needs within a constantly changing situation and the necessary demand for productivity and achievement of the vision and purpose. They meet these three needs and blend them together to help create a cohesive, productive team that achieves the common task and in the process respecting and developing each individual member. Do these circles overlap sufficiently in your organization to address the three areas of needs and the responsibility of the managerial leader's role? Are the tensions between them resolved by good communication, decision-making, and problem-solving?

It is possible to have a productive, organized, motivated team that accomplishes the task. It takes skilled leadership and motivated individuals to make it happen!

Leaders celebrate victories and successes.

Leaders take breaks and set aside time to think, relax, to be refreshed and renewed!

Code of Ethics of a Leader

1. I will treat everyone with respect and dignity.

2. I will be an active coach, mentor and example for others to follow.

3. I will maintain the highest standards of honesty and integrity.

4. I will insist on excellence and hold my people accountable.

5. I will build group cohesiveness and pride.

6. I will show confidence in my people.

7. I will maintain a strong sense of urgency and commitment to the cause.

8. I will be available and visible to my staff.

9. I will strive to develop myself to my highest potential.

10. I will strive to develop, empower and enable my people to reach their highest potential without yielding to status worship.

11. I will delegate wisely the proper amount of authority with responsibilities, training and empowerment and expect accurate accountability in return.

12. I will seek a time to be quiet with the Lord and listen to His still small voice speaking His word, His will, His commands, His challenges, His encouragement, His rebukes, His counsel, "This is the way, walk ye in it" (Is. 30:21).

13. I will seek to be involved in the lives of those around me just as Jesus the Servant Leader set the example.

14. I will seek to distinguish between the urgent and the important to avoid becoming overwhelmed by stress and pressures of life.

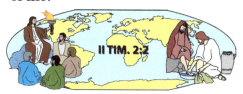

Jesus modelled servant leadership. He trusted ordinary men! He trained them and commissioned them to do the same. *Then He left!*

Styles of Leadership

A leadership style is a pattern of behavior in leadership situations exhibited over time as we influence other people.

Attitudes, attributes, and behavior influence style.

Be willing to understand and identify the predominant style of how we work with people—the bad ways as well as the good ways. This is necessary to find out our weak areas and to develop in ourselves a good blend of styles that doesn't destroy our unique God-given personality.

CAUTION: While growing up, many of us learned things we need to "un-learn" if we are going to work effectively with people today.

Basic Personality Tendencies
Doers
They tackle difficult tasks. They are motivated by challenges. They lead forcefully and persistently.

Influencers
They are articulate and use their verbal skills to convince others to get the job done.

Relators

They implement plans that have to do with people. They lead through relationships.

Thinkers

They analyze and lead through structure and methodology. They seek to implement the "right" plan.

Three Broad Categories

Task-oriented:

Task-oriented people place a strong emphasis on work results and rigid standards but they are weak on leadership principles and relationships.

People-oriented:

Those who are people-oriented have a strong concern for employees. Their focus is on motivating. They lack controlling and monitoring processes. They serve and care for others, but management skills often are missing.

Team-oriented:

Some people are focused on creating an effective team. Individualism is not part of their thinking.

> Teamwork: Coming together is a beginning…keeping together is progress…working together is a success! (John Maxwell)

Authoritarian and Exploitive Style

Activities and programs are emphasized. The false assumption is that the only worthwhile, productive commodities in any work situation are the tasks that are being done and that the only working relationship is that of superior to subordinate.

This style is a dictatorial manager or "master" approach. The "master" coordinates, controls, and directs all by himself. He is not accountable to anyone. He does what he wants to do (for example: He enforces guidelines, rules, policies to be rigidly obeyed but will not obey them himself.). He builds his own little "kingdom"; no one dares to interfere.

Subordinates must do their work exactly the way they are told to do it. No one challenges or questions his authority. The social nature of individuals must not interfere with the task to be done.

Vision, purpose, objectives, and people's needs are not fulfilled. Bad style! Eventually rebellion will occur.

Democratic Style

Assumption: The social nature and relationships of workers are the most important factors. If they are happy, they will be efficient and productive. Give them all they want and they will give back all you want.

People set the limits of their leader's authority and provide controls to maintain balance. Final authority remains with the people. (Not always the best way.)

Performance, attainment of goals, productivity, efficiency, effectiveness are lacking. (Not good!)

Minimum Effort Style

Assumption: "At all costs, avoid getting involved in anything!" The "leader" or "manager" simply avoids getting involved in work or worker problems.

Defeatists will not contribute to the organization or be motivated to improve operations.

You can't afford this kind of manager for his style is contagious. Your entire organization will soon get the same "virus"! NOT recommended!

Adequate Performance/Benevolent Authoritative Style

Assumption: A "leader" pushes just enough to get average results, but not so much that people will be upset. He issues orders and has a condescending attitude towards the subordinates. He lives in a world of never-ending compromise. He procrastinates. He does not really direct. The general attitude is: "All we want is a fair day's work, and you'll receive a fair day's pay! Just stay out of trouble! Do what the average worker around you does, no more!"

Subordinates have some freedom to comment on these orders. They are given some flexibility to carry out the tasks within carefully prescribed limits and procedures that might not even make sense. They may be rewarded if they meet or exceed their manager's goals.

Subordinates become cautious towards the managers. The "leader" or "manager" yields to a subordinate just enough to avoid problems of low morale or hostility. NOT recommended!

Consultative style

The manager sets goals. He issues general orders after discussing them with subordinates. The subordinates make their own decisions regarding the accomplishment of tasks. Only broad, major decisions are made by the higher levels of authority. Rewards rather than threats of punishment are what motivates subordinates. (Not bad!)

Supportive leadership style

The basic behaviour of the supportive leadership style is evident when there is consultation with subordinates as well as the "leader's" consideration of their opinions, expertise, skills, and suggestions.

The "leader" allows subordinates to participate in decision-making and problem-solving as well as planning, goal setting and other activities.

The result is that the subordinates feel they are "shareholders" of the organization and partners in the cause.

The leader does not abdicate his responsibility. It is necessary to have a designated leader. (Not bad!)

Ken Blanchard's Situational Leadership Model II®

Ken Blanchard's style emphasizes the practicing of different leadership styles with different people in different situations and at different times.

The leaders are flexible. They adjust their style according to the situations and people with whom they work.

"*Enthusiastic beginners*" need *directing* (how to start in a new activity).

However, the followers become "*disillusioned learners*" and find the task more difficult than they thought it would be. The situational leader will focus on coaching them, offering both direction and support.

As the followers develop in their positions, they become "*reluctant performers*". They know what they are supposed to do but they do not feel very confident about their ability. The situational leader will focus on supporting, encouraging, and motivating the followers to act on what they already know.

In the last stage, the leader activates the person's potential to become a "*peak performer*" who can move with competence and commitment. The leader delegates the tasks to him.

> "Jesus used a form of "situational leadership. He directed His disciples to listen and watch what He did. Then He put them in some situations—like the storm on the sea—where they were clearly be-

yond themselves. At that point He began to coach, and offered continued direction and support. Later, He sent them out to teach, preach, and heal as His representatives. They went out somewhat timidly, but came back with great

joy when they saw powerful results. Finally, after months of development—and success and failure—He prepared to go away and to delegate the ongoing task to them. In order to get them ready for full responsibility, we see Him 'setting the stage.' ...His worldwide mission could not be carried out if He did not delegate to them and leave them".

Flexible, adaptable leaders interact differently with their subordinates, as situations and personalities require, without favoritism.

Applying the supportive style and using the situational leadership model puts the pastor and church leaders on the same level as the laity.

However the situational leadership style does not emphasize the need for training and empowerment. There is a lack of effective delegation in which responsibility and accountability are not exchanged. It lacks the basic characteristic of servanthood in leadership.

You must understand that there are different ways of working with different people in different situations.

Jesus was a managerial leader who went beyond this situational leadership style and emphasized proper delegation and thorough training.

Authentic Managerial Leadership Style®
This is a notably visible style in an efficient, effective organization. It should be present at all levels with a strong emphasis placed on the three-fold needs within the organization: individual, team, and task needs.

Individual needs include one's relationship with God, godly character building with integrity, mentoring, training and growing the person.

Team needs include "the 20 characteristics of an effective team" (See "Team building".), people development, motivation, coaching, communication, conflict resolution, stress management, training and delegating.

Task needs include the effective and efficient practice of the seven functions of managerial leadership, as well as effective delegation giving authority, responsibility, empowerment, training in exchange for accountability and obligation.

An authentic managerial leader delegates and at the same time lives out godly values, vision and purpose to bring about change.

True delegation is the exchange of responsibility, authority, training and empowerment for an equal amount of obligation and accountability.

This must occur at every stage of the individual's and team's development. This will result in task development, and ultimately the vision will be attained, while each individual feels successful and fulfilled.

It takes work to use the authentic managerial leadership style® continuously. We often get stuck in one of the first three styles hindering us from accomplishing the vision and purpose effectively and efficiently. We succumb to being concerned with image building. So let's be strong "#4 leaders"!

Outcome: Increased willingness, ability & development of the individual and team with task accomplishment ⟶

DEVELOPMENT OF INDIVIDUALS AND TEAM; ACCOMPLISHMENT OF ORGANIZATION'S PURPOSE & VISION

HIGH / LOW

Actual Outcome of Different Leadership Styles

❹ The Managerial Leadership Style®

❹ • **Strong emphasis on the definition of managerial leadership, mentoring and the concept of true delegation.**
• **A workable concept that combines leadership principles with management skills in the development process of people and teams with task accomplishment**
• **a recognition that there are some positive traits in most other styles, however at the same time recognizing that negative, weak & sometimes dangerous tendencies exist in those same styles that can cause irreparable damage to individuals and organizations.**
• **a strong recognition that the ability to DELEGATE is a non-negotiable characteristic.**
• **a true authentic managerial leadership style® is practiced by those in charge as well as an embodied and practiced concept that characterizes the entire organization – not just the individuals in charge. It is a corporate, holistic and workable concept that appears *at all levels* from the board of directors to the custodian.**

❸ Leadership Style: Situational (Directing, Coaching, Supporting, Delegating)
Some team development and task accomplishment; emphasis on **individual development***; very good style, however, weak in emphasizing the need for training, empowerment & accountability in true delegation.*

❷ Consultive, sometimes Minimum Effort, Democratic, Supportive
Minimal Individual Development and Task Accomplishment; emphasis on **Team Development** *but it is temporary and the team is apt to disintegrate.*

❶ Leadership Style: Autocratic, Authoritarian Exploitive, Dictatorial (Benevolent…and sometimes not so benevolent!), Sometimes Minimum Effort, Directive *Minimal Individual and Team Development; Emphasis on forced* **Task Accomplishment** (must be avoided!)

A CHRISTIAN MANAGERIAL LEADER...

...is enabled by the Holy Spirit,
...serves with passion and purpose,
...models godly character, scriptural values and
   ethics,
...possesses and transfers a compelling vision

...TO WHOM?...
...to another person or group of people (a team)
...HOW?...
...by influencing, delegating, discipling,
(Equipping, training, coaching, encouraging, enabling,
facilitating, energizing, empowering, committing, challenging,
inspiring, motivating, edifying, developing, mentoring)
...BY WHAT MEANS?...
...by the 7 fundamental functions
(envisioning, planning, organizing, controlling, team building,
leading, learning)
...practised within the parameters of the Holy
Scriptures
...WHY?...
...to accomplish the vision, purpose, objectives
& goals in an effective, efficient manner, while
overcoming the perils & enjoying the blessings
and experiencing fulfillment and success
together as a team.

2 Tim. 2:2

Christ centered

Recognizing the need for godly leadership and management, effective Christian and authentic managerial leaders find, train and empower new leaders and managers to produce the necessary change and increased productivity to fulfill God's plan. The result is faithful, successful, fulfilled team members with a sense of individual significance who are accomplishing God's purpose in their lives and ministries, and who train faithful men and women to train others also. (II Tim. 2:2)

MANAGERIAL LEADERSHIP
balanced attention to:
INDIVIDUAL NEEDS
TEAM NEEDS
TASK NEEDS

Six Flaws of Ineffective Leadership

A number of significant flaws in leadership will create major problems in an organization. Ensure that the following six errors are not occurring in your organization and leadership.

1. *Incompetent*: The leader and at least some followers lack the will or skill (or both) to sustain effective action. When faced with an important leadership challenge, they are unable to create positive change.

2. *Rigid*: The leader and at least some followers are stiff and unyielding. Although they may be competent, they are unable or unwilling to adapt to new ideas, new information, or changing times.

3. *Intemperate*: The leader lacks self-control and is aided and abetted by followers who are unwilling or unable to intervene effectively.

4. *Callous:* The leader and at least some followers are uncaring or unkind. Ignored and discounted are the needs, wants, and wishes of most members of the group or organization, especially subordinates.

5. *Corrupt*: The leader and at least some followers lie, cheat and steal. Generally they put self-interest ahead of the public interest.

6. *Insular*: The leader and at least some fol-

lowers minimize or disregard the health and welfare of those outside the group or organization for which they are directly responsible. They insulate themselves from the rest of the group. They create a clique that prohibits others from participating in decision-making, problem-solving and other important aspects of the group's activities.

If you are a leader on a pedestal, you will not get much done up there! Jump down and get with the people! If you don't, God has ways and means to give you a big push off that pedestal that is in your mist of arrogance!

Summary

Every individual must give an account to God and that account will often be determined by how well the person in question was prepared, developed and motivated by his leader. Godly leadership activates the potential force and converts it into an active force, enabling and empowering individuals to use and develop their abilities and skills, giving a sense of fulfillment and success.

Leaders are concerned constantly with...

1. formulating a strategy of leadership development,

2. selecting those with leadership potential,

3. training leaders at every level,

4. formulating an efficient, effective organizational structure,

5. encouraging self-development of young "leaders-in-the-making",

6. developing and maintaining a warm, friendly organizational climate.

> Perceived Success without
> Successful
> Successive
> Successors
> is failure!

This is a basic principle in managerial leadership. Avoid the faulty thinking of having "success", when in reality it is not authentic success!

Assignment

1. Why is the Managerial Leadership Style® the best style for you as a leader?

2. To what three areas of *need* must a leader give equal and balanced attention?

3. Ask yourself some difficult questions and answer them as honestly as possible. You may want to ask your mentor to help you.

   a. Do I balance individual, task and team needs?

   b. Do I delegate appropriately?

   c. How am I preparing future leaders?

   d. Do I lead with integrity and honesty?

   e. Do I model Jesus' leadership style and values?

   f. Are the vision, purpose, and action plan being implemented effectively?

The Eagle

The eagles are the great teacher/trainers in the bird world. They make a fascinating study for aspiring leaders! Their nests are usually on the shelf of a sheer rock face where they raise their families.

A day comes when the mother eagle must train her eaglets to fly but she may be tempted to think, "Why does the thrill of soaring have to begin with the fear of falling?" Her love for each growing eaglet is tested by her concern that there is nothing but air to support the wings of each fuzzy little eaglet so warm, secure and cozy, cuddled under her wings... and what about the sharp rocks and ravines way below? What if her instinctive training methods don't work this time? But then, if they don't discover their wings there will be no purpose for their lives! They will never learn to soar or understand the privilege it is to have been born an eagle! So, from God-instilled eagle instinct, her supreme act of love and greatest gift to her family was to give each a push out of the warm and secure nest. At first the eaglet fluttered and plunged downward. Just before the eaglet is dashed to pieces on the rocks below, she dove below the falling eaglet and let it fall onto her back, saving it from certain death. She carried it back to the security of the nest. Each eaglet cuddled under the mother's wings for comfort, reassurance and security. Suddenly she pushed another one out of the nest! This process continues for several days... and then one day she pushed them all out again, one by one. But as her watchful eyes focused on the eaglets just as they came close to those dangerous rocks below, the eaglets rose and began to soar, and soon became distant specks in the sky above–just as eagles were created to do! She had fulfilled her mission. She led. She taught. She trained her successors until they too could soar. That's leadership in action!

(Adapted from David McNally. *Even Eagles Need a Push*)

FUNCTION #7: LEARNING

"Study to show yourself approved unto God…" (II Timothy 2:15)

"Wisdom is more precious than rubies, and nothing you desire can compare with it." (Proverbs 8:11)

"Knowledge is proud that it knows so much;
Wisdom is humble because it knows so little." (Howard Hendricks)

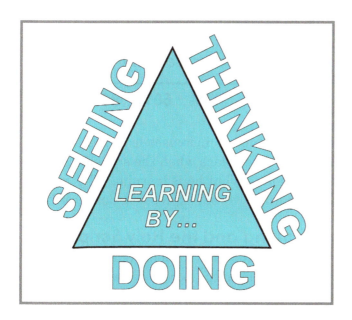

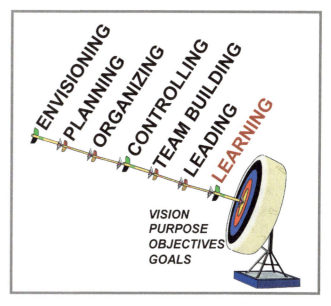

"And the things that you have heard me say in the presence of many witnesses entrust to reliable (faithful, trustworthy) men and women who will also be qualified (able, competent) to teach others also." (II Tim. 2:2)

"Change-The-Student Agent"

An authentic managerial leader is a "change-the-student" teaching agent!

One of the basic functions of being a leader is that of *teaching*—and teaching in such a way that real learning takes place. The purpose of teaching is to produce *change* by improving knowledge, skills, attitude, behaviour and even one's own ability to learn more.

> "To know and not to do is not to know at all" (Howard Hendricks).

A leader should be evaluated, not only on what he/she accomplishes personally, but on what his/her people achieve and how much they grow and mature under his/her leadership. Future leadership must follow the example of Jesus who said, "Follow Me, and I will make something out of you". The "Go ye…" (the doing) follows the teaching/ training process.

The Learning Process

"The mediocre teacher tells; the good teacher explains; the superior teacher demonstrates; the great teacher inspires" (Wm. Arthur Ward).

Respect the individuality of each person. Everybody learns through his or her own perceptions.

"Do not ask students to learn facts, but teach them to think" (W. E. McNeill).

IMPORTANT: Remember leadership has to do with people development. The major principle of skilled leadership is "delegation". People learn best by doing. The teaching leader delegates!

The following chart shows how much is learned in the teaching/learning process during a 24 hour period by what we *hear, hear and see,* and *hear, see and do.*

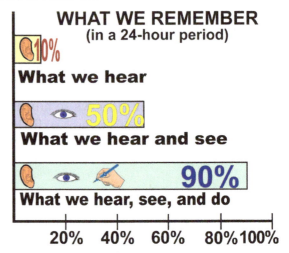

Delegated "doing" increases learning! The best learning takes place when the student can give expression to what he is learning. This may be in the form of verbal expression, doing, or both.

Learning and the Holy Scriptures

"Whoever finds me (wisdom) finds life and receives favor from the Lord. Whoever fails to find me (wisdom) harms himself; all who hate me (wisdom) love death" (Prov. 8:35).

"Take my yoke upon you and *learn* from Me; for I am gentle and humble in heart, and you will find rest for your souls" (Matt. 11:29, NIV)

"Ye shall know them by their fruits (by what they do)" (Matt. 7:16).

"Be doers of the Word and not hearers only" (James 1:22).

Doing is the ultimate step in evaluating one's

performance, character and learning—one reason why good leaders delegate! They get others doing—that's how they learn best! (See Deut. 4:10; Deut. 5:1; Deut. 31:12; Prov. ch.1-9)

The Teaching Process

a. Determine the changes that should occur in the student.
b. Develop a training program by selecting appropriate methods to achieve that change.
c. Bring the student to *learn* on his/her own.
d. Evaluate the changes that take place in the student.

Where there is no real learning,
       there is no true teaching.
Where there is no learning,
       there is no change.
Where there is no change,
       the teaching leader has failed his mission.

> perceived "teaching" + perceived "learning"
> = no change = failure
> – *in contrast* –
> true teaching + real learning = real change

Absence of Teaching Leadership

Why is the teaching of leadership skills frequently a low priority in Christian work?

a. The need for definite, progressive training is not fully recognized.
b. There is the misconception that because one is born with some natural tendencies, gifts and skills of leadership, there is no need for special training in this field. This is very faulty thinking!
c. Very few are trained in how to teach others to lead.
d. Those in administration may fear change because it may reveal weaknesses, limitations, outdated traditions and practices.
e. A person may resist adapting to new principles and techniques because he is comfortable and complacent with his present knowledge and way of doing things.
f. It upsets the "status quo". People fear being overtaken by others who may learn faster.
g. A person feels uncertainty in one's ability to grasp and implement necessary change.
h. The erroneous belief that leadership training is secular and therefore incompatible with Christian values is a very distorted view! Just read the Bible!

The Teaching Leader and the Learning Follower

"Let the wise listen and add to their learning; and let the discerning get guidance" (Prov. 1:5).

"Instruct a wise man and he will be wiser still; teach a righteous man and he will add to his learning" (Prov. 9:9).

A true leader is a "24-hour-a-day, seven-days-a-week" teacher whether he or she is conscious of this or not. As leaders, we must sharpen our skills and knowledge in the art of teaching. I often refer to the "teacher" as the "teaching leader" and the follower as the "learning follower." With the help of Dr. Howard Hendricks of Dallas Theological Seminary and others I want to review the seven keys or laws of the effective teacher.

1. The Law of the Teaching Leader

"If you stop growing today, you stop teaching tomorrow".

1) Know the content of what you teach! Your students will embrace the principles because they detect the authenticity of your own knowledge.
2) Be a learner. You cannot impart that which you do not possess.
3) Do not assume your student is interested in what you teach; you must create that interest.
4) Develop relationships that balance content and communication as well as the facts and form—the balance of what you teach and how you teach it.
5) The nature of the message determines the na-

INEFFECTIVE TEACHING

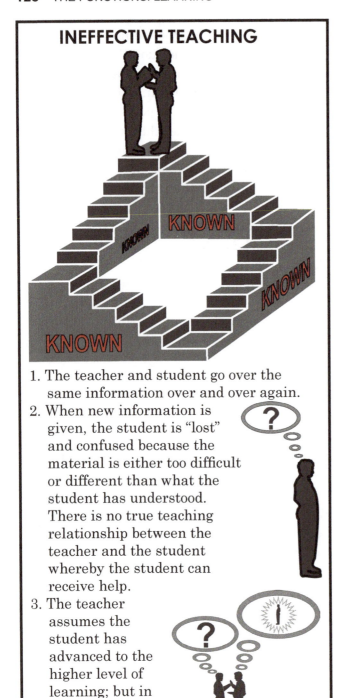

1. The teacher and student go over the same information over and over again.
2. When new information is given, the student is "lost" and confused because the material is either too difficult or different than what the student has understood. There is no true teaching relationship between the teacher and the student whereby the student can receive help.
3. The teacher assumes the student has advanced to the higher level of learning; but in reality the student has not advanced.

ture of the method to impart it.

6) Have a personal, consistent "reading" and "learning" study program.
7) Know your students; pray for them and their needs. Ask yourself, "How could I do it better?"

EFFECTIVE TEACHING

1. The teacher meets the student "where he is".

2. The teacher leads the student into the "unknown".

3. Interaction between the teacher and the student changes the "unknown" into the "known".

4. The student is now comfortable in the new "known" … on a higher level of knowledge.

Learning enables the student to CHANGE because he/she is STIMULATED to:
• know—make aware of new knowledge, seeing new insights, information, concepts
• understand—perceive the value, evaluate and think through the meaning and significance of the new information
• do—act on, use, and apply the knowledge that is understood.

2. The Law of Education

This law is the process of exciting and directing the self-activities of the pupil, learner, student, or follower. "Exciting" is an ignition word; changing the potential force in the learner to an active force.

The word "directing" has more to do with steering the follower in the right direction to learn. The two roles must be clear. The teaching leader must be a stimulator, motivator and coach. The student or follower must be allowed to be an investigator, discoverer and player!

The teaching leader must have three goals:

1. Teach people to *think* and to stretch their minds.
2. Assure the student or follower that he needs to learn how to learn. Learning is both a logical and a discovery process, opening his sight! It is important to remember the three components in the learning process,
   a) Present the whole in a preliminary synopsis.
   b) The next step is to analyze the parts
   c) Finally, go back to the whole with a clear synthesis.

3. Motivate the student/follower to learn by thinking and by doing. Don't do for him what he is capable of doing! This way you develop people who are self-directed, disciplined, and who do what they do enthusiastically and because they choose to do it!

3. The Law of Activity

Maximum learning is the result of meaningful and maximum involvement with reality.

- Practice makes permanent!
- Evaluated experience is the best teacher!
- We learn by doing the right things!
- The more you encourage involvement the greater the potential for learning. This process is completed when "change" takes place in the student and follower.
- The "doing" must be a meaningful activity that is characterized by:
  … stressing function and application,
  … planning activity with purpose,
  … providing direction without dictatorship,

… concerning itself with the process as well as the product,
… being practical and realistic,
… involving problem-solving situations.

4. The Law of Communication

To impart information effectively requires the building of bridges between the speaker and the listener.

1. *Bridges*: "Before we can communicate, we must establish commonness, commonality, and the greater the commonality, the greater the potential for communication".
   (a) concept/thought (*intellectual component*) – What do I know? What do I want my students to know?
   (b) feeling (*emotional component*) – What do I feel? What do I want my students to feel?
   (c) action (*volitional component*) – What do I do? What do I want my students to do?

2. *Words*: Take what you want to communicate and put it into words. Words are communication symbols which need to be arranged in a systematic order to convey a life message through the verbal forms of speaking and writing as well as the nonverbal such as expressions and gestures. They must be congruent. What you say must correspond with what people see! Research revealed how we communicate: by words (7%), tone of voice (35%), and body language (55%).

3. *Speech*: The presentation must be well prepared with a good introduction, conclusion, illustrations, and graphics. It must be clearly articulated and enunciated.

4. *Distractions*: Deal with those that are within the individual (attitudes, lack of sleep, health, etc.) and those within the environment/ surroundings.

5. *Listening*: The average person can listen 4 to 10 times as fast as the person speaking.

Keep the listener's attention. Combine your speaking with visualization, illustrations and analogies so that they see what they hear.

6. *Translation*: The words heard are often different than the words sent. Allow translation time for the hearer to apply them to himself as he should and make them his own.

7. *Test*: Be alert—not so much about how you think, but how the learning follower thinks; not how you feel, but how the learning follower feels; and not what you are doing, but what the learning follower is doing.

8. *Ask*: Allow the learning follower to ask perceptive questions that will show you, the teaching leader, whether he or she understands what you are teaching. You may have to repeat, re-explain and re-illustrate until it is understood.

5. The Law of the Heart
True teaching impacts from heart to heart rather than head to head. In the Scriptures, "heart" means that which embraces the totality or the whole of human personality including one's intellect, emotions and will.

As the teaching/learning process progresses, the teacher is to impart character, compassion, and content. The learner gains confidence, motivation and perception.

The focus in teaching is primarily upon what you do. The focus in learning is primarily upon what the student does. Therefore, test the teaching—not by what you do, but by what the student does as a result of what you do.

The teacher must know his students to meet their needs. To impact your students and earn the right to be their teacher and mentor, you need to be personally involved and close to your students. You can be sure that your students, followers, or mentorees will appreciate knowing you struggle with them as their teacher.

6. The Law of Encouragement
Teaching tends to be most effective when the learner is properly motivated. A motive is primarily that within (not without) which causes him or her to act.

Types of inappropriate motivation that can produce devastating results:
- *Enticement motivation* ("If you do this, then you will be rewarded with…!") Doing good things does not ensure good results; it is determined by the motivation.
- *Guilt motivation* (You aren't a very good Christian unless you do …!)
- *Deceit motivation*—intentional or unintentional (promising something that is not reality).

How do you motivate, encourage and inspire?
- Extrinsic or external motivation that comes from without needs to trigger intrinsic motivation that comes from within.
- Develop self-starters. The only place you can work is "outside" the student. Test all extrinsic motivation to see if it triggers "intrinsic motivation". If this doesn't happen, then your extrinsic motivation is not legitimate or effective!
- Teachers must take real needs and surface them so that they become felt needs. Develop responsibility with accountability using structured experience for growth and confidence on the part of the student or follower.

7. The Law of Readiness

The teaching-learning process will be most effective when both student and teacher are adequately prepared.

- Learning is most effective when a student or follower is adequately prepared – so build his or her learning interest before the class or training begins!
- Assignments precipitate thinking and provide a background or foundation to build on with the objective to develop habits of independent study.
- Good assignments are creative (not just work); they have clear-cut objectives and are well prepared.
- Recognize that people come with different sets of abilities.
- Look into the person's area of interest.
- Make the assignments thought-provoking. This builds a habit of self-study that keeps them going.

Improve your Learning Skills

- Turn knowledge into thoughtful opinions.
- Develop know-how to use new technology or do new activities/tasks, etc.
- Learn new preferences (likes and dislikes).
- Develop new dispositions (i.e. develop godly character).
- Learn new roles.
- Broaden your emotional range (when, how, etc. to express emotions).

Cultivate:

- Emotional resilience: Know when to explore and when to withdraw. Use in the face of uncertainty and difficulty. Tolerate a degree of strangeness.
- Mental resourcefulness: Be creative in searching for new ways to solve problems.
- Power of reflection: Stand back and evaluate situations objectively to determine the best approach.
- Immersion: Learn from reflection, analysis, direct experience and experimentation.
- Imagination: Create and explore hypothetical situations.
- Intellect: Use the skills of language and reasoning.
- Intuition: Listen to the inner deep-down small voice that provides ideas, solutions, etc.

In summary

1. In the final analysis, a good teaching leader will see that he/ she is reproduced and surpassed by others. As Howard Hendricks says, "A great teacher has always been measured by the number of students who have surpassed him".
2. A teaching leader must give the trainees the permission and the empowerment to use their own individual gifts and abilities as they develop their leadership skills.
3. Good leadership provides for and implements a skillfully designed teaching and learning process that brings about necessary change.
4. The Church spends very little time, effort and resources in the process of teaching, learning, training, doing! Let's change that!
5. A teacher is a patient person who understands that concepts are built like the layers of an onion. You often have to strip off erroneous ideas that way, and you replace them line upon line, precept upon precept.
6. So you tell, and they hear. You show, and they see. You provide controlled real life experience for them and they begin the "doing".
7. Motivation gets you started but it is habit that keeps you going.

> A teaching leader should be evaluated, not only on what he/she accomplishes personally, but on what his/her people achieve and how much they grow and mature under his/her leadership.

Self Learning and Expanding Your Personal Knowledge

In Chinese the word "learning" literally means "study and practice constantly". You have to make a sustained effort and even accept profound cultural shifts. You must constantly be getting out of your box. An authentic leader is a life-long learner on a life-long journey.

One would have to write many books to cover all the fields of learning applicable to leadership and management. Let me trigger your curiosity by suggesting just a few fields of study that will enhance your knowledge. These will complement your leadership and management expertise.

Read the books I've quoted from; however, always remember the Scripture, "*Examine all things and retain that which is good*". We must, by all means keep our learning, knowledge, personal actions, values and spiritual standing before God consistent with His inspired Word.

Learning and understanding "Emotional Intelligence" and the ability to see ourselves and the issue of self deception.

"Emotional intelligence is the ability to sense, understand, and effectively apply the power and acumen of emotion as a source of human energy, information, connection and influence."

It is a realm we are still largely in the dark. We need to not only become exceptional leaders and managers but also notable men and women. We need to engage not only the **analytical** mind but also the **emotions** and **intuition**. If you dig deeper you will find that "emotions are the primary source of motivation, information (feedback), personal power with humility, innovation and influence. In most cases, emotions are not at odds with good judgment and reasoning but can be linked to success. "Everything important that happens to us arouses emotion."

> "When you engage not only the analytical mind but also your emotions and intuition, your senses and emotional intelligence enable you to scan in moments through hundreds of possible choices or scenarios to arrive at the best solution in a matter of seconds instead of hours."

I highly recommend, "*Executive EQ, Emotional Intelligence in Leadership & Organization*" by Robert K. Cooper and Ayman Sawaf. They built

their research and study on what they call the Four Cornerstones of Emotional Intelligence, namely:

1. Emotional Literacy which focuses on building personal efficacy and confidence through emotional honesty, energy, awareness, feedback, intuition, responsibility, and connection.

2. Emotional Fitness that builds your authenticity, credibility, and resilience, expanding your circle of trust and your capacity for listening, managing conflict, and making the most of constructive discontent.

3. Emotional Depth in which you explore ways to align your life and work with your unique potential and purpose, and to back this with integrity, commitment, and accountability, which in turn, increases your influence without needing authority or an official position.

4. Emotional Alchemy (paradoxical results) through which you extend your creative instincts and capacity to flow with problems and pressures and to compete for the future by building your capabilities to sense more readily—and access—the widest range of hidden solutions and emerging opportunities. Emotional Intelligence is therefore the "ability to sense, act."

What most of the authors of studies and research in this secular field leave out is how our spiritual relationship with God is woven into the marvel of our creation. God created this complex, marvelous and wonderful creation, man and woman. The ultimate emotional intelligence comes from God. Ask Him to help you balance your analytical, intuitional and emotional intelligence.

Warning: It is not enough simply to explore the hidden recesses of the unconscious. Once we know in part how the mind works—and about the strengths and weaknesses of human judgment—it is our responsibility to build on our strengths and to buttress our weaknesses with the strengths of others and vice versa so that good judgment prevails.

Our self-concept is influenced by how we see ourselves, by what we do, say, hear, perceive and how the culture in which we grew up (family, church, religion, school, society, friends etc.) molded our thinking that resulted in a healthy self-esteem or a negative harmful one. Deeper growth is a change in self-concept without betraying one's values (based on the Holy Scriptures) and yet being realistic about one's self.

What finally counts is who you are, not what you know. By self examination you prepare for ground-breaking insight that forms the seeds of self-understanding. This slowly blossoms into changed behavior for the good. A life of potential and purpose unfolds. In spite of our biological programming, deficit-based thinking does not have to rule our minds, spirits, or actions. With concentrated, well-guided effort, we can regain energy, harness our inherent (albeit sometimes latent) optimism, and powerfully engage what life has to offer. All it takes is a shift (ever so slightly) in the way we see everything.

Created to learn

David Cottrell puts it well when he says, "LIVE IN THE LEARNING ZONE" by getting out of your comfort zone, reading, listening to people, giving back, setting goals and staying positive.

Ways of learning and knowing include common sense; naturally absorbing customs and traditions from others; authority; uncritical acceptance of another's knowledge; intuition/revelation; logical truths the mind grasps naturally; experience; trial-and-error learning; and deductive reasoning. It begins with general principles, then moves to specific applications developing over-arching statements of intent and purpose and then develops specific actions from these principles. Inductive reasoning goes from specifics to general principles synthesizing key concepts into a central truth; from particulars to generalizations. We MUST learn to think. Thinking has to do with the crucial characteristic or purpose which leads to the practical decision-making and problem-solving dilemmas. It can be positive or negative. Warning: *"Never accept as true anything we do not clearly know to be such."*

Learning courageous leadership

We need to embrace the God-inspired vision He has purposed for us and then translate it into a God-led plan that is courageously put into action with follow-through that sees the overall objective and mission accomplished. "A courageous leader might not be in a position to directly guide or conduct the activities of a specific group but could be *a leader who points the way for others—even millions of people—through writing, the arts, or other skills that are not connected to any official leadership position."*

Learning about the serious issue of self-deception

We need to identify in ourselves those areas where we have been deceived. It is so essential to our leadership. "To the extent we are self-deceived, our leadership is undermined at every turn".

We need to learn how to handle power. Power is an intoxicating, animating, life-sustaining narcotic. Many victims of this deadly narcotic worked hard to obtain power and are very reluctant to let it go. They lack conviction. Desperate shallowness, lack of real warmth, resistance to change, and insensitivity to the feelings and reactions of people around them are characteristics of these persons. Decisions are made undemocratically and in secret.

Those leaders who are able to combine action with reflection, who have sufficient self-knowledge to recognize the vicissitudes (uncertainty, unpredictability, fickleness) of power, and who will not be tempted away when the psychological sirens that accompany power are beckoning will in the end be the most powerful. They will be the ones who are remembered with respect and affection. They will also be the ones truly able to manage the ambiguities of power and lead a creative and productive life.

Learning How Entrenched Bureaucracies Hinder Authentic Leadership Development

An unconscious conspiracy in contemporary society prevents leaders—no matter what their original vision—from taking charge and making changes. Within any organization, an entrenched bureaucracy with a commitment to the status quo undermines the unwary leader. To make matters worse, certain social forces—the increasing tension between individual rights and the common good, for example—discourage the emergence of leaders.

We have ended the first decade of the 21st century. We have witnessed the consequences of bureaucracy with its unmerciful, ruthless and money-hungry leaders.

Learning How To Get Out Of Our Ruts

Stephen Covey put it this way,

We often get into ruts, on treadmills, caught up in patterns and habits that aren't useful. We keep doing the same things in our lives week-in, week-out, fighting the same alligators, struggling with the same weaknesses, repeating the same mistakes. We don't really learn from our lives. We don't stop to ask: What can I learn from this week that will keep next week from essen-

tially being a repeat of the same?

We function like a little dog going in circles chasing its tail... and getting nowhere!

The Learning Organization

Seriously consider getting the bestseller book, *The Fifth Discipline, The Art & Practice of the Learning Organization* by Peter M. Senge. He goes to great length showing how a learning organization should conduct itself. To entice you I will quote a couple of paragraphs that will convince you to study further.

It's just not possible any longer to "figure it out" from the top, and have everyone else following the orders of the "grand strategist". The organizations that will truly excel in the future will be the organizations that discover how to tap people's commitment and capacity to learn at **all** levels in an organization.

Learning organizations are possible because, deep down, we are all learners... not only is it our nature to learn but we love to learn.... The team that became great didn't start off great—it learned how to produce extraordinary results.

"This, then, is the basic meaning of a "learning organization"—an organization that is continually expanding its capacity to create its future.

For such an organization, it is not enough merely to survive. "Survival learning" or what is more often termed "adaptive learning" is important—indeed it is necessary. But for a learning organization, "adaptive learning" must be joined by "generative learning," learning that enhances our capacity to create."

I could go on and on! So much to learn! But just one more learning challenge!

Learn the Difference Between Spider Leadership and Starfish Leadership.

The spider has eight legs, a tiny head and eight eyes. The head runs the spider. Chop off the spider's head, it dies. In a **centralized** organization you ask, "Who is the head?" If you do not like the organization, you find the head and disable it. It is the head that gives good or bad command and you do not challenge it in fear of the consequences.

In a **starfish** organization the starfish does not have a head, there is no central command. Why do I like this comparison?

To answer this, I'll quote from *The Starfish and the Spider,* authors Ori Brafman and Rod A. Beckstrom. Get the book! They explain.

> The starfish's "central body isn't even in charge. In fact, the major organs are replicated throughout each and every arm. If you cut the starfish in half, you'll be in for a surprise: the animal won't die, and pretty soon you'll have two starfish to deal with.
>
> "Starfish have an incredible quality to them. If you cut an arm off, most of these animals grow a new arm. And with some varieties, such as the Linckia, or long-armed starfish, the animal can replicate itself from just a single piece of an arm. You can cut the Linckia into a bunch of pieces, and each one will regenerate into a whole new starfish. They can achieve this magical regeneration because in reality, a starfish is a neural network—basically a network of cells. Instead of having a head, like a spider, the starfish functions as a decentralized network. Get this: for the starfish to move, one of the arms must convince the other arms that it's a good idea to do so. The arm starts moving, and then—in a process that no one fully understands—the other arms cooperate and move as well. The brain doesn't "yea" or "nay" the decision. In truth, there isn't even a brain to declare a "yea" or "nay". The starfish has no brain. There is no central command."

The authors make the comparison of the spider versus the starfish or in other words the Catalyst versus the CEO.

While both are leader types, catalysts and CEOs draw upon very different tools. A CEO is The Boss. He's in charge, and he occupies the top of the hierarchy. A catalyst interacts with people as a peer. He comes across as your friend. Because CEOs are at the top of the pyramid, they lead by command-and-control. Catalysts, on the other hand, depend on trust. CEOs must be rational; their job is to create shareholder value. Catalysts depend on emotional intelligence; their job is to create personal relationships. CEOs are powerful and directive; they're at the helm. Catalysts are inspirational and collaborative; they talk about ideology and urge people to work together to make the ideology a reality. Having power puts CEOs in the limelight. Catalysts avoid attention and tend to work behind the scenes. CEOs create order and structure; catalysts thrive on ambiguity and apparent chaos. A CEO's job is to maximize profit. A catalyst is usually mission-oriented. But just because catalysts are different from CEOs doesn't mean that they don't have a place within organizations. Top-down hierarchy and structure can be repressive to the catalyst, but some situations are uniquely suited to catalysts.

So how does all this apply to ministries and the church? The church and its ministries have to get back to starfish leadership. There are too many spiders at the helm! The authors have applied this important and workable concept to business but it equally applies to the church!

A coercive system depends on order and hierarchy. There's always a pyramid, and there's always someone in charge. In short, if you see a CEO, chances are you're looking at a spider. An open system, on the other hand, is flat. There's no pyramid for anyone to sit on top of. ...Every spider organization has a physical headquarters. A headquarters is so integral that if we don't know whether a company is for real or not, we often check whether it has a physical address. No one orders priceless jewels, after all, from some company that has only a PO box. ...A starfish organization doesn't depend on a permanent location or a central headquarters. Yes, AA has a physical address and lists its offices in New York. But that's not really where AA exists. The organization is equally distributed across thousands of community centers, churches, even airports. AA is found wherever a group of members chooses to meet.

Using the above excellent illustration from nature, the authors made the following comments:

"...centralized organizations aren't good platforms. ...they won't be inspired to give it their all. Second, leaders in top-down organizations want to control what's happening, thereby limiting creativity. Third, and most important, centralized organizations aren't set up to launch decentralized movements. Without circles, there isn't the infrastructure for people to get involved and take ownership of an idea. Decentralized networks, however, provide circles and an empowered membership and typically have a higher tolerance for innovation."

So to conclude this point, examine thoroughly this concept and you will find the Holy Scriptures first taught this concept and principle and it worked—so lets get back to it! (Phil. 1:27b)

Summary

Real learning gets to the heart of what it means to be human. Through learning we re-create ourselves. Through learning we become able to do something we never were able to do. Through learning we re-perceive the world and our relationship to it. Through learning we extend our capacity to create, to be part of the generative process of life. There is within each of us a deep hunger for this type of learning.

Study the life of the Saviour, the greatest Teacher, and ask, "How did He do it?" Did he cram a lot of heads full of a collection of theological facts? Or did He involve them in the process so that the pagan world was compelled to testify, 'These are they who have turned the world upside down'? That's the challenge of Christian education. (Howard Hendricks)

"I hear, and I forget.
I see and I remember.
I do and I understand."
(Chinese Proverb)

Assignment

1. In a group setting, discuss how you take your followers from "knowing" to "doing".
2. Do you participate in activities that enable you to continue to learn? If so, what are the activities and how do they help you in your learning process? If not, what activities would you like to get involved in, so that you can continue learning new things?
3. How can you increase your learning, your world view and your relationships?
4. What are the seven laws of the effective teaching leader?

VI. THE SNARES

"Defeat is not the worst of failures. Not to have tried is the true failure." (George E. Woodberry)

"I know the price of success—dedication, hard work and devotion to things you want to see happen." (Frank Lloyd Wright)

"There is nothing I cannot master with the help of the One who gives me strength." (Phil. 4:13, Jerusalem Bible)

"For though a righteous man falls seven times, he rises again, but the wicked are brought down by calamity." (Proverbs 24:16, NIV)

Is the price too high?

Why do we Christians often shoot our fallen or wounded fellow Christians?

"And the things that you have heard me say in the presence of many witnesses entrust to reliable (faithful, trustworthy) men and women who will also be qualified (able, competent) to teach others also." (II Tim. 2:2)

We have divided up these snares or issues in the sections under character, individual, team, and task issues. However, in one way or another, most have a character issue at the root.

Recognizing and addressing the individual, team and task needs is essential for an effective authentic managerial leader. However, many *pitfalls await those of weak character and those who are caught off-guard*. Touched and changed lives validate a leader's ministry, not the accumulation of personal power, wealth, prestige, a clergy certificate or a seminary diploma.

Character/Heart Issues

"What a man thinks in his heart, so is he" (Prov. 23:7). Be careful what you think! It will be reflected in every aspect of your life (Phil. 4:8).

Pride-related Issues
- *Top-of-the-Pyramid Attitude*
  Using abusive authority, deplorable delegation; refusing to listen or let go; dictatorial in decision-making; egocentric (for example King Saul and many contemporary "leaders").

- *Know-it-all Attitude, Indispensability*
  No man is indispensable; there is more to learn. Do not be afraid to do a self-assessment (1 Cor 10:12).

- *Proud, Authoritative, Egotistic, Self-Centered*
  Leaders can become blind and numb to the feelings

of others, leading to decision-making devoid of understanding and compassion. These leaders are often defensive, resentful, negative and condemning (Matt. 23:6-12).

- *Image Building, Narcissism*
  We must be concerned about how we are perceived by God rather than by what people think (1 Tim. 4:16).

- *Celebrity Syndrome and Pedestal Complex*
  Too many clergy and "leaders" of para-church organizations see themselves as bosses, but not servants. Their followers eagerly, yet wrongly, reinforce that attitude (e.g. Jim Jones, David Koresh, and others).

- *Wanting to Be Always Right*
  (The wrongness of being right!) Guess what?! No one is right all the time! Listen to others! You might learn something!

It is good to have godly self-esteem (feeling good about what God has enabled you to do). However, be careful that it does not become distorted and any of the above issues surface.

God's Calling
- *Ignoring God's calling (James 4:17)*

- *Obsession with God's calling*
  The danger of becoming obsessed with God's calling in your life can create a disregard for other people, family relationships, etc. Such obsession becomes the idol that you worship. You lose God's true calling for you. Keep balanced!

Physical and Health Issues

- *Fatigue, Failure to Maintain Good Health*

  Maintain your health: spiritually, emotionally, physically, mentally and socially (1 Cor. 3:16,17).

- *Pressure and Facing Reality*

  Pressure will always be a part of leadership. Develop strategies such as taking necessary breaks to face the harsh realties of life (Phil. 4:13).

Emotional Health Issues

- *Emotional Instability and Immaturity*

  Often instability arises when we take our focus off God and place it on our circumstances (e.g. King Saul). Immaturity can cause self-doubt (1 Tim. 4:12).

- *Depression, Loneliness, Rejection, Discouragement*

  Not overcoming these emotions causes ineffectiveness (1 Kings 19: 3-5; 1 Sam. 30: 6).

- *Laziness, Procrastination, Lack of Motivation*

  Contributing factors are an unclear vision/calling/purpose, depression, self-pity, physical illness, stress, unresolved emotional issues and/or a fear of failure (Jonah 1:1,2).

- *Impulsive*

  Jesus taught Peter that to deal with his impulsiveness he needed to be humble, faithful, trusting, submissive to the authority of Christ, and to love God and others.

- *Jealousy/Envy (Prov. 27:4)*

Issues affecting Core Values

- *Failing to tell the truth*

  Keep your word (Eph. 4:15; Phil. 4:8).

- *Lack of Ethics, Standards of Honesty, Integrity*

  Does your life live your talk about integrity and honesty? (See Ps. 34: 12-16.)

- *Using your Managerial Leadership position for Personal Gain*

  Serve others. Fulfill your responsibilities. "If anyone wants to be first, he must be the very last, and the servant of all" (Mark 9:35).

- *Money, Possessions, Covetousness*

  Money is a useful tool, but loving it is sin and idolatry. Be content with what God has given (1 Tim. 6: 5b-10,17-19).

- In the short-term, it may "appear" to be advantageous to compromise godly core values. It is not worth it. You sell your soul.

Setting-an-Example Issues

- *Refusing to Set a Personal Example for Your People to Follow*

  People will give you their best, respect, confidence, willing obedience, loyal cooperation when you give them your best.

- *"Folie a Deux": Leaders Driving their Followers Mad*

  When a leader has a break with reality and influences a group to do the same (e.g. David Koresh, Jim Jones, and other current examples).

- *"Walk your talk"*

  Set a godly, Christ-like example for others to follow.

Relationship Issues

- *Marital Stress*

  Conflict of priorities, money-management, incompatibility with God's calling and a lack of support and encouragement are often at the centre of marital stress (e.g. Hosea).

- *Sexual Temptation*
  The devil loves to spoil a ministry and a marriage by using this powerful instinct that can easily get out of control (e.g. Samson, David and Solomon).

- *Joining the Wrong Crowd*
  Avoid separatist-type associates, contacts and friendships that bring out the worst in you. These include rebellious groups or other extremist cliques, etc.

Risk-Taking

- Taking foolish risks (excessive self-confidence)
- Taking no risks at all (excessive fear).
- Keep balanced. Make calculated decisions based on research and quality "think time" (Prov. 15:22).

Self-Assessment Issues

- *Refusing to Assess Your own Performance Realistically and to Accept Personal Responsibility*
  Be courageous at improving yourself. Become known as a "can-do" person, dependable in getting the job done, no matter what, with courage, integrity and persistence. "Whoever loves discipline loves knowledge, but he who hates correction is stupid" (Prov. 12:1).

- *Failing to Keep Abreast of New Ideas, Thinking, Training, and Development in Your Own Field*
  New ideas are the foundation for growth and development. "Examine all things, retain that which is good. Consider what I say and the Lord give thee understanding" (1 Thess. 5:21).

- *False Pride*
  Self-esteem is distorted and "gone bad"!

- *Failure and Inadequacy*
  Often leaders feel inadequate and limited. How wonderful that God doesn't use superhumans for his work but ordinary people like you and me who share common weaknesses! (Prov. 24:16).

Addressing Individual People Issues

"Am I my brother's keeper?" (Gen. 4:9). "Do to others what you would have them do to you" (Matt.7:12, NIV).

Training Your People

Perceived success without successful successive successors is failure

"Who am I mentoring to take my place?" The Apostle Paul modeled this principle of leadership training with Timothy (II Tim. 2:2).

Communication Issues

- *Chaotic Communication*
  Use organizational charts and job descriptions to clarify the chain of command, responsibilities, authority, accountability, etc. Ensure your words are consistent with your attitude and actions that speak loudly!

- *Failing to Keep your Criticism Constructive*
  Constructive criticism seeks to obtain peak performance, productivity and results (Eph. 4: 29).

Hidden Agendas

- *Manipulating People*
  Influencing people for your own personal gain is manipulation. It is selfish and destructive. Influencing people so that they have increased self-esteem and are fulfilled and successful in accomplishing a common purpose, is a goal of an effective godly authentic managerial leader.

- ***The Dark Side of Charisma***
Do not dominate and subjugate followers by using punishment and rewards to keep them weak, poor, uneducated and dependent. Use your influence to inspire your followers to accomplish a godly, worthwhile endeavor. Secular and religious history is full of examples of positive and negative charisma.

- ***Being a Buddy, Not a Leader and trying to be Liked Rather than Respected***
"…if we're not circumspect in our actions with our employees it is because we do not respect them. If we fail to respect them, they certainly will not and cannot respect us."
Being a "buddy-buddy" to one person may meet an emotional need but sacrifice the welfare of the organization.

Accepting People (1 Cor 12:1-13:13)

- ***Treating Everyone the Same Way***
Each person is different. Treat each one according to his/her own skills, abilities, personality, etc. If everyone is treated alike, they will be suppressed and stifled. They cannot develop their skills and gifts. They cannot become the people God intends them to become.

- ***Resisting and Avoiding Mavericks***
Mavericks (independent individuals who do not follow the crowd) are often gifted go-getters who save us from institutionalism and traditionalism. Jesus is our prime example. Nehemiah and John the Baptist are examples also.

- ***Recognizing Only Top Performers***
Treat everyone as a winner. Give rewards when goals have been met.

- ***Working in the Shadow of a Mentor***

Do not expect the junior colleague or the one you are mentoring to operate and function in exactly the same way you would. Do not try to press him or her into the same mold. He/she is a unique individual with a different personality, background experiences, skills (e.g. Elisha).

- ***Failing to Thank and Praise***
"Catch people doing something right! Then tell everyone about it!" (Kenneth Blanchard). "We always thank God for all of you, mentioning you in our prayers. We continually remember before our God and Father your work produced by faith, your labor prompted by love, and your endurance inspired by hope in our Lord Jesus Christ" (1 Thess 1: 2,3).

Addressing The Team Issues

"For we are God's fellow workers; you are God's field, God's building" (I Cor. 3:9).

- ***Understanding Organizational Culture***
Understand cultural fit, (who fits with the group and who does not). Be sensitive to the culture and help the team understand it. "I have become all things to all men so that by all possible means I might save some" (1 Cor. 9: 22b, NIV).

- ***Negative Synergism***
It is the combined action and activity of two or more individuals producing a total result less effective than that of the efforts of each individual separately. It is the result of individuals unwilling or unable to work together to accomplish the God instilled vision.

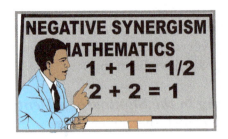

- *Faulty Delegation*
  Do not delegate a task and then meddle. "Make it your ambition to lead a quiet life, to mind your own business and to work with your hands, just as we told you" (1 Thess. 4:11). Meddling usually is the result of feeling insecure or needing to be in control.

"The best executive is one who has sense enough to pick good men to do what he wants done, and sense enough not to meddle with them while they do it!" (Theodore Roosevelt)

I have good people working for me! I don't want to meddle in their work!

- *Autocratic Bureaucracy*
  Autocratic bureaucracy results in ineffectiveness. It is often caused by a complex structure of legalistic regulations and wordy procedures. Eg: Pharisees, many denominations.

- *Leadership Backlash*
  Sometimes a leader's unpopular decisions or course of action creates a negative reaction to his leadership. The initial popularity turns to animosity (e.g. Moses).

- *Opposition*
  Opposition to leadership takes various forms such as mockery, scorn, anger, threats, internal strife and personal attacks (Neh. 4, 6).

Addressing The Task Issues

Jesus said, "It's like a man going away: He leaves his house and puts his servants in charge, each with his assigned task, and tells the one at the door to keep watch" (Mark 13:34, NIV). See also I Cor. 15:58, NIV.

- *Failing to Establish Good Standards*
  Ensure standards for behaviour are guidelines consistent with your values and vision. Ensure standards of procedures and methods produce effective, efficient results.

- *Failure to Envision, Look Ahead, Focus on the Future*
  Change is inevitable. Create vision and direction—the basis for effective planning, team-building, strategizing, and goal setting. "Where there is no vision, the people perish" (Prov. 29: 18, KJV).

- *Abuse of Power*
  Do not compromise your values and ethics to follow another who abuses his power. Be sure you don't abuse it yourself!

- *Stooping to a Dictatorial Style of Decision-making and Problem-solving*
  "The leaders who work more effectively…never say "I". They don't think "I". They think "we". They think 'team'". "Teach them…the duties they are to perform…that will make your load lighter, they will share in decision-making" (Exodus 18: 20, 22).

- *Concentrating on Problems Rather than Objectives*
  Focus on what you intend to achieve, rather than on problems. Have alternatives for reach-

ing your objectives. "...Forgetting what is behind and straining toward what is ahead, I press on toward the goal to win the prize..." (Phil. 3: 13).

- *Paperwork before People-work*
  Results take priority over relationships. Employees will never care how much you know until they know how much you care (Luke 10: 38-42, Mary and Martha).

- *Condoning Incompetence*
  If you are falling into this snare it could be that you feel the need to be loved or fear being called a task master. "Whatever your hands finds to do, do it with all your might" (Eccl. 9:10a).

- *Inappropriate Fund-Raising and Profit*
  Instead, provide for the continuation of the business/ministry as long as it fulfills a need. Ensure sufficient resources (people, money, equipment, etc.) for effective, efficient results— "the oil that keeps the wheels turning".

Is The Price Too High?

- Criticism—"Do not judge, or you too will be judged" (Matt.7:1). Give and accept "constructive criticism" well. Avoid destructive criticism. Judgmental criticism can be cruel (emotional persecution).

- Fatigue—Some rest is imperative (Mark 6: 31,32).

- Priorities and Think-time—Don't get behind in your "think-time"! (Matt. 14:23)

- Loneliness—Be willing to be alone. People will misunderstand or regard your leadership as a threat. Be strong. Withstand the temptation to give up.

- Identification—Identify with your team members (their emotions, victories, defeats, etc.)

- Unpleasant Decisions—They usually are unpopular and create isolation.

There are many who want the medals, but few who are willing to bear the scars.

- Competition—It can be healthy, but can create a fear of failure or fear of success; can create abuse of power, "steamrolling" or unethical procedures and philosophy.

- Humility—Prov. 16:19; Prov. 22:4; Prov. 29:23

- Rejection—John 4:44; Luke 4:24; Mark 6:4,5

- "For whoever wants to save his life will lose it, but whoever loses his life for Me will save it" (Luke 9: 24).

Your Rewards...

Practicing leadership principles and management skills is hard, but rewarding, *when you see the results in the lives of those you have led, taught, trained, and equipped.*

1. You will be rewarded as you see them **following** the scripturally sound pattern of practicing godly authentic leadership and management (Phil.3:17).

2. You will be rewarded as you see them demonstrate **quiet confidence** that things are under wise control.

3. You will be rewarded as you see them **planning** for anticipated changes, not just reacting to change.

4. You will be rewarded as you see them **maturing** in leadership and management, training others to practice these same skills and principles and maintaining a balance between leadership principles, management skills, technology and caring for the people.

5. You will be rewarded as you see them **moving away from** hierarchical, authoritarian and status-quo styles of administration to a team effort in which everyone has an opportunity to use and develop his/her gifts and talents and everyone shares in the difficulties and rewards.

6. You will be rewarded as you see them **coping with pressure**. They motivate their employees and followers. They have good relationships with peers/subordinates and the public. They create an environment that results in commitment and loyalty.

   • They articulate the vision, purpose, objectives and goals and keep the organization from straying from its mission.

   • They reach the finish line with a sense of fulfillment!

7. You will be rewarded as you see them build **effective teams** that work together synergistically and that accomplish more together than apart. (Synergism: 1+1= 3; 2 + 2 = 7!)

8. You will be rewarded as you observe them showing **excellence** in their actions, motivation, achievement of goals and the acceptance of responsibility and accountability. They demonstrate their newly sharpened skills as they practice authentic managerial leadership.

9. You will be rewarded as you see them **passing** the authentic managerial leadership torch to those they have trained and mentored and they in turn pass the torch to those they have trained and mentored.

Summary

Falling into one or more of the errors and snares in this study will destroy the integrity and character of your leadership.

Assignment

1. Identify the perils, snares or errors that most afflict you. What will you do about them?

2. Are you passing the leadership torch effectively and following authentic managerial leadership principles? How can you improve?

3. What errors, snares and perils are you facing within your organization? What steps need to be taken to become more effective?

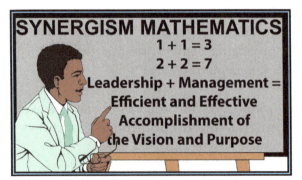

VII. PERSONAL AND ORGANIZATIONAL SELF-ASSESSMENT

"When an archer misses the mark, he turns and looks for the fault within himself. Failure to hit the bull's eye is never the fault of the target. To improve your aim, improve yourself." (Gilbert Arland)

"*And the things that you have heard me say in the presence of many witnesses entrust to reliable (faithful, trustworthy) men and women who will also be qualified (able, competent) to teach others also.*" (II Tim. 2:2)

Why do we need Self-Assessment?

It's time for personal and organizational self-assessment for you, your ministry, mission, church, or business. Yes, God uses business to support His work. Ask the question, "Are we (Am I) really heading in the right direction?"

Five steps to fulfil:
1. Plan purposefully,
2. Prepare prayerfully,
3. Proceed positively,
4. Purpose persistently,
5. Evaluate periodically.

Self-assessment is an integral part of planning and organizational renewal.

Good intentions are not enough! *Asking key questions forces us to think through what we are doing, why and how.* It helps us determine if we are hitting the target and the right target!

Note: Find a skilled facilitator to guide the participants and discussion groups; your aim:
1. To get to the *root* of the issues,
2. To deal with the issues and
3. To take appropriate steps to rectify the problem.

For every question, think deeply before answering yes or no, then explain.

Hold yourself responsible for a higher standard than anybody else expects of you. Never excuse yourself. (Henry Ward Beecher)

As human beings, we are endowed with freedom of choice, and we cannot shuffle off our responsibility upon the shoulders of God or nature. We must shoulder it ourselves. It is up to us. (Arnold J. Toynbee)

Personal Self-Assessment

1. Do I accept personal accountability and more responsibility?

2. Do I develop, equip and train people?

3. Do I influence thinking or control results?

4. Do I hang out with people that drag me down?

5. Do I manage others like robots rather than significant and unique people? Am I manipulative?

6. Do I expect reasonable productivity or allow incompetence?

7. Do I lose sight of the vision, purpose, and objectives and focus instead only on the problems?

8. Do I establish reasonable standards?

9. Do I praise and reward everyone, not just top performers?

10. Do I keep the respect flowing both ways without threatening the proper lines of authority?

11. Do I stay current on new developments while acquiring knowledge in other areas?

12. Do I make sound and timely decisions? Am I becoming a better troubleshooter?

13. Do I inspect and provide necessary controls in a non-threatening way? MBWA (Management By Walking Around)

14. Do I make sure that a person's job is understood, supervised properly, and accomplished? Have I developed a sense of responsibility?

15. Do I spend time on details and work that others should be doing?

16. Do I give my superiors problems or solutions?

17. Do I get all the facts first and pay careful attention to the details?

18. Do I base reports on results and facts?

19. Do I attempt to get the job done well, on time and, if possible, before the deadline?

20. Do I use my position for personal gain and disregard the needs of others?

21. Do I fear change or panic easily?

22. Do I give excuses to avoid problems and difficult situations?

23. Do I fail to tell the truth or keep my word?

24. Do I set a good example?

25. Do I cooperate with co-workers and maintain a team spirit?

26. Do I fail to ask my followers, peers, and superiors for their advice?

27. Do I emphasize rules rather than skills?

28. Do I criticize in non-constructive ways?

29. Do I consider reasonable complaints and positive input from my subordinates?

30. Do I keep my team informed?

31. Am I training an assistant to pass the leadership torch to?

32. Do I feel threatened by others' leadership gifts and abilities?

33. Do I "fit" into the role expected of me?

34. Do I agree with the vision, mission, and objectives? Are they missing?

35. Do I work to improve my leadership abilities?

36. Do I hold on to myths, traditions and old paradigms that hinder effectiveness?

37. Do I motivate my staff to their full potential? Can I do more (individually and collectively)?

38. Do I function as a leader, manager, administrator, or managerial leader?

39. How can I better serve my staff, community, and recipients of my organization's services?

40. How is my personal relationship with God? Is my faith growing?

41. How can I manage my time better?

42. What de-motivates me?

43. What is my action plan for next week, month, and year? (See "Action Plan Work Process", in "Function #2: Planning".)

44. What characteristics are my strengths? ... my weaknesses? How can I improve?

45. What do I want to be remembered for?

*"**Perceived Success without Successful Successive Successors is Failure.**"* (Yes or No?)

Organizational Self-Assessment
Often what we do fits only yesterday's realities. We must address what we should be doing today in view of tomorrow's needs!

1. What is our organization's current understanding of its mission and mission statement? Does it need reworking? Why? How? What problems might we encounter?

2. Why do we exist? Who are we targeting? What are we trying to achieve?

3. For what do we want to be remembered?

4. What changes have occurred in our environment, community, and resources? What technological, economical, political, national and international changes have occurred? How do they affect our organization?

5. What are our organization's major strengths and weaknesses?

6. What results is our organization seeking? Are we attaining them? Is this adequate for our efforts? Is it poor allocation of human and financial resources?

7. Do our competencies match the needs of the recipients? If yes, how? If not, why?

8. What ways have the recipients of our service changed? What are the implications?

9. What other groups should the organization be serving or stop serving? Why? Have their needs changed?

10. Are our resources too limited? Are other organizations more effective?

11. What supporters must be satisfied?

Those we serve usually behave in terms of their own realities and situations. We must identify their needs as accurately as possible and then determine how well we are meeting them. Here are some questions to assist in evaluating how well those needs are being addressed.

1. What do our *primary* recipients consider value? How well do we provide that?

2. What product or service can we alone offer? (What is our niche?)

3. What does our *supporting* constituency consider value?

4. Are we meeting the *real needs*?

5. How do we define results for our organization, unit, department, or group?

6. What is our ministry's criteria for success?

7. What are our major goals? Have we achieved them? To what extent?

8. Have we kept the goals in line with our purpose and mission?

9. What are the major activities that have helped (or hindered) results?

10. In what areas is our work only marginal? Why? How do we know that?

11. How well are we using our human and financial resources? How do we know that? What should be done?

12. What should we stop doing? Why?

13. What are the results of efforts to attract and keep donors supporting our ministry?

14. How does the organization define and share its results with donors? Should it change its procedures? Why?

Competency, opportunities, and commitment—our mission statement must reflect the results we are looking for. A clearly defined mission statement must translate into specific goals and objectives to achieve. We must focus on specific strategies for specific recipients who have specific "needs".

1. In what we are presently doing, can we do it better?

2. Is it the right thing to be doing? Does it still serve a need?

3. With our resources, where can we really make a difference?

4. Are we producing sufficient results to justify putting our resources into it? (What you do well– do more of! What you don't do well–abandon!)

5. If we were not already doing this and committed, would we start doing it?

6. Are we working in the right areas or need to change our focus?

7. Will this advance our capacity to carry out our mission?

Good intentions must become effective action! A decision is not effective until there is a commitment to ACTION!

1. What is our plan, focus and target date? Who is responsible?

2. What are our performance strengths (organization, departments, and individual)?

3. How well are we using our resources?

4. How can our strengths be exploited?

5. What are the end results we want to achieve?

6. Will our decisions, policies, programs and activities advance our capacity to carry out our mission? Which programs and activities should we focus our efforts on? Does each one fit our mission?

7. What should we do differently? Are there programs, activities, or recipient needs that the organization should add, abandon, or address later? Why? Should they be referred to other organizations, if we are unable to handle them effectively? Why?

8. What can we accomplish that will do the most for our organization in the short term and long term?

9. What are the current priorities for our organization and for my specific group or responsibility area? Do they help fulfill the mission, and goals of the organization, my group or responsibility area? Why are these priorities important?

10. What lessons have we learned and what do we recommend as action steps to take? Why?

11. What is our practical and achievable plan for positive results in our organization?

Effective, efficient use of resources + functions/ processes = accomplishment of the vision, purpose, objectives and goals.

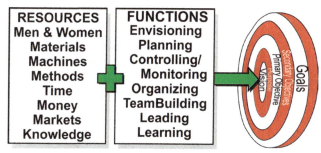

"In discussion of people (and) of the work of Christ, never set your sights too low. Dream the impossible, believe the unlikely, dare the difficult, stretch the imagination, live positively. The riches of God's resources are at the call of aggressive thinkers."
(Found on a wooden engraving in Haiti.)

The Managerial Leadership Chart

Where do you, as a managerial leader, plot yourself on the following Managerial Leadership Chart? The important thing is to be progressing along the line between [1,1] and [10,10]. You may honestly find you have plotted yourself somewhere "off" this line; do everything possible to get back on that line and move forward with the goal to reach the [10,10] quadrant.

Analysis of Team Effectiveness

Let's continue to examine your organization. Use the Belbin Team Analysis tool. You can review it in the section, *Function V. Team Building*.

Use the Worksheet to analyze an action plan for a particular project or to analyze the overall direction of your organization and team.

Sometimes asking someone you trust who is not a staff member can assist you in receiving an objective perspective.

Also, listen to your staff. Often you can glean information that will assist you in resolving problems or improving performance. Your focus is on the task, individual and team needs. You need to keep a balance that will result in effective and efficient use of resources and personnel and as a result have an organization or business that will be a win-win situation for the

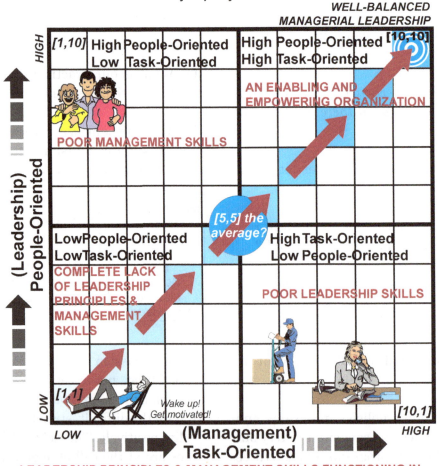

MANAGERIAL LEADERSHIP CHART

Where do you plot yourself on this chart?

LEADERSHIP PRINCIPLES & MANAGEMENT SKILLS FUNCTIONING IN HARMONY WITH EACH OTHER & REACHING THE (10,10) TARGET CREATES EFFECTIVE TEAMS THAT WORK AT THEIR FULL POTENTIAL

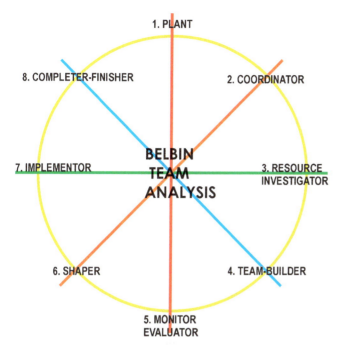

BELBIN TEAM ANALYSIS

1. PLANT
2. COORDINATOR
3. RESOURCE INVESTIGATOR
4. TEAM-BUILDER
5. MONITOR EVALUATOR
6. SHAPER
7. IMPLEMENTOR
8. COMPLETER-FINISHER

team and others to whom you provide a service or meet a need.

Analyze your organization. Write the names of those people who fill any of the eight roles. Indicate if it is a primary or secondary role. Also indicate their weak roles.

1. Plant (visionary):
2. Coordinator (focus is on the team):
3. Resource investigator (networkers):
4. Team-builder (focus is on the team members)
5. Monitor Evaluator (controlling/monitoring):
6. Shaper (take charge; give orders):
7. Implementor (putting the plan to work):
8. Completer-finisher (task-oriented):

Do you have a balance of all eight roles or do you need to make some adjustments? What do you need to do? Why do you need to make the changes? When will you do it? How will you make the changes? When will you evaluate the changes to ensure the changes are effective and efficient? Note: The leader is often the shaper.

Summary

"The gap of understanding between pulpit and pew has widened to such a degree that leadership is seen as a lofty fantasy, accessible only to those rare individuals having supernatural reserves of charisma and communication skill".

It is so wrong! Leadership can be learned and must be developed at every level for us to ultimately survive!

I can just sense your sigh of relief as you have reached the finish line in this exhaustive study! **You are to be commended for joining a select group of people who have taken this subject seriously for themselves and their organizations, and who are passing it on to their successors.**

"...conduct yourselves in a manner worthy of the gospel of Christ... stand firm in one spirit, contending as one man for the faith of the gospel without being frightened in any way by those who oppose you..." (Phil. 1:27,28. NIV).

Will you accept the authentic managerial leadership torch that is being passed to you?

Just one more thing...
Practice it!
Teach it!
Live it!
Pass it on to your successors!

"To know and not to do is not to know at all!" (Howard Hendricks)

"It is not the things we do not know
that get us into trouble.
It's the things we think we know
which aren't so".
Hugh White (Head of the Strategic & Defense Studies Centre at the ANU).

> *I pray above all things that you may prosper in good health, even as your soul propers (3 John2). May you become the authentic managerial leader that God purposed for you to become.*

Prayer of a Famous Leader

(Francis of Assissi)

Lord, make me an instrument of your peace!
Where there is **hatred**, let me sow **love**;
Where there is **injury**, **pardon**;
Where there is **doubt**, **faith**;
Where there is **despair**, **hope**;
Where there is **darkness**, **light**;
Where there is **sadness**, **joy**.
O Divine Master, grant that I may not so
　　much seek to be consoled, as to console;
To be understood, as to understand;
To be loved, as to love.
For it is in giving that we receive;
It is in pardoning that we are pardoned;
It is in dying that we are born to eternal life.

Assignment

1. Review and adjust the ACTION PLAN WORK PROCESS worksheet. (Review "Function # 2: Planning".)

2. In which of the seven managerial leadership functions (envisioning, planning, organizing, controlling/monitoring, team-building, leading, learning) are we strong or weak?

3. What will we do to improve?

4. How will we keep all seven functions working together, synergistically and unitedly to achieve the vision, purpose and mission?

ENDNOTES

I. THE CRISIS
A Leadership Crisis - Why?
(p.8) "We are...under-led." Bennis, Warren & Nanus, Burt. *Leaders*. (New York: Harper & Row, Publishers), p. 21.

Leadership Training and Church Growth
(p.11) "More than ever...about leadership." Kouses, James & Posner, Barry. *The Leadership Challenge*. (San Francisco: Jossey-Bass Inc., Publishers), p.xv,vii.

A Lack of Model Leaders
(p.13) The day was cold...send for me!" The Economics Press. *The Best of Bits and Pieces*. p.110.

The Supreme Biblical Model
(p.15) "A Christian leader...to take place." Barna, George. *Leaders on Leadership*. (Ventura. Regal Books.), p. 25.

"Shirtsleeve Christians" or "Roll-up-your-sleeves Christians"
(p.16) The late Dave Thomas, Founder of Wendy's Restaurants. From *The Christian Reader*, Nov/Dec.1994. p.81-85

II. THE DEFINITION
(p.20)"The leader, whenever... of the organization." James J. Cribbin. *Leadership: Strategies for Organizational Effectiveness*. p.12-14.
(p.20) "The sign of... need for leaders". Max DePree. *Leadership is an Art*. p.12-14,17,22.

People-Oriented
(p. 20) "...leadership involves a set...issues." Clemmer, Jim & McNeil, Art. The VIP Strategy. (Toronto: Key Porter Books Limited), p.3.
(p.20) "...is willing to develop...and ability." Manske, Fred. Spirit of Leadership. (Columbia Tx: Leadership Education and Development Inc.), p. 20.

Future-Oriented
(p.21) "A leader is...among executives." Manske, Jr., F.A. Secrets of Effective Leadership. (Germantown: Leadership Education and Development, Inc.), pp. 3,5.
(p.21) "...most significant contributions...prosper and grow." Kouzes, James M. & Posner, Barry Z. The Leadership Challenge. (San Francisco: Jossey-Bass Inc., Publishers), p. xxi.

Change & Development-Oriented
(p. 22) "Leaders work to...and each other." Clemmer, Jim & McNeil, Art. The VIP Strategy. (Toronto: Key Porter Books Limited), p. 113.

Influence & Motivation-Oriented
(p. 22) "Leadership is motivating...them feel successful." Baker, Don. Leadership. (Portland: Multnomah Press), p.4.
(p. 22) "...the ability to...worthy common goal". Engstrom, Ted W. The Making of a Christian Leader. (Grand Rapids: The Zondervan Corporation), p.20.
(p.23) "turn around...following you." Maxwell, John. Leadership 101. (Tulsa: Honor Books, 1994) p.120.

Action-Oriented
(p. 23) "Leadership is action, not position." McGannon, Donald H. Spirit of Leadership: Inspiring Quotations for Leaders. Compiled by F.C. Harrison (Columbia: Leadership Education and Development, Inc., 1989), p.19.
(p. 23) "...bridges the gap...makes things happen." Clemmer, Jim & McNeil, Art. The VIP Strategy. (Toronto: Key Porter Books Limited), p. 113.

Christian Leadership is...
(p. 23) "...is a person...for the group." Clinton, Robert. The Making of a Leader. (Colorado Springs: NavPress), p.197.

Management is...
(p.24) "...a set of activities...one or more goals." VanFleet, David D. Contemporary Management. (Boston: Houghton Mifflin Company), p.8.

What is the difference?
(p. 24) "Leadership captures concepts...it is done." Wagner, Peter. Leading Your Church to Growth. (Ventura: Regal Books), p.87.
(p. 24) "Most people confuse...foundation...leadership." Clemmer, Jim & McNeil, Art. The VIP Strategy. (Toronto: Key Porter Books Limited), p.32.

Managerial leadership is...
(p. 25) "...managers should not...to greater heights." Hickman, Craig R. Mind of a Manager Soul of a Leader. (New York: John Wiley & Sons, Inc.), p. 13.

Summary
(p.27) "one who guides...a desired end". Ted Engstrom. *The Making of a Christian Leader*. p.24.
(p.27) "The global economy...of managerial work." Robert E. Quinn, et all. *Becoming a Master Manager*. p.v.

III. THE CHARACTER
Courageous Risk-Taker
(p. 30) "The greatest achievements...calculated risks." Sanders, J. Oswald. (Compiled by Doug Nichols. 65 Quotes and Illustrations. #27.)

Lonely
(p.33) "Leaders are like...at a time." Successories Inc. Ottawa, Canada.
(p. 33) "If a man...or far away." Thoreau, Henry David. Used in: McCarthy, Kevin. The On-Purpose Person. (Colorado Springs: Pinon Press, 1992.) p. 69.

Complimentary, Encourager, Empower
(p. 34) "Catch people doing...everyone about it." Blanchard, Ken & Johnson, Spencer. One Minute Manager. (New York: Berkley Publishing Group).

Integrity (The Heart of Character)
(p. 35) "Blowing out your...many times over." Rush, Myron. The New Leader. (Wheaton: Victor Books, 1987), p.28.

IV. THE NINE PILLARS OF THE HOLY SCRIPTURES
Fulfilling the Great Commission
(p. 48) "He created the...success and prestige." Warren, Rick. The Purpose-Driven Church & The Purpose-Driven Life." (Grand Rapids: Zondervan, 1995, 2002).
(p. 48) "Not to listen...crime of commission." Schuster, John P. Answering Your Call. San Francisco: Berrett - Koehler Publishers, Inc., 2003.)

V. THE FUNCTIONS

FUNCTION #1: ENVISIONING

Why is Vision important?
(p. 57) "A vision with...build our lives." McCarthy, Kevin. The On-Purpose Person. (Colorado Springs: Pinon Press, 1992.) p. 84.

Setbacks and Hindrances
(p.58) "Although vision brings...often very lonely" (source unknown)

Guidelines and Principles
(p. 58) "...a special unique...intended for you." Taken from: McCarthy, Kevin. The On-Purpose Person. (Colorado Springs: Pinon Press, 1992.)

Did Jesus Christ have a vision?
(p. 60) "Jesus was able...order or change." Ford, Leighton. Transforming Leadership. (Downers Grove: Intervarsity Press, 1991). p. 15.

God's Purpose for You
(p. 61) "It is easier...common sense basis." Chambers, Oswald. My Utmost For His Highest. (Westword: Barbour and Company, Inc., 1963), p.64.

Uncle Cam's Leadership Style
(p. 61) Cowan, George. "Notes about Cameron Townsend; Uncle Cam's Leadership Style".

FUNCTION #2: PLANNING

Decision - Making
(p.67) "The wrong decision...time = success." Maxwell, John C. Your Attitude: Key to Success. p.66.

FUNCTION #3: ORGANIZING

(p.73) "A leader never...personalities and needs." Tracy, Diane. The First Book of Common-Sense Management. (New York: William Morrow and Company, 1989), p. 40.

Time Management
(p.75) Taylor, Harold. Harold Taylor's Time Management Tools and books may be purchased from 2175 Sheppard Ave. E., Suite 310, Willowdale, ON Canada M2J 1W8, 1-800-361-8463.

Principles and Guidelines of Delegation
(p. 78) "Jesus made truth...override our status." Gunderson, Denny. Through the Dust. (Seattle: YWAM Publishing, 1992.) p. 65.

Job Descriptions
(p.81)"A job description...their job exists." Hendrix, Olan. Management for the Christian Worker. (Libertyville: Quill Publications, 1976), p. 82.
(p.81) "It is my...the organizational structure.) Hendrix, Olan. Management for the Christian Worker. (Libertyville: Quill Publications, 1976), p. 87.
(p.82) "The best job...they are clear." Hendrix, Olan. Management for the Christian Worker. (Libertyville: Quill Publications, 1976), p. 88.

FUNCTION #4: CONTROLLING

(p.87) "Jesus...the Lord of...maintains control." Baker, Don. Leadership. (Portland: Multnomah Press), p. 23.

FUNCTION #5: TEAMBUILDING

Defining "Teamwork"
(p.92) "Teamwork is the...attain uncommon results." Successories Inc. Ottawa, Canada.
(p.92) "Teamwork divides the...doubles the success." Successories Inc. Ottawa, Canada.
(p.92) "...it is increasingly..units called team." Maddux, Robert B. Team Building: An Exercise in Leadership. Revised Edition. (Los Altos: Crisp Publications, 1988), p.4.
(p.92) "Now this is...is the pack." Kipling, Rudyard.
(p.92) "A strong leader...be even stronger." Lincoln, James E. Lincoln Electric Co.
(p.92) "Teamwork: Coming together...is a success." Successories Inc. Ottawa, Canada.

Selecting a Team Leader
(p.96) "The one who...face the music!" LeRoy Eims. *Be a Motivational Leader*. p.12.

Growing A Cohesive Team
(p.97) "The three circles...the three circles." Adair, John. Effective Leadership. (London: Pan Books Ltd., 1983), p. 36.

The Belbin Team Analysis
(p.99) Belbin, Meredith. www.belbin.com

Gangel's 5 Principles of Motivation
(p.102) "Gangel's 5 Principles of Motivation." Gangel, Kenneth O. Feeding and Leading. (Grand Rapids: Baker Books, 1989), pp. 169-171.

Conflict & Negotiation
(p.103) "Versatility: The ability...of the situation." Cook, Bruce. Leadership Dynamics.

Effective Communication
(p.103) "the act of...to communicate ideas." Cribbon, James. Leadership. AMACON. p.83.

Intuition
(p.103) "...What about intuition?...are in congruence." MacMillan, Pat. Hiring Excellence: 6 Steps to Making Good People Decisions. pp. 27, 34, 46, 47.

Perpetually Redefine Quality
(p. 104) "Excellence is dedicated...more rewarding kind." Wolf, Jill. Reflections Bookmarks.

Responsibilities Of The CEO
(p.108) "Wherever I've seen...work and responsibility." Drucker, Peter F. Managing the Non-Profit Organization. (San Francisco: Josey-Bass Publishers, 1992), pp. 157, 158, 178, 179.
The Animal School
(p.109) Swindoll, Chuck. Home where life makes up its mind. pg. 51.

FUNCTION #6: LEADING

Attributes
(p.112) "one who guides...a desired end." Engstrom, Ted. The Making of a Christian Leader. (Grand Rapids: The Zondervan Corporation), p. 24.

Traits & Characteristics
(p.114) "Policies without principles...worship without sacrifice." Donaldson, Canon Fredrick Lewis.

Responsibilities
(p.115) "...abandoning things that...are pushing for." Drucker, Peter, F. Managing the Non-Profit Organization. (San Francisco: Josey-Bass Publishers, 1992), p.48.

Ken Blanchard's Situational Leadership Model II®

(p.119) "Situational Leadership Model II®" Ken Blanchard and Paul Hersey originally developed the Situational Leadership Model. After testing, proving, and using this model, Ken improved on it and it is now known as the Ken Blanchard Situational Leadership II. Blanchard Training and Development Inc. publishes and extensive array of training materials [Blanchard Training and Development Inc., 125 State Place, Escondido, CA, USA 92025; 1-800-821-5332; 619-489-5005]

(p.119) "Jesus used a...not leave them." Ford, Leighton. Transforming Leadership. (Downers Grove: InterVarsity Press, 1991.) pp. 286, 287.

Managerial Leadership Style®

(p.120) "Managerial Leadership Style®" Goldore Consulting Inc., Box 590, Linden, AB, Canada T0M 1J0 (phone 403-370-6025); robertalexorr@yahoo.ca

The Eagle

(p.124) adapted from McNally, David. Even Eagles Need a Push. (New York: Dell Publishing, 1990.) p. xiv.

FUNCTION #7: LEARNING

The Learning Process

(p.126) Statistics based on the book: Teaching to Change Lives. Hendricks, Dr. Howard. (Sisters: Multnomah Publishers, Inc., 1987.) pp.58,59.

The Teaching Leader & the Learning Follower

(p.127) The 7 Laws of Teaching are based on the book: Teaching to Change Lives. Hendricks, Dr. Howard. (Sisters: Multnomah Publishers, Inc., 1987.)

Improve Your Learning Skills

(p.131) The 13 points are from an interview in Bottom Line Secrets with Guy Claxton, PhD. First published on January 1, 2001. He is the author of Wise Up - The Challenge of Lifelong Learning (Bloomsbury).

(p.131) "A great teacher...have surpassed him." Teaching to Change Lives. Hendricks, Dr. Howard. (Sisters: Multnomah Publishers, Inc., 1987.)

Self Learning and Expanding your Personal Knowledge

(p.132) "Emotional intelligence... and influence." Cooper, Robert K and Sawaf, Ayman. Executive EQ, Emotional Intelligence in Leadership & Organization. Pg. xiii.

(p.132) "emotions are...arouses emotion." Cooper, Robert and Sawaf, Ayman. Executive EQ, Emotional Intelligence in Leadership & Organization. pg.xv.

(p. 132) "When you engage...instead of hours. Cooper, Robert K and Sawaf, Ayman. Executive EQ, Emotional Intelligence in Leadership & Organization. Pg. xiv.

(p.132) "Emotional alchemy...to sense, act." Marcolm Gladwell. Blink. Pg. 276.

(p. 133) "What finally counts...see everything. Cramer and Wasiak. Change the Way You See Everything. pg. 13.

(p.133) "Live in the Learning...staying positive". Monday Morning Leadership. pg. 93.

(p.133) "Ways of learning...to be such". Kenneth O. Gangel. So You Want to be a Leader. pg. 66

(p.133) "A courageous leader...leadership position." Halcomb, Hamilton, Malmstadt,.Courageous Leaders. pg.1

(p.133) "To the extent...every turn". Leadership and Self Deception, getting out of the box. The Arbinger Institute. Pg. viii,

(p.134) "Those leaders...productive life". Leaders, fools, and impostors.Pg. 184.

(p.134) "An unconscious conspiracy...emergence of leaders." Warren Benis. Why leaders can't lead. Pg. xiv.

(p.134)"It's just not...capacity to create." Senge, Peter M. The Fifth Discipline.

(p.135) "The starfish's...no central command." Brafman, Ori and Beckstrom, Rod A.The Starfish and the Spider. Pg. 35.

(p.135) "While both are...suited to catalysts." Ibid. Pg 129.

(p.136) "A coercive system... chooses to meet." Ibid. Pg.46,47.

(p.136) "...centralized organizations...tolerance for innovation." Ibid. Pg.87.

Summary

(p.136) "Study the life...Christian education." Teaching to Change Lives. Hendricks, Dr. Howard. (Sisters: Multnomah Publishers, Inc., 1987.)

VI. THE REALITIES

Character/Heart Issues: Pride

(p.138) "Too many clergy...reinforce that attitude." Colson, Charles. The Body: Being Light in Darkness. (Dallas: Word Publishing, 1992.) p. 296.

Addressing the People Issues: Hidden Agenda

(p.141) "...if we're not...cannot respect us." Brown, W. Steven. 13 Fatal Errors Managers Make and How You Can Avoid Them. (New York: Berkley Publishing Group, 1985.) p.101.

Addressing the Task Issues

(p.142) "The leaders who...They think 'team'." Drucker, Peter F. Managing the Non-Profit Organization. (New York: HarperCollins Publishers, 1992.) pp. 18,19.

VII. PERSONAL AND ORGANIZATIONAL SELF-ASSESSMENT

(p.150) "Managerial Leadership Chart." adapted from Black, Robert R. and Mouton, Jane S. The Managerial Grid. (Houston: Gulf Publishing Company, 1994.) p. 10.

BIBLIOGRAPHY

Bibles and Study Helps:
The Holy Bible, New Internal Version, NIV. Copyright 1973,1978,1984 by International Bible Society.
The Leadership Bible, New International Version. Grand Rapids: Zondervan, 1998.
NIV Student Bible, Revised. Grand Rapids: Zondervan, 2002.
Women of Faith Study Bible, New International Version. Grand Rapids: Zondervan, 2001.
John C. Maxwell. *The Maxwell Leadership Bible New King James Version.* Nashville: Thomas Nelson, Inc., 2002.
The Holy Bible, New King James Version. Nashville: Thomas Nelson Publisher, 1982.
New Geneva Study Bible, Foundation for Reformation. New King James Version. Nashville: Thomas Nelson Publishers:1995.
Max Lucado. *He Did This Just For You New Testament. New King James Version.* Nashville: Thomas Nelson Publishers: 2001.
Eugene Peterson. *THE MESSAGE REMIX: The Bible in Contemporary Language.* Colorado Springs: NavPress Publishing Group, 2003.
The Living Bible. Wheaton: Tyndale House Publishers, 1971.
Complete Jewish Bible. Clarksville: Jewish New Testament Publications, Inc., 1998.
The Bible, Revised *Standard Version.* New York: American Bible Society, NT-1946, OT-1952.
Thompson's New Chain-Reference Bible. Indianapolis: B.B. Kirkbride Bible Co.,Inc., 1964.
THE HOLY BIBLE, The Berkeley Version in Modern English. Grand Rapids: Zondervan Publishing House, NT-1945, OT-1959.
The Comparative Study Bible presenting New International Version, New American Standard Bible, Amplified Bible, King James Version. Grand Rapids: Zondervan Publishing House, 1984.
The Jerusalem Bible, Reader's Edition. New York: Bantam Doubleday Dell Publishing Group, Inc., 1968.
Eight Translation New Testament-King James Version, The Living Bible, Phillips Modern English, Revised Standard Version, New International Version, Jerusalem Bible, New English Bible. Wheaton: Tyndale House Publication,1974.
James Moffat. *The New Testament, A New Translation.* New York: George H. Doran, 1922.
Charles B. Williams. *THE NEW TESTAMENT, A Private Translation in the Language of the People.* Chicago: Moody Press, 1949.
Wise, Micheal, Abegg Jr., Martin & Cook, Edward. *The Dead Sea Scrolls, A New Translation with Commentary.* New York: HarperCollins, 1996.
Holley, J.E. and Holley-Fizzell, Carolyn. *Holley's Visual Bible.* Los Angeles: J.E. & C.F. Holley,1937.
Torrey, R.A. *The Treasury of Scripture Knowledge.* Old Tappan: Fleming H. Revell Company.
Gray, James M. *Christian Workers' Commentary on the Whole Bible.* Old Tappan: A SPIRE BOOK Fleming H. Revell Company, 1977.
Young, Robert. *Analytical Concordance to the Bible.* Grand Rapids: WM. B. Eerdmans Publishing Company, 1973.
Willmington, H.L. *Willmington's GUIDE to the BIBLE.* Wheaton: Tyndale House Publishers, Inc.,1981.
Pfeiffer, Charles F. and Harrison, Everett F. *The Wycliffe Bible Commentary.* Chicago: Moody Press, 1962.
Unger, Merrill F. *Unger's Bible Dictionary.* Chicago: Moody Press, 1966.
Pfeiffer, Charles F., Vos, Howard F. and Rea, John. *Wycliffe Bible Encyclopedia Volume 1 A-J.* Chicago: Moody Press, 1975.
Pfeiffer, Charles F., Vos, Howard F. and Rea, John. *Wycliffe Bible Encyclopedia Volume 2 K-Z.* Chicago: Moody Press, 1975.
Find it Fast in the Bible: The Ultimate A to Z Resource. Nashville: Thomas Nelson Publishers, 2000.
Illustrated Family Bible Stories. Bath: Parragon Publishing, 2003.

Books:
Adair, John. *Effective Leadership.* London: Pan Books Ltd., 1983.
Adams, Jay E. *How to Handle Trouble God's Way.* Phillipsburg: Presbyterian and Reformed Publishing Co., 1982.
ADL Associates. *Back to Basics: Tried and True Solutions for Today's Leaders.* Lewisville: ADL Associates, 2002.
Alcorn, Randy. *The Treasure Principle.* Sisters: Multnomah Publishers, Inc., 2001.
Alcorn, Randy. *Money, Possessions and Eternity.* Carol Stream: Tyndale House Publishers, Inc., 2003.
Alexander, John W. *Managing Our Work.* Second Revised Edition. Downers Grove: Intervarsity Press, 1975.
Allender Ph.D., Dan B. *Leading With A Limp.* Colorado Springs: Waterbrook Press, 2006.
Anderson, Leith. *Leadership That Works.* Bloomington: Bethany House Publishers, 1999.
Andringa, Robert C. See National Center for NonProfit Boards.
Andringa, Robert C. and Ted W. Engstrom. *Nonprofit Board Answer Book.* Washington DC: National Center for Nonprofit Boards, 1997.
Ankerberg, John. And Weldon, John. *Cult Watch.* Eugene: Harvest House Publishers, 1991.
Ankerberg, John & Weldon, John. *The Facts On Why You Can Believe The Bible.* Eugene: Harvest House Publishers, 2004.
Arbinger Institute. *Leadership and Self-Deception.* San Fransisco: Berrett-Koehler Publishers Inc., 2002.
Armerding, Hudson T. *Leadership.* Wheaton: Tyndale House Publishers, 1978.
Badaracco, Joseph L, Jr. and Ellsworth, Richard R. *Leadership and the Quest for Integrity.* Boston: Harvard Business School Press, 1989.
Baker, Don. *Leadership: Learning To Make Others Succeed.* Portland: Multnomah Press, 1983.
Banashak, Brian. *The Little Book of Business Wisdom.* Mobile: Evergreen Press, 2003.
Bangs Jr, David H. *Entrepreneur Magazine's Business Plans Made Easy.* Entrepreneur Media Inc., 2005
Barker, Joel Arthur. *Paradigms: The Business of Discovering the Future.* New York: William Morrow and Company Inc., 1992.
Barna, George. *A Fish Out of Water.* Brentwood: Integrity Publishers, 2002.
Barna, George. *Leaders on Leadership.* Ventura CA: Regal Books/Gospel Light, 1997.
Barna, George. *Revolution.* Wheaton: Tyndale House Publishers, Inc., 2005.
Barna, George. *Turning Vision into Action.* Ventura CA: Regal Books/Gospel Light, 1996.
Bass, Bernard M. *Stogdill's Handbook of Leadership: A Survey of Theory and Research.* Revised & Expanded Edition. New York: The Free Press, 1981.
Batten, Joe D. *Tough-Minded Management.* Third Edition. New York: AMACOM, 1978.
Bender, Peter Urs. *Leadership from Within.* Toronto: Stoddart Publishing Co. Limited, 2001.
Bennis, Warren. *On Becoming a Leader.* Don Mills: Addison-Wesley Publishing Co., 1989.
Bennis, Warren. *Why Leaders Can't Lead.* San Francisco: Jossey- Bass Publishers, 1989.
Bennis, Warren and Nanus, Burt. *Leaders: The Strategies for Taking Charge.* New York: Harper and Row Publishers, 1985.
Berkley, E. Dale with Brendel, Doug. *The Disappearing Donor.* Akron: Berkey Brendel Sheline, 2005.
Best of Bits and Pieces. Fairfield: The Economics Press,1994.
Biehl, Bobb. *Increasing Your Leadership Confidence.* Sisters, Oregon: Questar Publishers, Inc., 1989.
Biehl, Bobband Ted W. Engstrom. *Boardroom Confidence.* Sisters, Oregon: Questar Publishers, Inc., 1988.
Blackaby, Henry T. & King, Claude V. *Experiencing God: Knowing and Doing the Will of God.* Nashville: LifeWay Press, 1997.
Blanchard, Ken and Hodges, Phil. *The Servant Leader.* Belgium: J. Countryman, Thomas Nelson, Inc., 2003.
Blanchard, Ken. And Muchnick, Marc. *The Leadership Pill.* New York: Free Press, 2003.
Blanchard, Ken and Cathy, S. Truett. *The Generosity Factor.* Grand Rapids: Zondervan, 2002.
Blanchard, Ken, Hybels, Bill and Hodges, Phil. *Leadership by the Book.* New York: William Morrow and Company Inc., 1999.
Blanchard, Ken. *We are the Beloved.* Grand Rapids: Zondervan Publishing House, 1994.
Blanchard, Kenneth, and Sheldon Bowles. *Raving Fans.* New York: Wm. Morrow & Co. Inc., 1993.
Blanchard, Kenneth. *The Color Model: A Situational Approach to Manging People.* Escondido: Blanchard Training and Development, Inc., 1994.
Blanchard, Kenneth. and Johnson, Spencer. *The One Minute Manager.* New York: Berkley Publishing Group, 1981.
Blanchard, Kenneth, William Jr. Oncken, and Hal Burrows. *The One Minute Manager Meets the Monkey.* New York: Quill William Morrow, 1989.
Bliss, Edwin C. *Getting Things Done: The ABCs of Time Management.* New York: Charles Scribner's Sons, 1976.
Block, Peter. *The Empowered Manager: Positive Political Skills at Work.* San Francisco: Jossey- Bass Publishers, 1987.

Bolman, Lee G. & Deal, Terrence E. *The Wizard and the Warrior*. San Francisco: Jossey-Bass, 2006.
Bossidy, Larry and Charan, Ram. *Execution: The Discipline of Getting Things Done*. New York: Crown Business, 2002.
Bottom Line Personal Book of Wisdom. Boardroom Inc., 1996.
Brafman, Ori and Beckstrom, Rod A. *The Starfish and the Spider*. New York: Penguin Group, 2006.
Brassard, Michael and Diane Ritter. *The Memory Jogger II*. Methuen, MA: GOAL?QPC, 1994.
Brendel, Doug. *7 Deadly Diseases of Ministry Marketing*. Fairlawn, OH: International Christian Publishers, 1998.
Briner, Bob. *The Management Methods of Jesus*. Nashville: Thomas Nelson Inc., 1996.
Briner, Bob and Ray Pritchard. *The Leadership Lessons of Jesus*. Nashville: Broadman & Holman, 1997.
Broom, H.N., and Longenecker, Justin G. *Small Business Management*. Third Edition. Cincinnati: South-Western Publishing Co., 1971.
Brown, Steven W. *13 Fatal Errors Managers Make and How You Can Avoid Them*. New York: Berkley Publishing Group, 1985.
Bruce, A.B. *The Training of the Twelve*. Grand Rapids: Kregel Publications, 1971.
Buckingham, Marcus and Curt Coffman. *First, Break all the Rules*. New York: Simon & Schuster, 1999.
Buford, Bob. *Half Time*. Grand Rapids: Zondervan Publishing House,1994.
Burke, H. Dale. *Less is More Leadership*. Eugene: Harvest House Publishers, 2004.
Burt, Steve, and Walrath, Douglas Alan, ed. *Activating Leadership in the Small Church: Clergy and Laity Working Together*. Valley Forge: Judson Press, 1988.
Butler, Phill. *Well Connected*. Waynesboro: Authentic Media, 2005.
Calvert, Gene. *High Wire Management*. San Francisco: Jossey-Bass Publishers,1993.
Capozzi, John M. *If You Want the Rainbow You Gotta Put Up with the Rain*. Fairfield: JMC Industries Inc. 1997.
Carlson, Richard. *Don't Sweat the Small Stuff about Money*. New York: Hyperion, 2001.
Carter, Jimmy. *Our Endangered Values*. New York: Simon & Schuster, 2005.
Carter, Violet Bonham. *Winston Churchill: An Intimate Portrait*. New York: Konecky & Konecky, 1965.
Carver, John. *Boards that Make a Difference*. San Francisco: Jossey-Bass Publishers, 1990.
Carver, John. *Strategies for Board Leadership*. San Francisco: Jossey-Bass Publishers, 1997.
Certo, Samuel C. *Principles of Modern Management*. Dubuque: Wm.C. Brown Company Publishers, 1980.
Chambers, Oswald. *My Utmost for His Highest*. Westwood: Barbour and Company Inc., 1963.
Champy, James. *X-Engineering the Corporation*. New York: Warner Business Books, 2002.
Chapman, Elwood N. *The New Supervisor*. Melno Park: Crisp Publications, Inc., 1992.
Charney, Cy. *The Leader's Tool Kit*. New York: AMACOM, 2006.
Childress, John R. *A Time For Leadership*. Los Angeles: Leadership Press, 2000.
Clemmer, Jim. *The Leader's Digest*. Toronto: TCG Press, 2003.
Clemmer, Jim. *Growing the Distance*. Toronto: TCG Press. 1999.
Clemmer, Jim, and McNeil, Art. *The VIP Strategy: Leadership Skills for Exceptional Performance*. Toronto: Key Porter Books, 1988.
Clinton, Dr. J. Robert. *The Making of a Leader*. Colorado Springs: NavPress, 1988.
Cloud, Dr. Henry. *9 Things a Leader Must Do*. Nashville: Thomas Nelson, 2006.
Cohen, Allan R. *The Portable MBA in Management*. New York: John Wiley & Sons, Inc., 1993.
Collins, James C. and Jerry I. Porras. *Built to Last*. New York: HarperCollins Publishers, 1997.
Colombo, John Robert. *Colombo's New Canadian Quotations*. Edmonton: Hurtig Publishers, ?.
Colson, Charles, and Vaughn, Ellen Santilli. *The Body: Being Light in the Darkness*. Dallas: Word Publishing, 1992.
Conger, Jay A. *Learning to Lead*. San Francisco: Jossey-Bass Inc., 1992.
Cook, Bruce. *Faith Planning*. Wheaton: SP Publications, 1983.
Cook, Bruce. *God's Secret for Getting Things Done*. Wheaton: SP Publications, 1983.
Cook, William H. *Success, Motivation, and the Scriptures*. Nashville: Broadman Press, 1974.
Cooper, Robert K. and Ayman Sawaf. *Executive EQ*. New York: Grosset/Putnam, Penguin Putnam Inc., 1996, 1997.
Cormack, David. *Team Spirit: A Management Handbook*. Grand Rapids: Zondervan Publishing House, 1989.
Cottrell, David. Monday Morning Mentoring. New York: HarperCollins Publishers, 2006.
Covey, Stephen R. *Principle-Centered Leadership*. New York: Simon & Schuster, 1991.
Covey, Stephen R. *The 7 Habits of Highly Effective People*. New York: Simon & Schuster, 1989.
Covey, Stephen R. and Merrill, A.Roger and Merrill, Rebecca R. *First Things First*. New York: Free Press, 1994.
Crabb, Larry. *The Safest Place on Earth*. Nashville: W Publishing Group, a division of Thomas Nelson, Inc., 1999.
Crabb, Jr., Lawrence J. *Understanding People*. Grand Rapids: Zondervan, 1987.
Crainer, Stuart. *The Ultimate Book of Business Quotations*. New York: American Management Association, 1998.
Cramer, Ph.D, Kathryn D. & Wasiak, Hank. *Change The Way You See Everything*. Philadelphia: Running Press, 2006.
Cribbin, James J. *Leadership: Strategies for Organizational Effectiveness*. New York: American Management Associations, 1981.
Crosby, Philip. *The Absolutes of Leadership*. San Diego: Pfeiffer & Company. 1996.
Cross, John R. *The Stranger on the Road to Emmaus*. Sanford: Good Seed International, Inc., 1996.
Dayton, Edward R. *Tools for Time Management: Christian Perspectives on Managing Priorities*. Grand Rapids: Zondervan Publishing House, 1974.
Dayton, Edward R., and Engstrom, Ted W. *The Art of Management for Christian Leaders*. Waco: Word Inc., 1976.
Dayton, Edward R., and Engstrom, Ted W. *The Christian Executive*. Waco: Word Inc., 1979.
Dayton, Edward R., and Engstrom, Ted W. *The Christian Leaders 60-Second Management Guide*. Waco: Word Books Publishers, 1984.
Dayton, Edward R., and Engstrom, Ted W. *Strategy for Leadership*. Old Tappan: Fleming H. Revell Co. Publishers, 1979.
Dayton, Edward R. and Engstrom, Ted W. *Strategy for Living*. Glendale: Regal Books Division, G/L Publications, 1976.
Dean, Dave. *Now is Your Time to Win*. Wheaton: Tyndale House, 1983.
Decision Making, Module 5. Atlanta: Leadership Dynamics International, 1977.
Decker, Bert. *The Art of Communicating: Achieving Interpersonal Impact in Business*. Los Altos: Crisp Publications, 1988.
Deere, Jack. *Surprised by the Voice of God*. Grand Rapids: Zondervan Publishing House, 1996.
Deems, Richard S., Terri A. *Leading in Tough Times*. Amherst: HRD Press, Inc., 2003.
Deir, Dr. Costa S. *Pocket Principles for Leaders, Vol. 1*. Columbia: Cityhill Publishing, 1989.
DePree, Max. *Leadership is an Art*. New York: Dell Publishing, 1989.
DePree, Max. *Leadership Jazz*. New York: Dell Publishing, 1992.
Dewert, Dick. *Lessons for Leaders, I & II*. ?
Dick, Ken. *What are You Doing with my Money?* Streetsville: Ken Dick Management Consultants. ?
DiLorenzo, Thomas J. *Lincoln Unmasked*. New York: Crown Forum, division of Random House, 2006.
Dingman, Robert W. *In Search of a Leader*. Westlake Village: Lakeside Books, 1994.
Dinnen, Stewart. *You Can Learn To Lead*. Fearn: Christian Focus Publications, 1998.
Dollar, Truman. *Building Blocks of the Faith*. Nashville: Fundamentalist Church Publications, 1977.
Douglas, Mack R. *How to Make a Habit of Succeeding: A 39-Step Program for Purpose, Creativity, and Action*. Grand Rapids: Zondervan Publishing House, 1966.
Douglass, Stephen B. *Managing Yourself: Practical Help for Christians in Personal Planning, Time Scheduling and Self-control*. San Bernardino: Here's Life Publishers, 1978.
Drane, John et al. *Death of a Princess*. London: Silvre Fish Publishing, 1998.
Drucker, Peter F. *Classic Drucker*. Boston: Harvard Business School Publishing Corporation, 2006.
Drucker, Peter F. *The Effective Executive*. New York: Harper & Row Publishers, 1967.

Drucker, Peter F. *The Five Most Important Questions You Will Ever Ask about Your NonProfit Organization*. San Francisco: Jossey-Bass Publishers, 1993.
Drucker, Peter F. *The Leader of the Future*. San Francisco. Josey-Bass Publishers, 1996.
Drucker, Peter F. *Managing the Non-Profit Organization*. San Francisco. Josey-Bass Publishers.
Easum, Bill. *Leadership on the Other Side*. Nashville: Abingdon Press, 2000.
Eddison, John. *Understanding Leadership*. London: Scripture Union, 1974.
Edwards, Gene. *A Tale of Three Kings*. Auburn: Christian Books, MCMLXXX.
Eims, Leroy. *Be a Motivational Leader*. Wheaton: SP Publications, 1981.
Eims, LeRoy. *Be the Leader You Were Meant to Be: Biblical Principles of Leadership*. Wheaton: SP Publications, 1975.
Eldredge, John. *Wild at Heart*. Nashville: Thomas Nelson, Inc., 2001.
Elliston, Edgar J. *Home Grown Leaders*. Pasadena: William Carey Library, 1992.
Engel, James F. *A Clouded Future?*. Milwaukee: Christian Stewardship Association, 1996.
Engstrom, Ted W. *Hooks, Lines & Sinkers*. Arcadia: The Workshop, 19?.
Engstrom, Ted W. *The Making of a Christian Leader*. Grand Rapids: Zondervan Publishing House, 1976.
Engstrom, Ted W. *The Pursuit of Excellence*. Grand Rapids: Zondervan Publishing House, 1982.
Engstrom, Ted W. *Reflections on a Pilgrimage*. Sisters: Loyal Publishing Inc., 1999.
Engstrom, Ted W. and MacKenzie, R. Alec. *Managing Your Time: Practical Guidelines on the Effective Use of Time*. Grand Rapids: Zondervan Publishing House, 1967.
Epp, Theodore H. *Christ Reflected in Bible Characters*. Lincoln: Back to the Bible Publication, 1959.
Epp, Theodore H. *Moses, Vol. 2: Excellence in Leadership*. Lincoln: Back to the Bible Publications, 1976.
Erickson, Kenneth A. *Christian Time Management: Investing God's Gift Wisely*. St. Louis: Concordia Publishing House, 1985.
Evans, Robert C. Moral Leadership. Whitby/Toronto: McGraw-Hill Ryerson, 1998.
Farkas, Charles M. and Philippe De Backer. *Maximum Leadership*. New York: Bertkley Publishing Group, 1996.
Farnsworth, Kirk E. *Wounded Workers*. Mukilteo: WinePress Publishing, 1998.
Farson, Richard. *Management of the Absurd*. New York: Touchstone Books/Simon & Schuster Inc., 1996, 1997.
Feinberg, Mortimer R. *Effective Psychology for Managers*. Englewood Cliffs: Prentice-Hall, Inc., 1965.
Fernando, Ajith. *Leadership Lifestyle: A Study of 1 Timothy*. Wheaton: Tyndale House Publishers, 1984.
Finzel, Hans. *The Top Ten Mistakes Leaders Make*. Wheaton: Victor Books, 1994.
Follett, Mary Parker. *Dynamic Administration*. New York: Harper & Row Publishers. 1941.
Forbes Inc. *Thoughts on Leadership*. Chicago: Triumph Books, 1995.
Ford, Leighton. *Transforming Leadership*. Downers Grove, IL: InterVarsity Press, 1991.
Fortune, Don & Katie. *Discover Your God-Given Gifts*. Grand Rapids: Chosen Books, 1987.
Friedman, Thomas L. *The World Is Flat*. New York: Farrar, Straus and Giroux, 2006.
Friesen, Garry. *Decision Making and the Will of God*. Portland: Multnomah Press, 1980.
Fritz, Roger. *Think Like A Manager*. Shawnee Mission: National Seminars Publications, Inc., 1991.
Fryar, Jane L. *Trust and Teams*. St. Louis: Concordia Publishing House, 2002.
Fryar, Jane L. *Servant Leadership*. St. Louis: Concordia Publishing House, 2001.
Gangel, Kenneth O. *Team Leadership in Christian Ministry*. Chicago: Moody Press, 1997.
Gangel, Kenneth O. *Competent to Lead: A Guide to Management in Christian Organizations*. Chicago: Moody Press, 1974.
Gangel, Kenneth O. *Feeding & Leading*. Grand Rapids: Baker Books, 1989.
Gangel, Kenneth O. *So You Want to be a Leader!*. Harrisburg: Christian Publications, 1973.
Gannon, Martin J. *Management: An Integrated Framework*. Second Edition. Boston: Little, Brown and Co., 1982.
Gardner, John W. *On Leadership*. New York: The Free Press, 1990.
Gaskiyane, Dr. I. *Polygamy*. Carlisle: Piquant, 2000.
George, Carl F., and Logan, Robert E. *Leading & Managing Your Church*. Old Tappan: Fleming H. Revell Co. Publishers, 1987.
George, Elizabeth. *A Wife After God's Own Heart*. Eugene: Harvest House Publishers, 2004.
Gibson, James L. Ivancevich, John M. and Donnelly, James H. Jr. *Organizations*. Fourth Edition. Plano: Business Publications Inc., 1982.
Gilbert, Rob. *More of...The Best of Bits and Pieces*. Fairfield: The Economics Press,1997.
Gitomer, Jeffrey. *Jeffrey Gitomer's Little Black Book of Connections*. Austin: Bard Press, 2006.
Gladwell, Malcolm. *Blink*. New York: Back Bay Books, 2005.
Glaser, Connie and Smalley, Barbara. *What Queen Esther Knew*. Rodale, 2003.
Goble, Frank. *Excellence in Leadership*. Caroline House Publishers Inc., 1972.
Godin, Seth. *Tribes*. New York: Penguin Group. 2008.
God's Words of Life for Leaders. Grand Rapids: Inspirio, The gift group of Zondervan, 1999.
Goodwin, Doris Kearns. *Team of Rivals: The Political Genuis of Abraham Lincoln*. New York: Simon & Schuster, 2005.
Gordon, Judith R., Mondy, R. Wayne, Sharplin, Arthur., and Premeaux, Shane R. *Management and Organizational Behavior*. Needham Heights: Allyn and Bacon, 1990.
Gordon, Thomas. *Leader Effectiveness Training: L.E.T.*. New York: Bantam Books, 1977.
Grace, Kay Sprinkel. See National Center for NonProfit Boards.
Green, Robert. *The 48 Laws of Power*. New York: the Penguin Group, 1998.
Greenslade, Philip. *Leadership, Greatness and Servanthood*. Minneapolis: Bethany House Publishers, 1984.
Grenz, Stanley J. and Smith, Jay T. *Pocket Dictionary of Ethics*. Downers Grove: InterVarsity Press, 2003.
Gunderson, Denny. *Through the Dust*. Seattle: YWAM Publishing, 1992.
Gunderson, Denny. *The Leadership Paradox*. Seattle: YWAM Publishing, 1997.
Gungor, Ed. *The Vow*. Nashville: Thomas Nelson Inc. 2007.
Habecker, Eugene B. *The Other Side of Leadership*. Wheaton: SP Publications, 1987.
Haggai, John. *Lead On! Leadership That Endures in a Changing World*. Dallas: Word Publishing, 1986.
Halcomb, James et al. *Courageous Leaders*. Seattle: YWAM Publishing, 2000.
Harari, Oren. *The Leadership Secrets of Colin Powell*. New York: McGraw-Hill, 2002.
Harmon, Dan. *Men of the Bible*. Uhrichsville, OH: Barbour Publishing Inc. 2001.
Harrison, Frederick C. (compiled by) *Spirit of Leadership*. Columbia, TN: Leadership Education and Development Inc., 1989.
Harvard Business Review. *What Makes a Leader*. Boston: Harvard Business School Publishing Corp., 2001.
Harvard Business Review. *Business Classics: Fifteen Key Concepts for Managerial Success*. Boston: Harvard Business School Publishing Corp.1991.
Harvard Business Review. *People: Managing Your Most Important Asset*. Boston: Harvard Business School Publishing Corp.1991.
Harvard Business Review. *Leading People*. Harvard Business School Publishing Corporation, 2006.
Harvey, Eric and Lucia, Alexander. *Walk the Talk...and get the Results You Want*. Dallas: Treeview Publishing books, 1993.
Harvey, Eric and Lucia, Alexander. *144 Ways to Walk the Talk*. Dallas: Performance Publishing Company, 1994.
Hedges, Charlie. *Getting the Right Things Right*. Sisters: Questar Publishers Inc., 1996.
Heim, Pat and Chapman, Elwood N. *Learning to Lead*. Los Altos: Crisp Publications, Inc., 1990.
Heller, Robert. *Learning To Lead*. New York: Dorling Kindersley Limited, 1999.
Heller, Robert, and Hindle, Tim. *Essential Manager's Manual*. London: Dorling Kindersley Limited, 1998.
Hendricks, Dr. Howard. *The Seven Laws of the Teacher*. Walk Thru the Bible Ministries. 1988.
Hendricks, Dr. Howard. *Teaching to Change Lives*. Sisters: Multnomah, 1987.
Hendrix, Olan. *Management for the Christian Leader*. Milford: Mott Media, 1981.

Hendrix, Olan. *Management for the Christian Worker*. Libertyville: Quill Publications, 1976.

Hendrix, Olan. *Three Dimensions of Leadership*. St. Charles, IL: ChurchSmart Resources, 2000.

Hersey, Dr. Paul. *The Situational Leader*. New York: Warner Books, 1984.

Hesselbein, Frances and Paul M. Cohen. *Leader to Leader*. San Francisco: Jossey- Bass Publishers, 1999.

Hesselbein, Frances and Marshall Goldsmith and Richard Beckhard. *The Leader of the Future*. San Francisco: Jossey-Bass Publishers, 1996.

Hiam, Alex. *The Starfish Files*. Amherst: HRD Press, Inc. 2005.

Hickman, Craig R. *Mind of a Manager, Soul of a Leader*. New York: John Wiley & Sons Inc., 1990.

Hickman, Craig R., and Silva, Michael A. *Creating Excellence: Managing Corporate Culture, Strategy, and Change in the New Age*. New York: New American Library, 1984.

Hiebert, Murray and Bruce Klatt. *The Encyclopedia of Leadership*. New York: McGraw-Hill Companies, 2001.

High, David R. *Kings & Priests*. Oklahoma City: Books for Children of the World, 1997.

Hocking, David L. *Be a Leader People Follow*. Glendale: G/L Publications, 1979.

Hoke, Steve and Taylor, Bill. *Send Me: Your Journey to the Nations*. Pasadena: World Evangelical Fellowship Missions Commission and William Carey Library, 1999.

Horne, Herman Harrell. *Teaching Techniques of Jesus*. Grand Rapids: Kregel Publications, 1971

Houtz, E.M. *Desktop Devotions*. Colorado Springs: NavPress, 1992..

Huber, Evelyn. *Enlist, Train, Support Church Leaders*. Valley Forge: Judson Press, 1975.

Hunter, James C. *The World's Most Powerful Leadership Principle*. Colorado Springs: Waterbrook Press, 2004.

Hybels, Bill. *Courageous Leaders*. Grand Rapids: Zondervan, 2002.

Hyde, Douglas. *Dedication and Leadership*. Notre Dame: University of Notre Dame, 1966.

Jenks, James M. and Kelly, John M. *Don't Do. Delegate!*. New York: Ballentine Books, 1985.

Johnson, Dwight L. *The Transparent Leader*. Eugene: Harvest House Publishers, 2001.

Johnson, Spencer. *Who Moved My Cheese?* New York: G. P. Putnam's Sons, 1998.

Jones, Bruce W. *Ministerial Leadership in a Managerial World*. Wheaton: Tyndale House Publishers, 1988.

Jones, Charles E. *Life is Tremendous: Leadership is for You!*. Wheaton: Tyndale House Publishers, 1968.

Jones, Laurie Beth. *Teach Your Team to Fish*. New York: Crown Business, 2002.

Jones, Laurie Beth. *The Path*. New York: Hyperion, 1996.

Jones, Laurie Beth. *Jesus CEO*. New York: Hyperion.1995.

Josefowitz, Natasha. *You're The Boss!*. New York: Warner Books, Inc. 1985.

Kahn, Steve. *The Secure Executive*. New York: The Berkley Publishing Group, 1987.

Karp, H. B., *The Change Leader*. San Diego: Pfeiffer & Company. 1996

Keith, Kent M. *Anyway*. New York: The Berkley Publishing Group, 2001.

Kellerman, Barbara. *Bad Leadership*. Boston: Harvard Business School Publishing, 2004.

Kets de Vries, Manfred F.R. *Prisoners of Leadership*. New York: John Wiley & Sons, 1989.

Kets de Vries, Manfred F.R. *Leaders, Fools, and Imposters*. San Francisco: Jossey-Bass Publishers, 1993.

Kilinski, Kenneth K. and Wofford, Jerry C. *Organization and Leadership in the Local Church*. Grand Rapids: Zondervan Publishing House, 1973.

King, Larry. *Future Talk*. New York: HarperCollins Publishers Inc., 1998.

King, Larry. *How to Talk to Anyone, Anytime, Anywhere*. New York: Crown Trade Paperbacks/Crown Publishers Inc., 1994.

Kise, Jane A.G., Stark, David and Hirsh, Sandra Krebs. *Discover Who You Are*. Minneapolis: Bethany House, 2005.

Knight, William Allen. *The Song of Our Syrian Guest*. Boston: Pilgrim Press, 1904...1945.

Knippel, Charles,T. *Joy in the Parish*. St. Louis: Concordia Publishing House, 2002.

Kouzes, James M., and Posner, Barry Z. *The Leadership Challenge*. San Francisco: Jossey-Bass Publishers, 1987.

Kouzes, James M., and Posner, Barry Z. *The Leadership Challenge Planner*. San Francisco: Jossey-Bass Publishers, 1999.

Kouzes, James M., and Posner, Barry Z. *A Leader's Legacy*. San Francisco: Jossey-Bass Publishers, 2006.

Kouzes, James M., and Posner, Barry Z. *Credibility*. San Francisco: Jossey- Bass Publishers, 1993.

Kriegbaum, Richard. *Leadership Prayers*. Wheaton: Tyndale House Publishers Inc., 1998.

Kutler, Stanley. *Abuse of Power*. New York: The Free Press, 1997.

Laken, Alan. *How to Get Control of Your Time and Your Life*. New York: NAL Penguin Inc., 1973.

Lanza-Bajo, Gloria. *The Thought-A-Week Guides: How to be a Better Manager*. New York: Ballantine Books, 1987.

Leadership. Carol Stream: Christianity Today.

Lawson, Ken. *Effective Leadership*. London England: Axis Publishing Inc. 2008.

Leadership Bible. New International Version. Grand Rapids: Zondervan.

LeBoeuf, Michael. *The Greatest Management Principle in the World*. New York: Berkley Book, 1989.

Lee, Mark. *How to Set Goals and Really Reach Them*. Portland: Horizon House Publishers, 1978.

Lencioni, Patrick. *The Five Temptations of a CEO*. San Francisco: Jossey-Bass Publishers, 1998.

LeTourneau, Richard. *Management Plus*. Grand Rapids: Zondervan Publishing House, 1973.

Lewis, Jonathan. *Working Your Way to the Nations*. Downers Grove: InterVarsity Press, 1996.

Lewis, Norm. *Priority One: What God Wants*. Orange: Promise Publishing, 1988.

Limerick, David, and Cunnington, Bert. *Managing the New Organization*. San Francisco: Jossey-Bass Publishers, 1993.

Lindgren, Alvin J., and Shawchuck, Norman. *Let My People Go: Empowering Laity for Ministry*. Nashville: Abingdon Press, 1980.

Lucado, Max. *Discovering the Cure for the Common Life*. Nashville: W Publishing Group, 2006.

Lucado, Max. *He Did This Just For You; New Testament*. Nashville: Thomas Nelson Publishers, 2001.

Lucado, Max. *He Still Moves Stones*. Dallas: Word Publishing, 1993.

Lutz, Lorry. *Women As Risk-Takers for God*. Grand Rapids: Baker Books, 1998.

Lutzer, Erwin. *Keep Your Dream Alive*. Wheaton: Victor Books/Scripture Press, 1991.

Lykins, Jay. *Values in the Marketplace*. R.C. Law & Co. Inc., 1991.

MacArthur, John. *The Book on Leadership*. Nashville: Thomas Nelson Publishers, 2004.

Mackenzie, Alec. *The Time Trap: The New Version of the Classic Book on Time Management*. New York: American Management Association, 1990.

Mackenzie, R. Alec. *The Time Trap: How to Get More Done in Less Time*. New York: McGraw-Hill Book Company, 1972.

MacMillian, Pat. *The Missions Recruiter*.

Maddux, Robert B. *Team Building: An Exercise in Leadership*. Revised Edition. Los Altos: Crisp Publications, 1988.

Malphurs, Aubrey. *Advanced Strategic Planning*. Grand Rapids: Baker Books, 1999.

Malphurs, Aubrey and Mancini, Will. *Building Leaders*. Grand Rapids: Baker Books, 2004.

Maltby, Dan E. *Team Problem Solving*. Nashville: Christian Management Association, 1998.

Mandel, Steve. *Effective Presentation Skills*. Melno Park: Von Hoffman Printing Company, 2000.

Manley, Patrick J. *How to Plan, Organize, and Control*. Scranton: International Correspondence Schools, Inc., 1991.

Manske, F. A. *Secrets of Effective Leadership: A Practical Guide to Success*. Germantown: Leadership Education and Development, Inc., 1987.

Manz, Charles C. *The Power of Failure*. San Francisco: Berrett-Koehler Publishers Inc., 2002.

Manz, Charles C., and Sims, Henry P. Jr. *SuperLeadership*. New York: Prentice Hall Press, 1989.

Marshall, Tom. *Understanding Leadership*. Lynwood WA: Emerald Books/Sovereign World Ltd., 1991.

Martin, Don. *TeamThink*. New York: Penguin Group, 1993.

Maxwell, John C. *Developing the Leader Within You*. Nashville: Thomas Nelson Inc., 1993.

Maxwell, John C. *Developing the Leaders Around You*. Nashville: Thomas Nelson Inc., 1995.

Maxwell, John C. *Leadership 101*. Tulsa: Honor Books, 1994.

Maxwell, John C. *The Right to Lead*. Nashville: J. Countryman, a division of Thomas Nelson Inc., 2001.

Maxwell, John C. *The 17 Indisputable Laws of Teamwork*. Nashville: Thomas Nelson Inc., 2001.

Maxwell, John C. *The 21 Indispensable Qualities of a Leader*. Nashville: Thomas Nelson Inc., 1999.

Maxwell, John C. and Jim Dornan. *Becoming a Person of Influence*. Nashville: Thomas Nelson Inc., 1997.

Maxwell, L.E. with Dearing, Ruth C. *Women in Ministry*. Camp Hill: Christian Publications, 1987.

McCarthy, Kevin W. *The On-Purpose Business*. Colorado Springs: Piñon Press, 1998.

McCay, James T. *The Management of Time*. Englewood Cliffs: Prentice-Hall, 1959.

McClain, Alva J. *Law and Grace*. Winona Lake: Moody Press Edition, 1967.

McGee, Robert S. *The Search for Significance*. Houston: Rapha Publishing, 1987.

McGinnis, Alan Loy. *Bringing Out the Best in People: How to Enjoy Helping Others Excel*. Minneapolis: Augsburg Publishing House, 1985.

McKenna, David L. *Power to Follow, Grace to Lead: Strategy for the Future of Christian Leadership*. Dallas: Word Publishing, 1989.

McNally, David. *Even Eagles Need a Push*. New York: Dell Publishing, 1990.

McNeil, Art. *The "I" of the Hurricane; Creating Corporate Energy*. Toronto: Stoddart Publishing Co. Limited, 1988.

McNeilly, Mark. *Sun Tzu and the Art of Business*. New York: Oxford University Press. 1996.

Meredith, Joel. *Meredith's Book of Bible Lists*. Minneapolis: Bethany House Publishers, 1980.

Migliore, Henry. *Common Sense Management: A Biblical Perspective*. Tulsa: Harrison House, 1988.

Migliore, Henry. *The Use of Strategic Planning for Ministry and Church Growth*. Tulsa: Harrison House, 1988.

Miller Jr., Arthur F. *Why You Can't Be anything You Want to Be*. Grand Rapids: Zondervan Publishing House, 1999.

Miller, Calvin. *Leadership*. Colorado Springs: NavPress, 1987.

Miller, Darrow L. *Discipling Nations*. Seattle: YWAM Publishing, 1998.

Millhouse, Paul W. *Enlisting and Developing Church Leaders*. Anderson: The Warner Press, 1946.

Morrison, Emily Kittle. *Leadership Skills*. Tucson: Fishers Books, 1994.

Mosley, Steve. *Secrets of the Mustard Seed*. Colorado Springs: Navpress, 2002.

Mouw, Richard J. & Jacobsen, Eric O. (Editors). *Traditions in Leadership*. Pasadena: The De Pree Leadership Center, 2006.

Munroe, Myles. *Becoming a Leader*. Lanham: Pneuma Life Publishing, 1993.

Munroe, Myles. *In Pursuit of Purpose*. Shippensburg: Destiny Image Publishers, 1992.

Munroe, Myles. *Understanding your Potential*. Shippensburg: Destiny Image Publishers Inc., 1991.

Murdock, Mike. *Secrets of the Richest Man Who Ever Lived*. Tulsa: Honor Books, 1998.

Murphy, John J. *Pulling Together*. Naperville: Simple Truths. 2010

Murren, Doug. *Leader Shift*. Ventura: Regal Books, 1994.

Murrow, David. *Why Men Hate Going to Church*. Nashville: Thomas Nelson, Inc., 2005.

Museveni, Yoweri K. *What is Africa's Problem?* Minneapolis: University of Minnesota Press, 2000.

Myers, Selma G. *Team Building For Diverse Work Groups*. Irvine: Richard Chang Associates, Inc. 1996.

National Center for NonProfit Boards. *The Executive Committee; The Planning Committee, The Chief Executive's Role in Developing the NonProfit Board* [#2]; *The Board's Role in Strategic Planning* [#6]. Washington DC, 1994, 1996, 1998.

National Institute of Business Management, Inc. *Creating & Motivating a Superior, Loyal Staff*. New York: NIBM, [date not given].

Nelson, Alan E. *Leading Your Ministry*, Nashville: Abingdom Press, 1996.

Nelson, Alan. *My Own Worst Enemy*. Grand Rapids: Fleming H. Revell, 2001.

Nelson, Alan E. & Toler, Stan. *The 5 Secrets to Becoming a Leader*. Ventura: Regal Books, 2002.

Nelson, Bob & Economy, Peter. *Managing For Dummies*. Foster City: IDG Books Worldwide, Inc., 1996.

New International Version. Grand Rapids: Zondervan.

Nolan, Timothy. *Plan or Die!* San Francisco: Pfeiffer & Co., 1993.

Northouse, Peter G. *Leadership: Theory and Practice, 2nd ed.* Thousand Oaks, CA: Sage Publications Inc., 2001.

Odiorne, George S. *How Managers Make Things Happen*. Englewood Cliffs: Prentice-Hall, Inc., 1961.

Olive, David. *No Guts, No Glory*. Toronto: McGraw-Hill Ryerson, 2000.

Oncken, William Jr. *Managing Management Time*. Englewood Cliffs: Prentice-Hall, 1984.

Orsborn, Carol. *Inner Excellence: Spiritual Principles of Life-Driven Business*. San Rafael: New World Library, 1992.

Osborne, Christina. *Dealing With Difficult People*. New York: DK Publishing, Inc., 2002.

Oster, Merrill J. *Vision-Driven Leadership*. San Bernardino: Here's Life Publishers Inc., 1991.

Owen, Jo. *How to Lead*. Glasgow: Pearson Education Ltd. 2005.

Oxford Dictionary of Quotations, The. Oxford: Oxford University Press, 1980.

Pagonis, Lt. General William G. *Moving Mountains: Lessons in Leadership and Logistics from the Gulf War*. Boston: Harvard Business School Press, 1992.

Palatnik, Lori with Burg, Bob. *Gossip*. Deerfield Beach: Simcha Press, 2002.

Palus, Charles J. and Horth, David M. *The Leader's Edge*. San Francisco: Jossey-Bass, 2002.

Patterson, Virginia. *Effective Delegation*. Diamond Bar: Christian Ministries Management Association, 1986.

Peter, Lawrence J. and Hull, Raymond. *The Peter Principle*. New York: William Morrow and Company, 1969.

Peters, Thomas J. and Waterman, Robert H. Jr. *In Search of Excellence*. New York: Warner Books, 1982.

Peters, Tom. *Leadership*. New York: DK Publishing, Inc., 2005.

Peters, Tom. *Reinventing Work Series: The Project 50*. New York: Alfred Knopf Inc., 1999.

Peters, Tom. *Thriving on Chaos: Handbook for a Management Revolution*. New York: Harper and Row Publishers, 1987.

Pillai, Bishop K.C. *Light through an Eastern Window*. New York: John Speller & Sons. 1963, 1977.

Pollard, C. William. *The Soul of the Firm*. Downers Grove: The ServiceMaster Foundation and HarperBusiness and Zondervan Publishing House, 1996.

Pollock, David R. *Business Management in the Local Church*. Chicago: Moody Press, 1992.

Posner, Mitchell J. *Executive Essentials*. New York: Avon Books, 1982.

Powell, James Lawrence. *Pathways to Leadership*. San Francisco: Jossey-Bass Publishers, 1995.

Pringle, Dr. Phil. *Top 10 Qualities of a Great Leader*. Tulsa: Harrison House Publishers, 1982.

Prior, David. *Jesus and Power*. Downers Grove: Intervarsity Press, 1987.

Prior, Kenneth. *Perils of Leadership*. Downers Grove: Intervarsity Press, 1990.

Pritchett, Price. *Fast Growth*. Dallas: Pritchett & Associates, Inc., 1997.

Pritchett, Price. *Culture Shift*. Plano: Pritchett Rummler-Brache, 199?

Pritchett, Price. *New Work Habits for a Radically Changing World*. Dallas: Pritchett & Associates Inc., 1994.

Pue, Carson. *Mentoring Leaders*. Grand Rapids: Baker Books, 2005.

QUALITY, SERVICE, TEAMWORK, and the quest for EXCELLENCE. Lombard: Celebrating Excellence Publishing Company, 1992.

Quinn, Robert E. et al. *Becoming a Master Manager*. New York: John Wiley & Sons Inc., 1996.

Rendall, T.S. *Nehemiah: Laws of Leadership*. Three Hills: Prairie Press, 1980.

Robbins, Stephen P. *Essentials of Organizational Behavior*. Second Edition. Englewood Cliffs, 1988.

Robinson, Maureen K. see National Center for Nonprofit Boards

Rogers, Jenny. *Influencing People*. New York. American Management Association, 1999.

Rosenberg, Michael. *The Flexible Thinker*. Canada: Orange You Glad Inc., 1998.

Rush, Myron. *Management: A Biblical Approach*. Wheaton: SP Publications, 1983.

Rush, Myron. *The New Leader: A Revolutionary Approach to Effective Leadership*. Wheaton: SP Publications, 1987.

Ryrie, Charles C. *Object Lessons: 100 Lessons from Everyday Life*. Chicago: The Moody Bible Institute, 1991.
Sanders, J. Oswald. *Spiritual Leadership*. Chicago: Moody Press, 1980.
Schaeffer, Francis A. *The Mark of the Christian*. Downers Grove: Intervarsity Press, 1970.
Scholtes, Peter R. *The Leader's Handbook*. New York: MacGraw-Hill Companies Inc., 1998.
Schuster, John P. *Answering Your Call*. San Franciso: Berrett-Koehler Publishers, Inc., 2003.
Schwartz, David J. *The Magic of Thinking Big*. New York: Fireside, 1965.
Scott, Susan. *Fierce Conversations*. New York: Berkley Publishing Group, 2004.
Senge, Peter M. *The Fifth Discipline*. New York: Currency Doubleday, 1990, 1994.
Sherman, Doug, and Hendricks, William. *Your Work Matters to God*. Colorado Springs: NavPress, 1987.
Shula, Don and Blanchard, Ken. *Everyone's a Coach*. Grand Rapids: Zondervan Publishing House. 1995.
Sider, Ronald J. *Rich Christians in an Age of Hunger*. Dallas: Word Publishing, 1990
Simon, Henry A. *Mentoring: A Tool for Ministry*. St. Louis: Concordia Publishing House, 2001.
Slater, Robert. *Get Better or Get Beaten*. Buff Ridge IL: Irwin Professional Publishing, 1994.
Smallman, William H. *Able to Teach Others Also*. Pasadena: Mandate Press, 2001.
Smith, Lawrence R. *Journal of Innovative Management*, Vol.1 Number 4, Summer 1996. Methuen: GOAL/QPC, 1996.
Smith, Timothy. *Donors Are People Too*. Akron: Berkey Brendel Sheline, 2003.
Soundview Editorial Staff. *Skills for Success*. Middlebury: Soundview Executive Book Summaries. 1989.
Soundview Executive Book Summaries. Middlebury: Soundview Executive Book Summaries.
Spangler, Ann. *Praying the Names of God*. Grand Rapids: Zondervan Publishing House, 2004.
Spikes, Brian. *Boss is a Four-Letter Word*. Toronto: Stoddart Publishing Co. Limited, 1987.
Stackhouse Jr., John G. *Humble Apologetics*. New York: Oxford University Press, Inc., 2002.
Stahlke, Les. *Affirmed for Success*. Edmonton: PS Communications, 1998.
Stanley, Andy. *The Next Generation Leader*. Sisters: Multnomah Publishers, Inc., 2003.
Stone, Dave. *Keeping your Head above Water*. Loveland: Flagship Church Resources, 2002.
Stoner, James A. F. *Management*. Englewood Cliffs: Prentice Hall, Inc., 1978.
Strategies for Success. Cambridge, MA: Sloan Management Review, 1996.
Sutterfield, Ken. *The Power of an Encouraging Word*. Green Forest AR: New Leaf Press, 1997.
Swenson, Richard A. *Margin: Restoring Emotional, Physical, Financial, and Time Reserves to Overloaded Lives*. Colorado Springs: NavPress, 1992.
Swindoll, Charles R. *Hand Me Another Brick*. Nashville: Thomas Nelson Inc., 1981.
Taylor, Harold L. *Delegate: The Key to Successful Management*. Don Mills: Stoddart Publishing Co., 1989.
Taylor, Harold L. *Making Time to Sell: A Salesman's Guide to the Effective Use of Time*. Toronto: Time Management Consultants, 1985.
Taylor, Harold L. *Making Time Work for You*. Toronto: Stoddart Publishing Co., 1986.
Taylor, Harold L. *Personal Organization: The Key to Managing Your Time and Your Life*. Toronto: Harold Taylor Time Consultants Inc., 1988.
Taylor, William D. *Too Valuable to Lose*. Singapore/Wheaton: World Evangelical Fellowship, 1997.
Team Memory Jogger. Methuen: GOAL/QPC and Joiner Associates Inc., 1995.
Terry, George R. *Principles of Management*. Seventh Edition. Homewood: Richard D. Irwin Inc., 1977.
Terry, George R. *Supervisory Management*. Homewood: Richard D. Irwin Inc., 1974.
Tinker, Melvin. *Alien Nation*. Fearn: Christian Focus Publications, 2001.
Towns, Elmer. *The 8 Laws of Leadership*. Lynchburg: Church Growth Institute, 1995.
Townsend, Patrick L. and Joan E. Gebhardt. *Five-Star Leadership*. New York and Toronto: John Wiley & Sons Inc. 1997.
Tracy, Diane. *The First Book of Common-Sense Management*. New York: William Morrow and Company, 1989.
Tunnicliffe, Geoff. *101 Ways to Change Your World*. Colorado Springs: Victor Books/Chariot Victor.1997.
Two Seekers, *No Jesus, No Peace – Know Jesus, Know Peace*. New York: Warner Books, Inc., 2002.
Tzu, Sun. *The Art of War*. Trans. Thomas Cleary. Boston: Shambhala Publications Inc., 1991.
"V". *The Mafia Manager*. New York: St. Martin's Press. 1996.
Van Ekeren, Glenn. *Speaker's Sourcebook II*. Englewood Cliffs: Prentice-Hall, Inc., 1994.
Van Fleet, David D. *Contemporary Management*. Boston: Houghton Mifflin Co., 1991.
Van Fleet, James K. *Power with People*. West Nyack, Parker Publishing Co., 1970.
Van Fleet, James K. *The 22 Biggest Mistakes Managers Make and How to Correct Them*. West Nyack, Parker Publishing Co., 1973.
Wagner, Peter. *Leading Your Church to Growth*. Ventura: GL Publications, 1984.
Walton, Mary. *The Deming Management Method*. New York: Putnam Publishing Group, 1986.
Ward, Ruth McRoberts. *Self-Esteem: Gift from God*. Grand Rapids: Baker Book House, 1984.
Wareham, John. *The Anatomy of a Great Executive*. New York: HarperCollins Publishers,1991.
Warren, Rick. *The Purpose Driven Life*. Grand Rapids: Zondervan Publishing House, 2002.
Warren, Rick. *The Purpose Driven Church*. Grand Rapids: Zondervan Publishing House, 1995.
Water, Mark. *The Bible Made Easy*. Carlisle: Hunt & Thorpe, 1999.
Water, Mark. *The Bible and Science made easy*. Peabody: Hendrickson Publishers, Inc. 2001.
Water, Mark. *Bible Teachings made easy*. Carlisle: Hunt & Thorpe, 1998.
Water, Mark. *World Religions made easy*. Peabody: Hendrickson Publishers, Inc., 2002.
Weiss, W. H. *The Art and Skill of Managing People*. West Nyack, Parker Publishing Co., 1975.
Weems, Lovett H. Jr. *Church Leadership: Vision, Team, Culture, and Integrity*. Nashville: Abingdon Press, 1993.
White, Jerry. *Making Peace With Reality*. Colorado Springs: Navpress, 2002.
White, John. *Excellence in Leadership: Reaching Goals with Prayer, Courage and Determination*. Downers Grove: Intervarsity Press, 1986.
Willingham, Ron. *The People Principle*. New York: St. Martin's Press, 1997.
Wilkes, C. Gene. *Jesus on Leadership*. Nashville: LifeWay Press, 1996.
Wilkinson, Bruce. *A Life God Rewards*. Sisters: Multnomah Press, 2002.
Wilkinson, Bruce. *The Prayer of Jabez*. Sisters: Multnomah Press, 2000.
Willmer, Wesley K with Smith, Martyn. *God & Your Stuff*. Colorado Springs: Navpress, 2002.
Willmer, Wesley K. ed. *Money for Ministries: Biblical Guidelines for Giving and Asking*. Wheaton: SP Publications, 1989.
Wilson, Susan B. *Goal Setting*. New York: AMACOM, 1994.
Woodbridge, John D., ed. *Great Leaders of the Christian Church*. Chicago: Moody Press, 1988.
Woods, John. *The Quotable Executive*. New York: McGraw-Hill, 2000.
Yancey, Philip. *Soul Survivor*. New York: Doubleday, 2001.
Yandian, Bob. *Decently & In Order*. New Kensington: Whitaker House, 1987.
Yukl, Gary A. *Leadership in Organizations*. Second Edition. Englewood Cliffs, Prentice Hall, 1989.
Yount, William R. *Created To Learn*. Nashville: Broadman & Holman Publishers, 1996.
Zaccarelli, Herman E. *Training Managers to Train: A Practical Guide to Improving Employee Performance*. Menlo Park: Crisp Publications Inc., 1988.
Zenger, John H. The Handbook for Leaders. New York: McGraw-Hill Co., 2007.
Zigarelli, Michael A. *Management by Proverbs*. Chicago: Moody Press, 1999.
Ziglar, Zig. *Steps to the Top*. Gretina: Pelican Publishing Co., 1985.
Zondervan. *God's Words of Life For Leaders*. Grand Rapids, 1999.

Index

Additional copies of

Authentic Managerial Leadership

are available through

Barnes & Noble

Amazon.com

Espresso Book Machine

For special prices on bulk orders, contact

Xulon Press

1-866-381-2665

or

Robert A. Orr, c/o Goldore Consulting Inc.

Box 590, Linden, AB Canada T0M 1J0

Phone: 403-370-6025

E-mail: robertalexorr@yahoo.ca

CPSIA information can be obtained at www.ICGtesting.com
Printed in the USA
LVOW01s1614250814

400817LV00005B/23/P